Back Door Java

Back Door Java
State Formation and the Domestic in Working Class Java

Jan Newberry

UNIVERSITY OF TORONTO PRESS
Toronto Buffalo London

© University of Toronto Press 2006
Toronto Buffalo London
utorontopress.com

Reprinted 2021

ISBN 978-1-55111-689-1

Originally published by Broadview Press © 2006 Jan Newberry

LIBRARY AND ARCHIVES CANADA CATALOGUING IN PUBLICATION

Newberry, Jan
Back door Java: state formation and the domestic in working class Java/Jan Newberry.

(Broadview ethnographies & case studies)
Includes bibliographical references and index.
ISBN 1-55111-689-8

1. Housewives—Java—Social conditions. 2. Working class women—Java—Social conditions.
3. Urban women—Java—Social conditions. 4. Community life—Java.
5. Women—Government policy—Java.
I. Title.   II. Series.

HD6194.Z6J387 2006   305.43'6408624095982   C2006-901471-X

We welcome comments and suggestions regarding any aspect of our publications—
please feel free to contact us at news@university of Toronto Press or visit us at
utorontopress.com.

Unversity of Toronto Press acknowledges the financial assistance to its publishing
program of the Canada Council for the Arts and the Ontario Arts Council, an
agency of the Government of Ontario.

Cover design by Zack Taylor

Printed in the U.S.A.

Contents

List of Figures

Acknowledgements

The initial research for this project was supported by two grants from the Southeast Asia Council of the Association for Asian Studies and a grant from the University of Arizona Graduate School. I would like to thank the Lembaga Ilmu Pengetahuan Indonesia (LIPI) for permission to conduct this research, and the American-Indonesian Exchange Foundation (AMINEF) for all their support. My special thanks to Dr. Tony Sadjimin at the Clinical Epidemiology and Biostatistics Unity (CEBU) at Dr. Sardjito General Hospital in Yogyakarta, who agreed to sponsor my research, and to all the great staff there, including particularly Dr. Yati Soenarto and Nurwicaksono. My research was greatly enriched by the invaluable help of my research assistant and little sister, Mei Sugiarti, who translated more than just language for me. Thanks to her family who extended innumerable acts of hospitality to me.

My work in Java would not be possible without my friends and neighbors. My very special thanks to the Suyono family who are now my family too. They have fed me, watched over me, and kept me safe in Java for fifteen years. My fieldwork would not have been possible without the support and friendship of Joan Suyenaga, Suhirdjan and their wonderful children, Lani, Rio, and now, Santi. I thank all these families for their unselfish friendship, as well as all the great food and the laughs. They were my first and best teachers about what "homemaking" really means in Java.

On this side of the world, I would like to thank my teachers in anthropology, Tad Park, Jim Greenberg, Mark Nichter, Jane Hill, Bob Netting, Ellen Basso, Helen Henderson, to name only a few. Many thanks to my Canadian research assistant, Elizabeth Chant, for all her help in manuscript preparation. It is deeply saddening to me that I had no chance to adequately thank Daniel Nugent for everything he taught me before he died. Much in this book is a result of his influence. Rest in peace, Daniel.

My family has been my bedrock in life as well as in scholarship. The work of women in holding the universe together is amply demonstrated to me by my mother, my sister, my niece, and now my daughter, Ana.

One last pair of women have earned my eternal gratitude. Christine Koggel and Catherine Kingfisher are two scholars whose work inspires me and whose support of my own work has been immeasurably important to this project. The best of this work is due to all these influences; all mistakes are my own doing.

Finally, this dissertation is dedicated to the one who is dedicated to me. Steve Ferzacca is not only my first and last editor, but my partner in knowing Java and anthropology.

Chapter One

Through the Missing Back Door, an Entrance

Much of what houses are and imply becomes something that goes without saying (Carsten and Hugh-Jones 1995:4)

Returning to central Java three years after my initial fieldwork, I found the house that I had lived in with my husband and fellow fieldworker, Steve Ferzacca, empty. This was surprising because the house was a beautiful one. Small but tiled in white with modern cement walls and pane glass windows, it was something of a standout in the part of the working-class neighbourhood where we had lived. Our nearest neighbours had houses that incorporated some cement but still made heavy use of bamboo. Few had an indoor well and pump, and none the bright, shiny newness of our house. Steve and I had been pleased to be the first tenants in this small house. We had not planned to do fieldwork in this type of urban neighbourhood known as a *kampung*, but we did want to live in a modest way and not in the fancier districts to the north of town. We were happy to have a few modern conveniences and such a pleasant house (see Figure 1.1).

Figure 1.1
View of my house to the right of Bu Sae's renovated house. (Photo by S. Ferzacca.)

It occurred to me that a suitable tenant had not been found in the intervening years because the house was just too nice for this middling section of Yogyakarta, one of the court towns of Central Java. Still, many of our neighbours had improved their houses since we had left, and our little house was no longer such an exception. Later, as I visited with our old next-door neighbours, I discovered the local theory on the continued vacancy in our house: it had filled up with ghosts.

I was sitting in Bu Sae's family room when a loud thump was heard from the back. Both Bu Sae and Bu Apik, two women who had been my close neighbours and mentors, looked to the back and then at each other.[1] Bu Sae told me that ever since we had left the house next door there had been strange noises from the back part of the house, near the well. We had already heard from several neighbours that our old rental house was haunted, that *setan masuk* (Satan had entered).[2] We heard stories about a white-faced man with wild hair dressed in clothes from *zaman kuno* (ancient time) who had been seen sitting by our well. Another time, a young boy sleeping in the house had heard a loud thump next to his head only to find no one there when he awoke. Many of these accounts were told in a joking fashion. Bu Bambang had cuffed her son, Mas Yoto, who had often played at our house, and said he was the only *setan* that was involved.

Ghost stories were not unusual in the *kampung*. We already knew that the open area with bamboo trees across the street from us was considered to be haunted as was the area around the ruined royal house down the street. We heard from the *kampung* kids several longstanding stories about disembodied heads that rolled around scaring people and about little people who lived in various places in the *kampung* (*tuyul* who steal money or *setan gundul*, or bald-headed Satan; see Koentjaraningrat 1989:342; Geertz 1960). Empty and unused areas tended to fill up with ghosts, and since our house had been left too long empty, it was no wonder that it had attracted ghosts.

This explanation for our empty house did not seem particularly satisfying to me because people in the *kampung* had managed to live surrounded by ghosts for some time. It was only on further discussion that we realized that the ghosts were only a manifestation of the deeper structural problem with our house: it had no back door. It would have been easy to dismiss these comments if this were the first time I had heard about this lack of a back door. But in fact, the back door had been a continuing issue during my fieldwork in this *kampung* and to hear about it after three years' absence, brought home its significance again.

DOMESTIC SPACE

My original research interests had concerned the relationship between agrarian communities and the state. Trained in peasant studies, I was eager to find resistant agrarian heroes holding off the state and global forces.

Instead, I found myself spending time in urban Javanese kitchens among poor and working class people who were making do. I spent my time in Java, not among rice farmers, studying changing rural communities, but among urban housewives, studying a national housewives' association, PKK, *Pembinaan Kesejahteraan Keluarga*. My goals shifted as I faced the necessities of a field site that chose me rather than the other way around. My plans to work in the Javanese countryside had to be modified, and I settled down to make do myself by studying what I saw around me.

The ubiquitous national program aimed at housewives that my neighbours all belonged to, whether willingly or unwillingly, seemed an obvious choice for a focus. My old-fashioned sense of fieldwork meant to me that I should try to live like the people whom I was studying and so it was that I decided to act and study as a housewife. My new research focus was conceived very vaguely as the household and its connection to state programs as evident in the local practice of PKK.

What I found to my own surprise was that domestic space, defined for me and by me in fieldwork, was significantly about community, too. I spent months as a housewife-in-training, ostensibly studying the development of the category of *ibu rumah tangga*, or housewife, as a relatively recent category of social and economic experience. Yet, community, as an official nationalist idea and as a lived practice in the *kampung*, kept insinuating itself as an intervening variable. In the months and years since that original fieldwork, I have struggled to make sense of where the household stopped, the community began, and the state intervened. Early on, I had to change my definitions of family and household. Although I did not make the mistake of seeing them as the same thing as earlier anthropologists often had, I nonetheless had not clearly defined for myself what the domestic unit was that I was studying. As I continued to try and isolate the domestic from the communal from the state, I was foiled at every turn. It wasn't until I analyzed separately the various components of the domestic, and considered them along with the community and state, that I began to understand what I was seeing.

NATIONALIZED HOUSEWIVES

The government will support PKK which we hope will be a spearhead for the development of society from below, 'motored' by women. I ask that the various activities programmed at the national level be channelled through PKK. We can have many programs for women to enhance the role of women in development. But it should not be forgotten that these programs' are aimed and to be implemented by women in the villages, whether in the urban or rural areas. If there are too many organizations, it is not in accordance with their simple desires and way of thinking, and will only serve to confuse them. (Presidential meeting on the occasion of the National Working Meeting of P2W-KSS, 2 March 1981, cited in and translated by Suryakusuma 1991:57.)

It may indeed be possible to live in Java and not know the significance of PKK but it would be impossible to live there and not be aware of its presence (see Figure 1.2). It seems that every village hamlet entrance and every urban *kampung* walkway is emblazoned with a PKK plaque, outlining the ten principal programs of PKK (*10 Program Pokok PKK*):

> 1) comprehension and practical application of *Pancasila*,[3] 2) mutual self-help, 3) food, 4) clothing, 5) housing and home economics, 6) education and craft skills, 7) health, 8) development of cooperatives, 9) protection and conservation of the environment, 10) health planning (read as family planning).

Figure 1.2
PKK marker for cooperative garden. (Photo by S. Ferzacca.)

The very prevalence of this list of ideal female domestic activities may render it invisible to some. In fact, the level of PKK activity in any given locale varies in terms of a complex mix of factors, for example, the relative wealth of the area, the history of PKK organization, and the personality of the local PKK leaders. Yet no place should be without PKK and its programs by a government decree of 1971, which extended this successful program to all of Indonesia after its original genesis in Java. The origins of PKK were more humble, however.[4]

PKK, *Pembinaan Kesejahteraan Keluarga* (Support for the Prosperous Family, sometimes translated as The Family Welfare Movement[5]) began as a 1957 home economics seminar held in Bogor, West Java. The seminar was conducted by the Education Section and Community Nutrition Institute of the Ministry of Health. Based on a mimeograph from the government's

Ministry of International Affairs, a list of education topics thought to be appropriate for a developing society was compiled by an interdepartmental committee between 1960 and 1962. This committee included the Ministry of Culture and Education, the Ministry of Agriculture, the Ministry of Manpower, Ministry of Religion and the Ministry of Internal Affairs. This was how the ten programs of PKK were originally conceived (Suryakusuma 1991:56).

The Governor of Central Java included PKK as part of regional development efforts in the mid-1960s. Originally, PERTIWI, one of the first organizations for wives of government officials, was given the job of promulgating PKK and its principles. *Pusat Latihan PKK* (PKK training centres) were begun in all the districts of Central Java, and in the early 1970s, these were funded from district budgets. It was at the end of 1971 that the Minister of Internal Affairs suggested that PKK be implemented throughout Indonesia. In 1973, PKK became a main program of the LSD (*Lembaga Sosial Desa*, Village Social Institution). The LSD was later changed to the LKMD (*Lembaga Ketahanan Masyarakat Desa*, Institution for the Maintenance of Village Society; see Chapter Two) in 1980, and in the same year, responsibility for PKK shifted from the Ministry of Social Affairs to the Ministry of Internal Affairs. At this time, PKK also began receiving some of the money granted to villages through INPRES (Presidential Instructions).

It was in 1982 that PKK became one of the working sections of the LKMD structure and was put under the charge of the village head's wife who also served as the "functional" second deputy chairman (*Ketua II*) of LKMD. This change would prove to be very important in the incorporation of wives into local administration as the helpmeets of their official spouses. Suryakusuma also notes the shift in 1982 that moved the *Pancasila* state ideology courses to the first of the PKK programs, putting the state's unmistakable stamp on PKK. She goes on to say that the inclusion of PKK in the GBHN (*Garis Besar Haluan Negara*, State National Guidelines) in 1983 marked the zenith of PKK's state approval; "[n]ow as one of the ten sections of LKMD, in theory at least, PKK is supposed to be implemented in all the 70,000 villages in Indonesia" (Suryakusuma 1991:56–57). While PKK has been incorporated within the structure of village and *kampung* administration through the LKMD, the structure of PKK itself is also broken into sub-sections: social projects, sport and art, education, community relations, family planning, equipment, credit-savings program (*simpan pinjam*), and area commissioners (Gerke 1992:33). A final shift in PKK administrative and bureaucratic position has to do with its inclusion as the main voice for the government's family planning program (*Badan Koordinasi Keluarga Berencana Nasional*, BKKBN, Coordinating Board for National Family Planning).

PKK, which by some accounts arose out of the vibrant women's movements around the time of independence, has become a public organization of the national government (Branson and Miller 1988; Gerke 1992; Wieringa 1993). All adult (i.e., married) women are considered members and are urged to attend local monthly meetings. What the nationalization of PKK has ultimately accomplished, is the state-sponsored promotion of a new social category—the *ibu rumah tangga* (housewife)—and the conscription of Indonesian women, particularly those of the lower classes, as unpaid social welfare workers.

KAMPUNG HOUSEWIVES

For most *kampung* inhabitants, PKK is experienced most directly through the monthly meetings at both the RT (*rukun tetangga*, harmonious neighbours) and RW (*rukun warga*, harmonious citizens) level of administration (the RT division typically comprises some 20–40 households, and there are some six RT divisions in a single RW). These two administrative units are the lowest rungs of state administration.[6] Some women choose to be more active, such as Bu Apik who was a local birth control officer, and hold other administrative offices in the RW. Perhaps the most famous PKK-sponsored activity is the *Posyandu*, a local government-supported clinic which operates once each month, sponsored by each RW. Most RW groups have some sort of public meeting building, although it is possible to host the *Posyandu* in any home or open space in the neighbourhood. In my own RW, the *Posyandu* was held in the community building near the entrance to the *kampung*. In the neighbouring RW, the *Posyandu* was held at a small private kindergarten in the house yard of its director.

At the *Posyandu*, all children five years of age and under are brought to be weighed and receive a vitamin pill and a free meal. The vitamin and food are little more than symbolic since the *Posyandu* meets only once a month, but the monthly weighing is significant because records are kept to track whether children are gaining or not. If not, mothers are directed to go the local PUSKEMAS (*Pusat Kesehatan Masyarakat*, or public health clinic) where they can see a doctor and/or nurse for little or no money. This kind of direct access to health care is one of the great successes of Indonesia's public health system, and it is directly related to the decrease in infant mortality in Indonesia. Each *Posyandu* is organized by the local PKK group, directed by the Ibu RW, the wife of the local RW headman. The food that is served is cooked by RT groups on a rotating basis, and this is organized by the Ibu RT, the wife of the RT headman.

In this, its most public program (along with the birth control program), PKK is a well-organized community outreach program run with the labour of community women as housewives. Other notable programs of PKK include hygiene and general health education, mosquito prevention, craft instruction, training for small-scaled and home-based industry, fund-raising for the poor and ill in the area, and more recently, elder healthcare. The much-loved *arisan*, or credit lottery, is also a central piece of any PKK meeting. The work involved and the ethic of PKK is explicitly aimed at housewives, and it is clear that the work of married women who stay at home is the central mechanism for its organization. What is not clear is how well this picture matches the realities of *kampung* women.

The practice of PKK administration implies much overlap between the male and female sides of administration, particularly in rural areas where, for example, a PKK leader will use the facilities for transport, communication, and administration provided by her husband's office (Suryakusuma 1991:63). In 1984, PKK was standardized throughout Indonesia, and PKK offices were instituted at all administrative levels with a complete set of PKK data to be displayed on a special board devoted to PKK activities. These offices are typically housed within the male-dominated local administrative structure. "These [PKK] programs are designed to fit in with the development efforts and ideological aims of the state ... PKK officials claim that the implementation of PKK is achieved by integrating government efforts with community efforts" (Suryakusuma 1991:65).

The legacy of community governance and politics in Indonesia is outlined in the next chapter. The work of social scientists, administrators, and historians in organizing the village based on the romantic ideal of the natural community has produced this social form—the idealized village community, which is also promoted through the structure and practice of PKK. Although it might seem paradoxical since the move toward the nuclear family in industrial Europe is often seen to signal the end of community, for Indonesia, the family is seen as the prime unit of social organization which articulates with the community and hence, the state. The roles assigned to women through PKK not only valorize the nuclear family ideal with a stay-at-home mom, they also enforce and enhance local exchange practices presumed to be traditional to Javanese society. The five roles of women that usually accompany the ten primary programs of PKK illustrate the contemporary view of women's appropriate roles; note the order:

1. loyal backstop and supporter of her husband [helpmate]
2. caretaker of the household
3. producer of future generations
4. the family's prime socializer
5. Indonesian citizen

(translation from N. Sullivan 1983:2)

EVERYDAY FORMS OF STATE FORMATION

State formation is typically taken to refer to the first appearance in human civilization of the state as a political form. Using it here to suggest something in the process of occurring rather than as a descriptive statement of something that has already been achieved serves to highlight the ongoing nature of political rule. The central goal of any political order is to secure its reproduction through the continual consent to be ruled. The reproduction of that order and consent is a cultural process, both grand and mundane, and only virtually accomplished, in-the-making, continually in the process of being achieved.

The transit of people as housewives, mothers, fathers, daughters and sons, their labour, their kinship practices, their services, and their things through domestic space, and in response to nationalist programs aimed at domestic life, made up the everyday acts of state formation that I studied. I use "everyday acts of state formation" (Joseph and Nugent 1994; see also Corrigan and Sayer 1985) to describe what I saw through the back door in Java, because the creation and definition of the domestic is a state project. The making of the state is intimately bound up with domestic life, and as is clear in Indonesia, with community organization.

PKK places working class housewives at the forefront of developing Indonesia. As a result, the domestic activities of women and their roles in community have become, in a sense, a form of governmentality, an extension of government programs aimed at social welfare through the informal and formal labour of women and hence, the extension of a rationality of self-management in aid of producing self-regulating, moral communities that are modernizing. Simultaneously, governance through community organization and women's work has been coloured by local cultural practices of community support and exchange. My participation in the local community as a housewife ethnographer demonstrated that the rituals of community in Java represent the dispersion of state power through local discourses, the result of the ongoing formation of the relations of rule in Indonesia. Significantly, this process of state formation as an everyday dispersion of state power through forms of governance is subject to modification as local communities use state resources to their own ends. Domestic space thus becomes extended through the community and simultaneously reinforced as the proper site of women's work.

In the following pages, the relationship of domestic space to community and its importance to state formation will be considered by looking very closely at one corner of one *kampung* neighbourhood in one part of one central Javanese city in Indonesia. No argument for the universal applicability of this work will be made, or to my way of thinking, is even necessary. Instead, I offer a micro-view of state rule in terms that are mundane but visible. This is state formation on a human and daily level. By attempting to slow the process and isolate some of the elements, our understanding of state formation, its pervasiveness and its ordinariness, is deepened. There is no need to believe that the same elements are evident everywhere equally in Indonesia. Instead, I propose that state formation is consummately a form of bricolage, a making and re-making with local materials.

BACK DOORS

When we first arrived in the neighbourhood, most houses were very simple. A few were remnants of older, more elaborate Javanese houses, and some were new, "modern" style houses. Most were small with some mixture of bamboo and wood and perhaps some cement. Yet, the simplicity of the architecture does not betray the complexity of social relations that it makes possible, a fact made abundantly clear by the effects of our missing back door.

When we rented our house, we were blind to some of the signals given about the status of the house and what it represented in the small area of the *kampung* where we would live. Looking back now, it's easy to see that the house was troubled from the first by family tensions (and now by ghosts) although it had originally been seen as a promise to the extended family living around it—a promise ultimately unfulfilled as a brief history of our house shows.

The corner of the *kampung* where our house stood was dominated by a large extended kin group. Over the course of doing fieldwork and living in the *kampung*, it became clear that the area served as an extended family compound around which several households were organized into a larger domestic group. The centre of this compound was a ramshackle wood and bamboo house, to the immediate right (east) of our house, that belonged to the senior couple Bapak and Ibu Cipto. Bu Sae, a cousin of Pak Cipto, lived in the house on the other side of our own. Although Bu Sae, her husband and four children had lived for many years in a leased house to the east of the Cipto family compound, for the last decade they had lived in the dilapidated bamboo and wood house west of the Cipto's that had been Bu Sae's natal house.

Our own house belonged to an elder daughter of Bapak and Ibu Cipto, but it was something of an anomaly in the extended family compound. Not only was it newer than the surrounding houses, with cement walls and tiled floors, but it was the only house to be available for *kontrak* (lease). When we first looked at the house, the back portion was unfinished. Initially, we had been taken to see the back of the house by going through the house of the owner's parents, Bapak and Ibu Cipto. At that time, the back of the house was open and one could easily pass from the parent's backyard to the new house and on to the back of Bu Sae's house. We agreed to lease the house for a year with the stipulation that it would be finished by the time we moved, in two month's time. Pak Widodo, the son-in-law who owned the house, asked at the time of our agreement if we would like a wall in the back of the house. Not understanding completely, we had replied that it was not necessary, although we did want an electric pump installed for the well. Pak Widodo insisted again, "wouldn't it be nice to have a wall in the back?" So without understanding the nature of the wall or the need for it, we agreed—since it cost us nothing and the owner himself seemed to want it so much.

We were very surprised when we returned to move in at the changes that had occurred in the house. Before it was completed, the door at the back, past the *mandi* (bathing area, in this case including the toilet) had opened onto an open backyard area from which one could easily pass into the Sae and the Cipto backyards and back doors. When we returned, the whole area had been completely walled in with bricks, and a roof had been extended over half of the area that now had a kitchen with sink, tiled floor, and piped water. Most significantly, this back area was now completely cut off from the neighbours by walls that were over seven feet high. To us, this new space seemed a welcome, very private area in the back of the house away from the prying eyes of others. To our neighbours, the new wall not only signalled a break in usual *kampung* and family relations, but it also rendered our house incapable of functioning within the *kampung* community.

The faction of the family that was doing better financially, Ibu and Bapak Widodo, had evidently built this house so that it would not function communally; it was shut off from both family and community activities. Bu Sae herself had complained to me about the house because she could no longer get to her cousin's house from her back door to his. The new house with its long cement and cinder block walls had shut out the breeze that used to flow through her house. Our new house blocked not only the flow of wind but of people and things. Once the back portion of our house had been completed, it was a solid piece of construction from the *gang* (narrow street) in front to the brick wall at the back, effectively driving a wedge into what had been a more open family compound.

Yet, the house did have a door letting onto the back yard area, which was half given over to the kitchen. What was missing was a door out to a narrow alley that allowed access to the street to the west. The lack of a back door was significant not only for what it meant about kinship relations in the compound, but because of the message it sent about involvement in *kampung* exchange relations and community and the changing socio-economic fortunes of *kampung* dwellers. As it turns out, the front door and back door are equally important to social relations in the *kampung*, but in vastly different ways.

Great emphasis is placed on receiving guests in Java, and to receive them well, they must be served at the very least a drink. It is very poor form to be unprepared no matter who comes or how many guests attend. I saw this ethic in practice many times, but perhaps the most telling episode was when I received guests and ran short of sugar for the tea. I turned to Mas Yoto, one of the children who were our constant companions, and sent him to buy sugar, little realizing what I had asked him to do. It wasn't until he walked back into the house with the bag of sugar stuffed up under his shirt, an act forced on him because he had to enter through the front door, that it became obvious to me that our lack of a back door was keenly felt as a social deficiency, even on the part of a ten year old boy.

The role of the front door and the required openness to potential visitors is characteristic of *kampung* homes. Most descriptions of visiting in Java (Geertz 1960; Keeler 1984) place the male head of the household in the front of the house to receive guests and the female in the back, often behind a curtain or door, to prepare food and drink. There have been changes in *kampung* houses due to rising incomes, but this division between a formal open front room and the more enclosed family room to the back remains. While this is not much different from traditional Western homes with their receiving rooms and parlours, the difference at this time in *kampung* Java is that the front room must be open to any guest. That is, *kampung* doors are always open, unless the people in the house are sleeping, it is late in the evening after the appropriate time for visiting, or the residents are gone. In visiting a Javanese house, a guest usually approaches the doorway and leans forward, calling *kula nuwun* (literally, "I request" or "ask" in polite Javanese). This call is repeated until the guest hears an answering *mongo* (the mark of Javanese politeness which means generally "if you please"). At this point, the guests hesitate until asked to enter again, and then typically shedding their shoes and saying again *nuwun,* they step over the threshold. The key thing is that guests may approach a house at almost any time and expect to be received. The general lack of telephones has left this Javanese convention relatively unchanged, although it varies by class and area.[7] In contrast to the front door, the back part of a *kampung* house typically is approached only by family and close neighbours, and even then, adult males often will not approach the back door of a house unless they live in it.

The front and back doors of a *kampung* house are crucial to maintaining the ties that make community. Their use goes to the heart of the house and its role in the symbolic order, in the gender and kinship systems, and in the reproduction not only of the household but the community.

HOUSE/HOUSEHOLD/HOME

The back door in Java opens onto and out of domestic space, a space whose constitution is bound up with local exchanges, national projects, *kampung* kin networks, gendered labour, and the everyday work of the state. And yet, the domestic proves to be a difficult space to define. Its components include the complications of kinship, the constraints and freedoms of built form, and the moral valence of appropriate home life. As I sorted through the complications of the domestic in Java, I encountered three separate, but frequently overlapping, literatures that can be summarized as dealing with the house, the household, and the home. Naming these literatures in this way is not meant to imply that these are always coherent subdisciplines or fields of study but instead to gloss the relatively separate issues analyzed.

The house as a structure that has a symbolic as well as an actual form has been the subject of much recent work, particularly in Southeast Asia.[8] Some researchers have analyzed the house as a particular kinship system, while others have concentrated on the built form of houses, a line of inquiry in keeping with recent work on space and place in anthropology. *Kampung* houses, the spaces between them, and their relationship to community and kinship are considered in Chapter Three.

The term "household" is used widely in economic anthropology as well as development literature. The word serves as a historical marker for the change from treating the family as a functioning economic unit with unified goals to the acknowledgment that the family may actually comprise different economic strategies, not to mention purses, by generation and gender, among other things. The critiques of feminists and the failure of development schemes has led to the frequent use of household as the preferred designation for a site of complex economic and exchange strategies. Chapter Four takes up the description of the *kampung* as a form of social reproduction responsive to state-driven development initiatives and an international division of labour. The role of the household as an economic unit is considered. Both the *kampung* and the individual household are treated as sites of mediation, contention, and conformity. Particular emphasis is devoted to the effects of Indonesia's national housewives organization and local government administration.

Home is used here to invoke the sentimental and moral aspects of domestic space. As its use in the English language suggests, the home is more than the house and the household. The Indonesian national housewives organization, PKK, has goals as diverse as disseminating birth control, increasing literacy, and promoting household crafts production. It also includes a powerful message about the contours of the morally appropriate Indonesian home with its stay-at-home mother and two children, not to mention its embrace of *Pancasila* (the government ideology), proper hygiene, and reproduction of state values. In Chapter Five, the ingredients of the appropriate Indonesian home are described along with the moral map of the *kampung*. The historical trajectory of domesticity in Europe and Anglo-America and the contrast between *kampung* sentiment and state ideologies of proper domesticity, citizenship, and motherhood confirms the centrality of social reproduction in human life, and what is at stake in controlling it.

This triptych of approaches that I have glossed as house, household, and home, is a set of partial ingredients for understanding domestic space in Java and Indonesia. As I suggested above, however, domestic space cannot be isolated from pull of community and the practice of the state, and that is the larger goal of the following ethnography: to understand how domestic space, community, and state produce a particular lived culture in the *kampung*.

It was living in a house in a Javanese *kampung* that gave me the purchase I needed to understand how my neighbours were living in the state, the community, and family. It was through watching them negotiate the complications of kin, the requirements of national citizenship, and the ties of *kampung* community that I came to see the domestic project at the centre of state formation and the state rule at the centre of the domestic.

As it turns out, our missing back door was an entrance. It was through this door and its importance to our *kampung* neighbours that I gained the most important glimpses of *kampung* community and family life.

NOTES

1. *Bu* is the short form of the honorific *Ibu*, or mother, used for older and respected women. *Pak* is the short form of *Bapak* or father; *Mbak* is sister, and *Mas* is brother. All the names used here are pseudonyms.

2. Unless indicated otherwise, all foreign words are in Bahasa Indonesia, the national language of Indonesia.

3. *Pancasila* is the state ideology of Indonesia which includes five principles that are used to guide all official action: monotheism, nationalism, humanism, social justice, and democracy. In 1983, legislation was introduced requiring all political parties to adopt *Pancasila* as their sole ideological basis (Robison 1993:44).

4. Before beginning a description of the origins and evolution of PKK, it should be noted that the sources on PKK are not consistent, including the government's own publications, and the majority of women I interviewed, even those involved in PKK, were similarly fuzzy on the details. It is clear that PKK has gone through various bureaucratic shufflings, and a completely accurate picture of these shifts is probably impossible given the contradictory sources. The following discussion follows closely Julia Suryakusuma's 1991 article, which appears to be the clearest presentation of the general chronology of events around the development of PKK. Other sources included various PKK mimeographs and publications and Gerke (1992), Wolf (1992) N. Sullivan (1994), and Wieringa (1993).

5. *Pembinaan Kesejahteraan Keluarga* has been defined in various ways. A common translation has been Family Welfare Movement, but it is more literally translated as Guidance for the Prosperous Family. The second translation is more in keeping with PKK's character as a public administrative structure with quasi-private aims. In fact, the name actually changed at one point from "program" to "*pembinaan*," "implying more guidance and control and indicating clearly the role that state had in mind for PKK" (Suryakusuma 1991:56). PKK does not have the character of popular activism suggested by the term movement. Instead, it represents an organizational structure that extends from the President of the Republic of Indonesia down to very small units of local administration.

6. See Chapter Two, p. 35-36, for fuller description of administrative structure.

7. Quite the opposite of the Western experience, televisions have appeared in Javanese homes in advance of the telephone. Indeed, most *kampung* houses I visited in 1992–93 had a radio or a television, but only one or two had a telephone. This lack of a phone culture has worked to preserve some forms of community and politesse that are missing now in the West, where the drop-in visit is relatively rare.

8. See Fox (1993); Waterson (1990); Carsten and Hugh-Jones (1995); Gillespie (2000); and MacDonald (1987).

Chapter Two

Kampung

In the earliest morning a clean white lighthouse on an islet was seen ahead, and as the sun rose, bluish mountains came up from the sea, grew in height, outlined themselves, and then stood out, detached volcanic peaks of most lovely lines, against the purest pale-blue sky; soft clouds floated up and clung to the summits; the blue and green at the water's edge resolved itself into groves and lines of palms; and over sea and sky and the wonderland before us was all the dewy freshness of dawn in Eden. It looked very truly the "gem" and the "pearl of the East," this "Java Major" of the ancients, and the Djawa of the native people, which has called forth more extravagant praise and had more adjectives expended on it than any other one island in the world. (Scidmore 1986[1899]:17)

ORDINARY PEOPLE

The people I worked and lived with were ordinary. They were not dancers, musicians, mystics, or court people. They were not the movers and shakers of the modern Indonesian nation-state. Neither were they the desperately poor. They were not the quintessential Javanese peasant toiling in a rice field. They could not have been less noteworthy, in terms of the usual Javanese ethnographic subject. They were the every man and every woman of modern Indonesia. They were neither spatially nor economically marginal. They were and are the innards of Java and of Indonesia. People such as these working class citizens of a *kampung* neighbourhood in Central Java have profound importance for what Indonesia is today and where it is going. It is their very normality, typicality, ordinariness—and thus ethnographic invisibility (Rosaldo 1989; Smith 1974)—that makes them of interest to me.

KAMPUNG RUMAH PUTRI

If you arrive in Yogya, as it is known colloquially, at the main railroad station or at the airport and ask to be taken to *Rumah Putri*, your request will be understood immediately. If not, you must only explain that it is near the southwest corner of the sultan's palace and your driver will know where to go. Although Yogya is filled with *kampung*, the locations of established *kampung* are a matter of common knowledge critical to understanding the social map of the city. *Kampung Rumah Putri* is not the most well known area of the city by any means, but it does form part of the established memory of most city dwellers.

Kampung have a variety of faces. In one sense, they are neighbourhoods, spatially defined as residential in contrast to the busy city streets that bound them. In another sense, they are part of an administrative structure that includes both urban and rural areas and extends from small groups of contiguous households up to the provincial level. Just as significantly for residents, these named spatial units are markers of a particular style of life, one whose meaning differs to insiders as opposed to outsiders.

Kampung Rumah Putri, by all definitions, is anchored at its northeast corner by the intersection at the southwest of the Yogyakarta *kraton*. This busy intersection sees heavy traffic south to the productive agricultural areas of Bantul and north towards the city centre, with its administrative buildings, Dutch colonial architecture, and monuments to Yogya's role in the war for independence. The long stretch of the famed street Jalan Malioboro reaches from the Sultan's palace due north toward Merapi, the active volcano that serves as a powerful symbol of Yogya's special mystical and cultural status. The main east-west road near *Kampung Rumah Putri* is likewise a large, heavily trafficked one which serves as part of the bus routes around the city with connections to the main routes beyond it. As a transportation hub for the region, Yogya is the link between the rural countryside and the network of rail and bus lines to other regions in Java. The city itself calls to mind a kind of crossroads between Dutch colonial charm, a nostalgia for high Javanese culture of the court, and a pragmatic modern approach to the social and economic changes in Indonesia since Independence.

Most of the city's *becak* (pedicab) drivers know *Rumah Putri* as a spot on a well-defined tourist route that includes a long-running daily *wayang* performance and a puppet maker's shop in the *kampung*. Yogyakarta is famous as a centre for the arts, including performing arts, such as *gamelan* (gong-based orchestra), *wayang* (shadow puppets), and dance, as well as craft industries of silver and batik. The Yogya *kraton* (sultan's palace) actively supports such court arts. The *kraton* itself is the seat for one of the last remaining sultanates in Indonesia. For this reason, Yogya is a frequent destination for tourists. The city is also known as *kota mahasiswa*, or city of students, because of the number of colleges in the area, particularly Universitas Gadjah Mada, the oldest and second largest public university in Indonesia.

The named unit *Kampung Rumah Putri* has a number of official coordinates, and *kampung* insiders are proficient in moving between the various definitions of the *kampung* known as *Rumah Putri*, depending on the context. For example, the name *Rumah Putri* is used for two levels of administrative units, the *lingkungan* (sub-village unit) and the *kelurahan* (village unit).

The name *Rumah Putri* was also used for the *rukun kampung* (RK), a defunct administrative unit with a continued resonance that adds to the confusion about the name and the limits of *kampung* community.

Neither the general area known to outsiders nor the official definitions of *lingkungan* and *kelurahan* entirely correspond to the area defined by residents as *Rumah Putri*, who are nonetheless aware of both the official definitions and the vaguer definitions of outsiders. *Kampung Rumah Putri* is often identified by its residents with its presumed connections to the *kraton* as witnessed by a decaying house structure at the end of my street, what had once been a large, imposing house of royal design within a walled compound. Popular opinion was that the name of the *kampung* comes from this house, and it has been variously interpreted as evidence for a direct connection to the *kraton*.[1]

According to an official history of the area (Salamun 1989/1990), *Rumah Putri* was the seat of a *Nayaka*, a high ranking cabinet minister, in 1855. Reportedly this minister along with several others were under the supervision of a *Bupati Nayaka Lebet*, a regency cabinet minister responsible for the city of Yogyakarta. The house associated with the *Nayaka* was built for his daughter during the reign of Hamengkubuwana VII (1877–1921), according to her great grand-daughter, who still resides in the *kampung*. Royal succession runs through the males (although this is not always true in Java by any means), and as the story goes, the house was given back to the *kraton* on the *Nayaka*'s daughter's death. Other residents reported various versions of this story, and the royal connections of the *kampung* figure prominently in all accounts.

According to some *kampung* residents, early inhabitants were *abdi dalem*, the loyal servants of the *kraton* responsible for everything from serving tea to lighting lanterns (*abdi dalem* come in all ranks, and presumably those living in the *kampung* were lower ranking servants). One older woman, Bu Hartono, recalled the days when these *abdi dalem* were a common sight, in their traditional *batik* sarongs, walking through the *kampung* on the way to the *kraton*. Back then, she said, people used polite Javanese, saying *mongo, mongo* to those passing by, which can be translated in this instance as "please, go ahead," as a response to someone asking forgiveness for passing in front of someone else.[2]

Several *kampung* residents reported their own royal connections, typically through relatives who had worked as *abdi dalem*. We were introduced early on to Pak Parno who volunteered to teach us Javanese including the highest level, *krama inggil*, the register commonly used at the *kraton*. He was able to do this because he too had served as an *abdi dalem* at one point. His abilities were the object of much pride on the part of his relatives. Loyalty and pride in the *kraton* are typical of Yogyakarta, and as in many *kampung*, its royal connections, however tenuous, are critical to how *Rumah Putri* is understood by its residents.

Kampung Rumah Putri extends south and west from the *kraton* and city, blending into rice fields to the west and south. In addition to work in the palace, early residents of the *kampung* were involved in agriculture, mixing court and countryside in their daily lives. This *kampung* provided a place to keep a foot in both worlds, agricultural as well as crafts and service industries.

One important aspect of *Kampung Rumah Putri*'s local history is the presence of a large Catholic Church just outside the main entrance which is marked by an archway bearing the *kampung's* name. A residence for Catholic sisters is located within the kampung as well. Like the rest of Indonesia, Muslims are the majority in this *kampung*, but the Catholic community is large and noticeable. Residents described how a particular priest (*romo*) shielded residents from the Japanese during their occupation of Java. For this reason, the sense of loyalty to the church is quite strong. Neighbourhood Catholic prayer meetings are held on a rotating monthly basis throughout the *kampung*.

Although the administrative units identified with *Rumah Putri* and its *kraton* connections have meaning for residents, the limits of *Kampung Rumah Putri* for its inhabitants are, in the final instance, ineffable. What follows here is an attempt to chart how "*kampung*" has come to mean home community with connections both to particular histories of the state administration and to the experience of everyday life in these neighbourhoods. While administrative units have structured the limits of *kampung* in some contexts, networks of exchange, support, family ties, face to face relations, and habitual use define *kampung* limits as well.

MAPPING THE *KAMPUNG*

Before coming to Java, I had never heard of *kampung* and I had no idea what they were. The only *kampung* I had seen before coming to *Kampung Rumah Putri* had been the congested areas downtown, where houses and shacks were squeezed behind the big houses and stores lining the main streets. In Yogya's centre, for example, there is a bridge that allows one to see the stratigraphy of wealth and poverty, from the luxury of the street-level houses to the crowded small lean-tos that border the polluted waters of the river. This kind of densely packed poverty is the conventional reference for the word *kampung*.[3] Entering *Rumah Putri* along its wide main street, I had no impression of the dense neighbourhoods I had glimpsed down the narrow alleys or *gang* that lead off the main streets in the centre of Yogya where the major arteries feed a "labyrinth of lesser alleys threading through the body of the block, gradually dwindling to a web of dim dirt paths that can only be traversed single file with shoulders brushing the walls to each side" (J. Sullivan 1992:42).

After passing the public meeting house and the market near the entrance to *Kampung Rumah Putri*, I could see that the houses along its main street were large and permanent, many made of concrete with permanent tiled roofs and having space between neighbours (see Figure 2.1). The overall impression of the area was of a calm and peaceful neighbourhood. Its lanes and alleys were shaded by many trees. Although most of the roadways were much narrower than that from the main entrance, the *kampung* was crossed by several roadways that were wide enough for a single car. Unlike the more densely packed *kampung* in the centre of Yogya described by Guinness (1991), J. Sullivan (1992), and N. Sullivan (1994), *Kampung Rumah Putri* seemed almost rural; there were still areas of open space absent from the downtown *kampung*. In fact, there was an open space across from the rental house with a substantial growth of papaya and bamboo, and within easy walking distance, there were the terraced padi rice fields, or *sawah*, so emblematic of the Javanese countryside.

Figure 2.1
View of the street in *Kampung Rumah Putri*. (Photo by S. Ferzacca.)

Living in the *kampung* became a project of learning to see it differently, of learning to see the social sediments manifest in the houses, lanes, doorways, corners, and open spaces. Just as I would come to understand the significance of both the social and physical architecture of our own house, I would come to see the neighbourhood in a different way: not from the outside in but from the inside out. I would come to see beyond the nice, shady middle-class neighbourhood with permanent houses along wide streets, to the complex network of narrow, dirt paths running behind and between houses leading to small lean-tos of bamboo housing large families. I would no longer be able to see the cement-walled house of the seamstress at the end of the street without also seeing its one-roomed, dirt-floored bamboo extension that housed a widower relative and his two children. His bare dirt front yard was approximately five metres square, larger than the actual shelter, and taken up with the family's well and his *becak* or pedicab, the means of his occasional livelihood. It was at the corner of two main alleyways, and yet initially, I literally did not see his dwelling and had no idea that three people lived there.

My social mapping of the *kampung* and my ability to see what was before my very eyes developed along with my social relations and experience in the *kampung*. As time went on and my fieldwork came to centre on *kampung* life, my vision adjusted to see how many people lived in small nooks and crannies in and around these homes eking out marginal incomes and making do. I was no longer able not to see the tiny kerosene lights at night that revealed the numbers of people pressed into small areas of the *kampung*. As my census interviewing continued I stopped feeling surprised to find a tiny home with a family or perhaps a single elderly woman in a place I had not even identified as habitable. The open spaces of my initial impression gave way to a complex cartography of larger homes and yards with smaller homes accreted around them. In many ways, this pattern reiterates the *wong cilik* (little people) versus *wong gedhe* (big people) or *wong gedhongan* pattern (*gedhong* is the Javanese word meaning building in the sense of a permanent cement structure; J. Sullivan 1992; Guinness 1991). Instead of the larger homes defining the outside boundaries of the *kampung*, the interior of the *kampung* revealed a pattern of larger homes with smaller homes crowded around and in-between them. This pattern of occupation suggests not only the complex mix of lives hidden behind large houses in *Kampung Rumah Putri*, but it reiterates metaphorically the reality of urban life hidden by government rhetoric of ideal community life as organized in the city (Graaf and Pigeaud 1984:172; Pires 1967 [1512–1515]:173; Raffles 1978[1817]:83; Scidmore 1989[1899]:37).

THE GREAT ARCH OF *KAMPUNG* FORMATION[4]

To talk about *kampung* in Java is more than to talk about an urban neighbourhood, although that is perhaps its simplest referent. The history of its meaning describes a transit from ethnic enclave and wealthy neighbourhood, to royal guild areas and protectorates of nobles, to village-like native quarters and conduits of administrative and political control, to walled-in slums and cohesive urban community. In some fashion, all of this historical residue remains within *kampung* culture, and a capsule history of the term *kampung* shows that it includes notions of separation by ethnicity, occupation, and class. For example, *wong kampung* or *kampung* person can suggest humbleness and community spirit or it may connote poverty and a clannish, inward-looking attitude towards others. It equally calls to mind notions of rural consensus and cooperation and hotbeds of political fervour among the disenfranchised: devout Muslims, the unemployed, the very poor. *Kampung* life evokes a safe haven from the pressures of modern life and an emphasis on old patterns of mutual care and attentiveness, but it likewise suggests a narrow and suspicious watchfulness by neighbours and kin.

While *wong kampungan* (Javanese), or people with a characteristic *kampung* mentality, carries pejorative connotations for those who live in newer suburbs or in suburban housing areas known as *perumahan*, for its inhabitants, *kampung* resonates with the sense of safety, neighbourliness, and a home made through daily practises of exchange and interaction. What emerges most strongly from both accounts, is the sense of boundedness, of external differentiation and internal homogeneity.

As I began my analysis of the *kampung* and tried to explain it to others, I realized that *kampung* exist on a number of levels: as an administrative unit, a set of streets and houses, a group of people living in close association, a lifestyle, a social formation, a class fraction, a structure of feeling (Williams 1977), and a space where all of these combine. Although the word itself does not gloss the meaning of both people and place as does pueblo, for example, it does resonate with place, class, and people. Picking apart its significance proved to be a difficult part of my work, and it remains unfinished here. The brief history of its usage offered in the following is only the barest indicator of its complexity.

Ethnic Enclave

> The Tjina, or China, and the Arab kampongs, are show-places to the stranger in the curious features of life and civic government they present. Each of these foreign kampongs, or villages, is under the charge of a captain or commander, whom the Dutch authorities hold responsible for the order and peace of their compatriots, since they do not allow to these yellow colonials so-called "European freedom"—an expression which constitutes a sufficient admission of the existence of "Asiatic restraint." Great wealth abides in both these alien quarters, whose leading families have been there for generations, and have absorbed all retail trade, and as commission merchants, money-lenders, and middlemen have garnered great profits and earned the hatred of Dutch and Javanese alike. (Scidmore 1989[1899]:37)

A 1948 New Century Dictionary's etymology of compound refers to the Malay word *kampong*, meaning enclosure, from which this definition is derived: "In the East Indies, etc., an enclosure containing a residence or other establishment of Europeans." In a similar fashion, the first meanings of *kampung* in the pre-colonial and colonial era in Java and surrounding islands were associated with the neighbourhoods of foreign trading populations (Chinese, Arab, South Asian, Persian, and other Southeast Asian) in port cities along Java's north coast and in other places.[5] "Harbor towns contained mercantile communities of mixed ancestry, dwelling in wards

of their own and maintaining more or less friendly relations among themselves" (Graaf and Pigeaud 1984:172). Deepening Dutch occupation reinforced this trend. In the sixteenth century, as the trading port of Jacatra,
as it was known at the time, became the city of Batavia, its planner, Jan
Peterzoon Coen, "began to lay out a new town on the model of a fortified
European city" (Cobban 1976:48). Ethnic enclaves developed in a fashion
reminiscent of a medieval Dutch city with a network of canals and "stuffy
tightly packed and many storied houses" (McGee 1967:49) designed "to
recall the images of Amsterdam in the minds of Europeans" (Cobban
1976:49).

Farther inland, a mix of defined foreign and indigenous residential
areas were present in native areas such as the fourteenth century Majapahit kingdom, although the Chinese and Moorish neighbourhoods were
not yet called *kampung*, but instead, *pacinan* and *pakojan*, respectively
(Pigeaud 1960:477). Raffles noted in the nineteenth century that Chinese
dwellings (*umah gedong*) doubled as residence and place of business and
were built of brick, in stark contrast to the native dwellings of rattan and
bamboo (Raffles 1978[1817]:90).

Guild Neighbourhoods and Royal Protectorate

> The Malay word kampung is generally taken to mean 'village' but in Java it
> is more commonly applied to urban entities, to parts of towns and cities.
> Initially, it meant 'compound', most typically the walled yards, gardens, and
> residences of well-to-do families (Reid 1979:5) and it was long used thus in
> Yogyakarta for the residential compounds of princes, nobles, and other dig-
> nitaries. In fact, the Sultan's palace itself was once recognized as a complex
> of kampungs. (J. Sullivan 1992:20)

For both the inland native capitals and the cosmopolitan port cities, *kampung* appear to have been associated with urban centres. Yet, urbanism was
not a straightforward phenomenon in Java. Early travellers noted the
blurred boundaries between city and country. Raffles reported "an assem-
blage or group of numerous villages, rather than what in European countries would be called a town or city" (1978[1817]:92), and according to
Reid, early European arrivals to the coastal cities of Southeast Asia
remarked that the boundaries between "city and countryside seemed
almost non-existent" (1988:240). This may explain why, despite its early
usage as the walled-in residential compounds of well-to-do urban families
of various ethnic identities, the Malay usage of *kampung* means village.

Yet another influence on the meaning and weight of *kampung* comes
from its association with the occupationally stratified neighbourhoods
associated with the sultanates of Central Java and their palaces. The Sultan's palace in Yogya was built after the Giyanti Treaty of 1755 (Koentjaraningrat 1989; J. Sullivan 1992) when the separate sultanates of
Yogyakarta and Surakarta (Solo) were established. During its construction,

enclosing walls were built as fortification around various court structures including the living quarters of queens, concubines, servants, the military, crafts people, artisans, and musicians. These living quarters were referred to as *kampung*, according to Steinberg (1971:82), and the occupationally differentiated areas of this "town within a town" (Rutz 1987:74) were named for their specific function or duty in relationship to the Sultan. So for example, the *abdi dalem* or servants to the Sultan who were responsible for palace lamps (*silir*) lived in a *kampung* known as *Siliran*.

Although the areas outside the *kraton* walls may have retained a distinctly rural flavour, *kampung* associated with the Chinese merchant community (*pacinan*) developed along the north-south road to the north of the *kraton*. This area eventually became the famed *Jalan Malioboro*, favoured shopping spot for tourists and the busiest street in Yogyakarta. These early *kampung* outside the walls were also associated with specific occupations or services offered. Their early functions are likewise shown in the names they carry to this day: "Pajeksan—the place of the palace prosecutors (*jaksa*); Gandekan—home of the court heralds (*gandek*); Dagen—the woodworkers' quarters (*undagi*); Jlagran—the stonemasons' quarter (*jlogro*) (J. Sullivan 1992:23; Selosoemardjan 1962). In addition, there were *kampung* associated with military encampments and several other ethnic enclaves for people such as the Bugis from Sulawesi, South Asians, and later Dutch colonials. Separate *kampung* existed for Muslim officials, those who helped take care of the mosque, and the "descendants of Muhammad" (J. Sullivan 1992:23).

In addition to an association with ethnic and occupational difference, the internal administration of *kampung* was established early on as a consequence of the tax farming of the surrounding countryside. *Nagara* (realm or city) refers to the exemplary court centres found in Yogyakarta and Solo, including the Sultan's palace and the area within the walls of the *kraton*. The area outside the *nagara*, known as the *nagaragung* (greater realm), was not administered by the court but instead was split among princes and high nobles (*patuh*) whose control over their lands or *kabekelan* was mainly confined to tax farming through their professional *bekel* (tax collector and manager; C. Geertz 1960, 1965; Koentjaraningrat 1989; J. Sullivan 1992). The nobles themselves were required to live within the *kraton* or on nearby lands granted to them by the king. In part this "honour" resulted from royal fears that these loosely allied nobles could quickly become potential competitors (cf. Adas 1981), and thus they were not permitted to live outside the *nagara* because of the danger they posed as potential rivals to the sultan. They relied instead on their *bekel*, who also maintained official compounds (*kampung krajan*) in the city, to see to their lands (1992:24).

Kampung in Yogya may have always existed as "elements of a rational administrative plan and de facto units of a state system" (Sullivan

1992:24), despite the fact that the *kampung* outside the *kraton* walls were considered the same as all the surrounding countryside and had no formal administrative structure and no tax base to provide it. These *kampung* were expected to be self-contained and to govern themselves internally. The *nagara* and its *nagaragung* are represented as two concentric spheres, the former surrounded by the latter. Yet, the area of *kampung* outside the *kraton* walls also served as buffer and mediation between the court and the countryside. This nested configuration lends credence to observations of no absolute or discernible division between rural and urban spatially, administratively or sentimentally.

Village Administration

> As before, the kampung chiefs were neither formally appointed nor paid and owed their positions primarily to their social ranking, popularity, or other personal entitlements to deference. They needed the approval of the *assisten wedono* and their superiors but they also needed the approval and backing of the kampung members who selected them. They had to secure that civil order was maintained in their neighbourhoods and to assist with other bureaucratic chores—securing and providing information, passing on government directives—but they were also expected to speak for kampung members, and to mediate for them with higher authorities. (J. Sullivan 1992:33; see also Dipodiningrat 1956:39–40)

Over time the city of Yogya grew through expansion. The *kampung* outside the walls expanded with growing numbers of state functionaries, courtiers, and their servants, and the *kraton* served to attract various producers and service-producers. Eventually, this growth led to what J. Sullivan calls the "vulgarization" of the *kampung*. "[A]t some stage they lost their original cachet and gained their present-day caste [sic] as residential quarters of the 'little people' (*wong cilik*); 'home communities' in the view of the *wong cilik* themselves, 'slums' in the view of many 'big people' (*wong gede*) (J. Sullivan 1992:25).

There is not much evidence for how such a transition occurred because court chroniclers had little interest in urban *kampung*. The change in the nature of *kampung* was, in some measure, a function of changing relations between the *kraton* and *kampung* as new *kampung* emerged based not on function or occupation but merely on residence. As such, *kampung* lost their "genteel connotations," and eventually those who lived in *kampung* became known as *wong kampung*, "which, in elite circles translates as 'slum dweller' and in *kampung* circles denotes membership of a revered community" (ibid., 26).[6]

The association of *kampung* with urban poverty and benign rusticity was evident among the Dutch colonialists. A 1920's report on town development in the Indies, described the urban masses as "still three-quarters agrarian in their thinking," not yet fully urban but rather, attempting "to find expression for their rustic simplicity within an urban setting (cited in J. Sullivan 1992:31). Various reforms subtly changed structures of administration as well as sentiment for rural areas and their urban reincarnations, the new *kampung*. For example, during the British interregnum of 1811 to 1816, Thomas Stamford Raffles, Lieutenant-Governor of Java, launched a comprehensive modernization of traditional property rights and land-tenure practices (J. Sullivan 1992:29; Furnivall 1976:67–78). It was Raffles, according to Furnivall, who consolidated the position of the village as the basic rural administrative unit outside the *kraton*, although this process was begun before his tenure and continued after the end of British rule.

Two other important moments in the development of *kampung* were the successive elaborations of administration outside the *kraton* by the Dutch and then the changes made during the Japanese occupation. It was during the liberal period of reforms by the Dutch that an attempt was made to standardize administrative structures in the rural areas and also in urban *kampung*, yielding two effects: (1) the constitution of units that were not commensurate in size but in power, and (2) the establishment of a level of administrative power that was two-faced. It was during the reforms of 1917 and 1918 that a fundamental disjuncture between power oriented upward toward formal administrative structures and that oriented downward toward an imagined community of equals was established (Anderson 1991). The character of political power in the *kampung* and its relationship to idealized peasant communities will be considered in another section below. For now a brief description of the current structure is helpful.

At the time of my fieldwork, 1992-93, the Republic of Indonesia was divided into 27 *propinsi* or provinces. Each province is headed by a governor, and the subdivisions of the province, the *kabupaten* or regencies, are headed by *bupati*. Regencies correspond to large cities, as in the case of the Yogyakarta area, and sometimes comprise a large rural area. Within the *kabupaten*, therefore, there may be several towns and hamlets. The *kabupaten* are further divided into *kecamatan*, equivalent to wards, administered by a *camat*. The wards are then divided into *kelurahan* or "villages" administered by a *lurah* (this summary of the offices follows J. Sullivan 1992:134; see N. Sullivan 1994:63 for placement of PKK within the local government).

Below the *kelurahan*, the lowest level of paid civil service in Indonesia, are the RW (*rukun warga*, harmonious citizens) and the RT (*rukun tetangga*, harmonious neighbours) divisions of the city (the countryside differs slightly). The RT division typically comprises some 20–40 households, and there are some six RT divisions in a single RW. The precursor of the RW was the RK (*rukun kampung*, harmonious *kampung*), a larger division that comprised several RW in one large unit, but this had changed in the mid-1980s, at least in Java. The RT, RW, and formerly the RK, are headed by unpaid volunteers who are conceived by the government and most residents to be popularly elected *kampung* figures.

John Sullivan describes the civil-administrative system as ending at the level of the village or *kelurahan*, and the two tiers below the level of *kelurahan* (formerly equivalent to RK and RT and now RW and RT) as being "completely outside the state apparatus" and purely "non-political" (1992:135). He goes on to say that from the perspective of the state, the *kampung* sphere is an entirely separate entity from the government, although *kampung* may support higher tiers of government. Yet, he cites a 1983 Ministry of Internal Affairs regulation to the effect that these lower levels or tiers are "social organizations acknowledged and founded by government to maintain and perpetuate the values of Indonesian social life ... also to help increase the smooth execution of governmental, developmental, and social tasks" (cited in J. Sullivan 1992:136).

From my own work in the *kampung* (and indeed from Sullivan's own quote), it was clear that these lower levels of administration are nonetheless part of the administrative structure since these popularly selected leaders perform official functions for the Indonesian government. Moreover, they are highly political because they involve not only perceived prestige and status in the *kampung*, but also because the Pak RW (Father RW) and Pak RT (Father RT) are presumed to be conduits to government help and also to serve as redistribution points for other *kampung* social goods. The articulation between these lower level unpaid officials and the civil service administration is also demonstrated in the elections of officials. The heads of the RT choose the head of the larger RW section but this "process takes place under the direction of the Lurah, including the final approval of candidates" (J. Sullivan 1992:136). That is, a member of the paid civil service has oversight over these popularly selected officials.

It is at the most local levels of administration that differences between rural and urban sectors are apparent. This point of slippage between paid civil service and local positions held due to prestige and status becomes a key point in the articulation between local and extra-local power, which in turn has major effects for the functioning of communities in the wider polity.

The Stated Community

> The head of this group of neighbouring families assumed leadership in their own affairs, was responsible for their good behaviour, had to turn in reports of any doubtful acts and surrender any wanted individual to the government. (Benedict 1946:82–83)

The administrative structure evident in the *kampung* is the legacy of many attempts at defining community and effective governance in Indonesia, perhaps particularly in Java. Groups of neighbours organized for cooperation and administrative control owe more than a little to a long history of colonial imaginings about the existence of the cooperative peasant village as a kind of natural community. Indeed, the relevance of the ideal community has been re-"stated" across colonial governments, Japanese war-time occupation, the newly independent national state, and the modernizing New Order regime.

Arguments about the antecedents and influences of the neighbourhood system are not unrelated to arguments about the presence of an autonomous, self-governing, egalitarian Javanese village. Whatever its antecedents, this urban administrative structure fits rather too nicely with both colonial conceptions of village administration and sociological perceptions of the pre-colonial past. It is no coincidence that the pre-colonial *negara* (state) of C. Geertz (1980) and the galactic polity described by Tambiah (1985) are premised on a powerful central authority with tributary relations that reach only to the level of the autonomous community. This model bears a striking resemblance to the colonial forms of rule, which were also based on control only to the level of the village headman. This idea of village and state persists despite critiques of its basis in faulty historical analysis and orientalist models (Dumont 1966; Goh 1998; Kemp 1988; Rigg 1994).

The classic statement about the Javanese village's relative autonomy and inward cohesion is Clifford Geertz's theory of agricultural involution (1963). The elegance and simplicity of his argument is one of the reasons for its persistence. In essence, he argued, the Javanese rural sector did not innovate because rice terraces could absorb more and more labour as they were driven harder under colonial administration. Instead, they became more internally elaborate, or involuted, because they were organized through egalitarian, cooperative rural groups. Geertz's theory has been thoroughly critiqued for its hypostasised model of peasant cooperation that left out the differentiation within agricultural production.[7] That is, Geertz's idea of shared poverty implied more homogeneity and equality than actually existed in the *desa* (countryside), and it was here, in the proposition that peasant production was egalitarian, communal and locally integrative that Geertz elides the historical character of these relations (cf. Lansing 1991 on Bali).

As more recent historical analysis on Java demonstrates, "[c]olonial authorities saw what they wanted to see, and this differed from era to era, historical justification being sought for each new interpretation" (Breman 1988:5). The work of Jan Breman on pre-colonial Java (1980, 1983, 1988) and that of Michael Adas on peasant resistance in pre-colonial and colonial Southeast Asia (1981) suggests that the nature of the pre-colonial state was such that the village level and the household were never entirely penetrated by the state's reach. Consequently, an intermediate level of authority was needed to account for peasant production and taxation under colonialism. What this more recent work suggests is that there was never an autonomous, egalitarian, closed, corporate peasant community sharing its poverty in pre-colonial Java but rather, a complex pattern of dependency relations (cf. Wolf 1957).[8] In other words, Dutch colonial administration created the phenomenon of a timeless rural village that was democratic and cooperative by instituting a level of administration based on its existence. More complex relationships of inequality, mixed land tenure, and patronage were then concealed by the institution of villages for colonial counting and control (Goh 1998).

The effects of Japanese wartime occupation on the administration of urban areas show some interesting parallels with the ideal peasant village. According to most sources, the RK/RT system is a remnant of Japanese occupation. According to J. Sullivan, the Japanese Sixteenth Army introduced this "precursor of the *rukun tetangga* to Java in 1944" (1992:136). The Japanese found this organization of neighbor groups to be invaluable in Japan and thus a likely candidate for Java as well. These small residential groups were organized to facilitate "tasks of maintaining social order, gathering taxes, controlling and deploying labour forces" (J. Sullivan 1992:136).

The *rukun tetangga* or RT grouping has been compared to the Japanese *goningumi*, a group of five to ten households, later replaced by the *tonarigumi* or neighbourhood group. "[T]here were around ten households to each *tonarigumi* and every 10–20 *tonarigumi* were formed into *burakukai* (village associations) in rural areas, *chonaikai* (neighbourhood associations) in urban areas" (J. Sullivan 1992:138). J. Sullivan, concludes that this cell organization "probably gave rise to the classic image of Japanese neighbourship ... which means roughly that your best friends are the households to the immediate right and left and the three directly opposite," a concept still acknowledged in parts of modern Japan (1992:137; see also Bestor 1989; Falconeri 1976). Such groups of contiguous households have been described as a longstanding pattern of administrative organization in Japan and China (Antlov 1995; Benedict 1946; Bestor 1989; Falconeri 1976; Garon 1997; Kasza 1995; Keyes 1995; Reid 1988; J. Sullivan 1992).

In China, Japan, and then Java, this clustering of households into small groups was for the purposes not only of counting and control, but for the dissemination of information quickly and for mutual defence. In rural areas, it was also a system for gathering taxes and labour service. And yet, like the egalitarian village, these small neighbourhood groups were based on the presumption of state administration penetrating only to the level of a group of cooperating and contiguous households. Indeed, some argue that the *tonarigumi* system was merely an overlay on a much older traditional system of household cooperation and exchange that defined the autonomous village in Japan (Bestor 1989).

The crucial issue here, in addition to uncovering the imaginary in the stories of the Javanese peasant community, is the identification of a zone of slippage between the most local levels of social organization and any centralized political authority. The Janus-faced articulation between local community and the state is what creates its very mixed heritage. This middle ground where authority from above reaches down and local self-government rises up from below has had contradictory effects for Java. For example, the neighbourhood system implemented by the Japanese was actually used to shield individual Javanese from the worst abuses of the Japanese. Because local headmen were responsible for the head counts within their units, they were easily able to manipulate the number to hide people who could then be absorbed without detection into the community. In stark contrast, during the horror of the wave of killings that followed the alleged communist coup in 1965, neighbours reported suspected communists to local leaders who then reported their presence to the authorities. In this way, not only did local community administration serve to control and police neighbours, but petty, local grievances could become the justification for accusing another of being a communist. In the first case, the community closed to shield its members from repression; in the second, it opened itself to the worst of state terrorism.

A further reason why the idea of the self-governing small community with ties to the better, truer Javanese culture of the countryside (*desa*) persists was its re-creation and reproduction first through grassroots organizations in the era of independence and subsequently, in government programs of the New Order government of Suharto (1967–98). Schulte Nordholt (1987), in a nicely detailed piece on the creation of the *Lembaga Sosial Desa* (LSD, Village Social Institution) and its transformation into the *Lembaga Ketahanan Masyarakat Desa* (LKMD, Institution for the Maintenance of Village Society), highlights some of the contradictions in the construction of post-Independence community and its political relevance. In original intent, the LSD was supposed to be in the hands of rural people, and there was no connection to official administration. The post-World War II desire to return to simple agrarian values made sense in a time of drastic, dislocating social change, and it shared much with colonial and pre-colonial imaginings of rural Java as discussed above. Begun in the 1950s as a private effort to help poor rural villages help themselves, the LSD evolved from the efforts of several exceptional individuals to "activate the populace" on its own behalf (Schulte Nordholt 1987:49). The program was based on presumptions about "traditional" models of village cooperation and leadership with a thoroughly sociological view of "social institution" (which can be literally translated into Indonesia as *lembaga sosial*) lifted from Dutch social science (Schulte Nordholt 1987:50).

Ultimately, this organization of the countryside was taken over by the newly independent Indonesian state under its first president, Sukarno, and the LSD became the LKMD, part of a suite of programs developed to promote modernization. Today, the LKMD is conceived to be a grass-roots organization to mobilize the village populace for government programs. The ten sections of the LKMD are:

1) Security, defence and order, 2) Education and the comprehension and practical application of Pancasila, 3) Information, 4) Economics, 5) Development of infrastructure and environmental protection, 6) Religion, 7) Health population and family planning, 8) Youth, physical education, and art, 9) Welfare, and 10) PKK. (Suryakusuma 1991:58)

The state's imprimatur is clear in the inclusion of the state ideology, *Pancasila*, as it is in the very formalization of what was originally conceived to be a popular movement.

Under the New Order's developmentalist regime, the administration of community organization became a prime way to modernize, and the community form has been so useful in part because of its association with the ideal of the Javanese village. In the emergence of the LSD, the private work of a few dedicated people on behalf of the rural poor drew upon ideas of ideal communal self-help. This approach was taken up by the Indonesian government as a way to solve its problems building infrastructure, organizing development work, and delivering necessary social and infra-structural goods. Not surprisingly, the revolutionary potential of this community-level organization was diffused by its connection to official governance. Thus, its presumptive origins notwithstanding, the cooperative, cohesive, homogeneous, and democratic village assumed a bureaucratic life of its own, and until 2001, the LKMD structure was the prime vehicle for delivery of state programs to the rural populace. As suggested in Chapter One, PKK would come to be part of the LKMD structure. In this way, official government organization of the local was used to co-opt independent organizations of the countryside and women in order to administer these domains. Kasza (1995) has called such state order organizations formed through quasi-public means "administered mass organizations," which he sees as reflexive of state goals and directives. Despite its contradictory origins, the ideal community organization is now used to prevent popular power that might be contrary to state desires.

The association of *desa* life with the good and true Javanese culture is inherent in the Indonesian government's programs for local administration and development, such as PKK and LKMD. One lynchpin for this association is captured in the emphasis on *gotong royong*, a principle of mutual self-help generally associated with rural life that is actively embraced by sociological research and government propaganda (Bowen 1986). *Gotong royong* serves as a potent moral indicator for the city as well. *Gotong royong* and similar phrases such as *tolong-menolong* (mutual aid) are used frequently in government rhetoric to inspire cooperation and community spirit. The traits of cooperation and *gotong royong* are in fact built into Pancasila and the Ten Principle Programs of PKK.

The appeal to this sentiment for cooperation is not just official nostalgia for the rural past, it also serves to prod people into accepting this form of community as inherently Javanese and thus, inherently good. The breakdown of *gotong royong* was often cited by my *kampung* neighbours as an indicator of the changes in contemporary urban life. By referring to the rural past rhetorically, *gotong royong*'s emotional valence for the populace is heightened while it serves to validate the state's insistence that local communities are self-sustaining, and of course, it simultaneously allows greater state access and control. Even more, the ideal community so conceived is based on the presumption of equality which masks internal differentiation.

What I saw in my time in *Kampung Rumah Putri* was a mix of historical residue and sediments that, both administratively and imaginatively, produced a self-governing community of equals with popularly selected leaders. Citizens of so-called developed democracies frequently do not have the kind of representation and connection to administration represented by the RT/RW system as well as the LKMD and PKK. Yet, the uses of this administrative structure and lived social organization are never predictable. In many ways, *kampung* are a kind of "stated" community, and I use that term here to suggest two things. First, the image of the ideal community has been significantly tied up with state rule, whether it be the pre-colonial, colonial, occupying, post-independence, or modernizing state. In all cases, state rule seems to have required both the real community, as a form of social organization and administrative unit, and the imagined community, as a way to mobilize the populace. Second, these communities are stated as a rhetorical map of a nostalgic past and a modern future. The first meaning refers to the state-driven organization of local communities, and the second to the ideal community being pronounced by the state. Yet, whatever the original character and intent of the formation of this ideal type of community, it is the connection to *kampung* sentiment and its local use that gives it meaning in the life of local residents.

Home Community

The outgroup and the general distinction tend to be described by kampung people in rather simple spatial and economic terms. The outsiders, who mainly, though not exclusively, inhabit the better streetside homes in the neighbourhood, are classed as rich by the kampung which tends to view itself as not-rich if not exactly poor (which has unpleasant connotations in the kampung). While it is generally true that kampung people are poorer than most of their on-street neighbours, and packed into the spaces behind the on-street buildings, it is impossible to separate the two groups neatly on spatial or income lines. (J. Sullivan 1992:20)

Popular culture in Java is *kampung* culture in many ways. The modern *kampung* is typically associated with the lower-class. Patrick Guinness (1986) describes an opposition between so-called streetside society associated with the larger, more elaborate houses of the Dutch and the Chinese and the domain of the lower class *wong cilik* (Jv. little people) in the smaller crowded neighbourhoods behind them. Norma Sullivan (1994) emphasizes the self-definitions of *wong kampung* who set themselves off from *wong gedhongan* (*gedhong* meaning house in this instance and referring to larger, masonry houses that line larger streets). As John Sullivan describes the downtown *kampung* he studied, it was "a middling, unremarkable, unheroic sort of place" (1992:42). In urban Java, *kampung* have two aspects, an inward face and an outward one. Although conventionally understood as the densely populated settlements of the lower classes in Java, as well as many other parts of Indonesia and Southeast Asia, the boundaries of *kampung* are often defined as much through a kind of popular cognitive mapping based on everyday life of residents in their home community

The inhabitants may range from wealthy to poor, but the majority are informal sector workers, a significant number working at or near home. More recent descriptions of class in Indonesia suggest the continuing invisibility of the majority of *kampung* residents. Robison describes a segment of the middle class as populist, which includes "the sprawling mass of clerks, teachers and lower-level civil servants" (Robison 1996:88). Although many of the *kampung* folk I worked with correspond to Robison's description, many more are poorer people, working in a mix of informal and service sector jobs.[9] While not always the poorest in Indonesia's urban centres, *kampung* dwellers often lie at the boundaries of the formal and informal economies, in some cases resembling Marx's lumpenproletariat of prostitutes, beggars, and street performers, and at others, the labourers and home workers of early phases of industrialization, or ironically, the labour associated with the end of national industrial organization in late capitalism. In the neighbourhood where my work was centred, occupations ranged from market seller to puppet-maker, masseuse, seamstress, fibreglass statute maker, prostitute, bank clerk, teacher, small food stall owner, maker of traditional health tonics, day labourer, and house-based industry worker. In terms of home ownership, *kampung* residents may own land and houses but these are frequently fragmented into smaller and smaller pieces as parents die and split inheritance among children. Often, residents rent rooms or small houses on *kontrak.*

I use the term working class here quite deliberately, despite what seems its awkward fit with Indonesia's social and economic structure. Often depicted as displaying a feudal class structure, with royalty and the elite *priyayi* class at one extreme and the impoverished peasantry at the other, Indonesia's class composition has been changing since Independence in 1945. In its usage here, the conservative connotations of "working class" serve to mark this class fragment as distinct from the very poor and any putative middle class (cf. Robison 1996; Hadiz 1997). The lack of a true land-owing middle class or bourgeoisie is characteristic of Indonesia and many other parts of Southeast Asia. Signs of the emergence of a more broadly based "middle" class prompted Robison's analysis as it did Kahn's preliminary remarks on the anthropology of the emerging middle class in Southeast Asia (1991). Yet *kampung* class is a relevant social and economic category as much for how it captures a felt sentiment of social unity by *kampung* residents as for what it accomplishes for the Indonesian national economy.

Indeed, whatever the analytical perspective from the outside, from the inside, *kampung* resonate with ideas of a tradition of intimate home community, friendly cooperation, and mutual support. This particular idea of community reiterated in successive state administrations also has been enshrined in classic ethnographic descriptions of Java (Geertz 1960; H. Geertz 1961; Jay 1969; Keeler 1987). It is no exaggeration to suggest that Clifford Geetz's (1963) notion of shared poverty, whatever its limitations as a description of actual social relations, is an apt description of the how *kampung* dwellers describe life in these neighbourhoods. That is, masses of lower class and poor people share minimal resources while placing value on common social position and neighbourly exchange.

My own neighbours in *Rumah Putri* describe *kampung* life as better than life in other parts of the city. People help one another in the *kampung*, they would say, and if someone else does not have enough to eat, there are neighbours who will share with them. The sense that *kampung* are the place for poorer people, and are better for that fact, was evident in the daily conversations of the *kampung*. At the same time, in other contexts, the description *wong kampung* (*kampung* people) meant the dismissal of these enclaves as slums and refuges of the disenfranchised and dangerous.

One topic of continued discussion among our neighbours in *Rumah Putri* was about who had got above themselves and who did not take part in *kampung* life. One local standard was whether a person or a family came out in the evening to talk to neighbours, to *ngobrol*, or shoot the shit. Those who came home from their work, left their front doors closed, and never were seen in front of the house were particularly pointed to as not being *kampung*. One should appear at least occasionally or have the door open so that guests can call if one wants to stay in *kampung* exchange networks.

When I first began talking to my neighbours about the RT/RW system and PKK, some of the older residents talked about how in the old days every family was expected to give some rice (it varied from a cup to a teaspoon) toward the community's stock, to be used for those who were poor or sick or for the times when the community needed to celebrate together. The *dana sosial* or social fund that is one of the key parts of any RT/RW or PKK meeting is based on this idea. This notion of shared goods was often described as true Javanese culture and a remnant of rural ways where everyone helped. When I spoke to women who had been involved with PKK for many years, they often talked about the social fund and the goods (such as glasses, spoons, and mats) needed for any meeting as being something that each group must have. They saw this as having little to do with official programs, but instead as basic to a neighbourhood group that functioned.

Whatever the historical basis for community in urban Java, there remains a powerful local ideology concerning mutually supportive community that in daily practice is reinforced by the felt obligation for people to help one another in times of need. My former neighbours made continual reference to the life of friendly cooperation and support to be found in the *kampung*, and it was not uncommon to hear people discuss not only the merits of *kampung* life, but also the disadvantages of living in some other setting. Like the very idea of community, this notion of shared burdens and goods is encoded in the words *gotong-royong* of New Order propaganda. The history of imagining the ideal community is a long one, and it is given life when *kampung* residents make reference to an ethic of sharing burdens and extending help to neighbours.

Kampung, in their moral resonance with an idyllic rural past, are meaningful for their residents, not just because the state insists on it, but because they connect to ideas about how authentic Javanese people live together, work, and exchange. In this way, the *kampung* might be understood as a kind of a "moral economy" (Scott 1985). For many, the mosque-based community is the key ingredient in this moral economy and another sense of mutually supportive, integrated community, especially in Yogya (Woodward 1989). Likewise, the rural *peasantren* schools devoted to Islamic education embody another image of the ideal community. While the influence of Islam in Java has been tremendous, the details of that influence are beyond the scope of this work.[10]

KAMPUNG AS STRUCTURE OF FEELING

The streets of Solo describe the boundaries of vast residential neighbourhoods. Alleyways that run off the main streets penetrate these neighbourhoods. The architecture of the residential areas manifests strong concern for safety. Its distinguishing feature is the prevalence of walls that surround houseyards, occasionally reaching twenty feet in height. The purposes of these walls are description of property boundaries and protection against thieves and whatever else undesirable might enter. They help to achieve the tone of calm and security that often prevails inside Javanese households. One might speculate that they work to create the same tone on the street. Javanese neighbourhoods, especially those in the centre of the city, are not homogeneous. They contain the places of the wealthy and the noble as well as the shanties of the poor, and also, often, small factories, repair shops, and other businesses. The walls, then, hide what they protect, and they protect a great variety. To someone who is not familiar with the neighbourhood, what is behind the walls is unknown. They create a pervasive sense of a "somewhere else" ... a pleasant mystification. (Siegel 1986:125–26)

This capsule history of the term *kampung* (by no means exhaustive since the word has been used for some time throughout Southeast Asia) shows that it includes notions of separation by ethnicity, occupation, and class. It also bears traces of attempts at civil administration and the control of localities. Its modern meaning in urban contexts such as Yogya and Jakarta retains some of its polysemy. For example, a *wong kampung* or *kampung* person can suggest humbleness and community spirit or it may connote poverty and a clannish inward attitude towards others. *Kampung* life evokes a safe haven from the pressures of modern life and an emphasis on old patterns of mutual care and attentiveness, but it likewise suggests a narrow and suspicious watchfulness by neighbours and kin. While *wong kampungan*, or people with a characteristic *kampung* mentality, carries pejorative connotations for those who live in newer suburbs, for its inhabitants, *kampung* resonates with the sense of safety, neighbourliness, and home. What remains strongly in both accounts is a social formation resonant with the historical trajectory of these areas and the general tension that results from formation and reformation over time.

The reference above to Williams's "structure of feeling" is meant to suggest that the consciousness of *kampung* life cannot be reduced to fixed forms and to show that, as he says in reference to social forms in general, "they become social consciousness only when they are lived, actively, in real relationships" (1977:130). There is always a fundamental tension between "received interpretation" and "practical experience." Yet, these forms do not require definition, classification, or rationalization to "exert palpable pressures" and set limits on experience and action. In looking to the competing ideas and practices of community it is important to keep in mind that "[s]tructures of feeling can be defined as social experiences in *solution*, as distinct from other social semantic formations which have been *precipitated* and are more evidently and more immediately available" (Williams 1977:133–34).

What is important in the development of the *kampung* as a social formation is the association of *kampung* with particular moral sentiments. Once the domain of foreigners and the elite, *kampung* have come to be associated with lower class neighbourhoods known as much for their poverty as for their political positioning. They have served at times as barely controlled sites of political pacification, at others, as the seat of political revolution and oppositional culture, and occasionally, as the staging area for conservative and reactionary grassroots politics. And always, they have been the point at which popular politics and state control meet. *Kampung* are the places and the spaces where the creation of political culture and its citizens can be seen with some clarity, because not only are *kampung* one of the places where local power must be reconciled with state power, but the working class inhabitants of the *kampung* in their adjustments and adaptations to this reconciliation reveal the class contradictions emerging rapidly in Indonesia today (Kahn 1991).

And yet, as Ferzacca points out "the absence of the *kampung* in historical and ethnographic studies of Java, and for that matter, elsewhere in Indonesia … is conspicuous" (1996:45). Ricklefs (1981) in his *A History of Modern Indonesia*, a standard guide to Indonesia's past, does not mention *kampung* and neither does Koentjaraningrat (1989), Indonesia's own pre-eminent ethnographer. Selosoemardjan in his 1962 *Social Changes in Jogjakarta* defined *kampung* in a footnote only as a dwelling place of the lower classes. This lack of interest in *kampung* is interesting in light of their enormous influence on the lives of most urban Javanese.

The idyllic rural community "[f]or whatever century, it always seems to have recently disappeared or to be in the process of disappearing" (Roseberry 1989:57). Both city and the country are ever-changing qualities that must be understood in the context of specific histories. The images of the rural Javanese countryside and the ideal community are then a way of looking to the past as well as to the future, on the part of state and people alike.

As Corrigan and Sayer say, the secret of the state is the way it works within us. And this is true for the idea of community in Java. This moral sentiment is extended into and imbricated with the stated ideology of community and family evident in PKK. In the chapters that follow this one, the coordinates of domestic space will be considered. Yet as this chapter ends, it must be said clearly that the domestic is never separate from the community. My work on PKK and its relevance for the residents of *Kampung Rumah Putri* is based on my residence in a community of women. It was the lives of these women, fitted in and around state-sponsored forms of community and domesticity, that illustrates both the reach of the state and its limits.

WOMEN'S WAYS OF WALKING

> Women complained that their everyday responsibilities kept them from visiting and travelling as often as they wished. With limited opportunities to travel, women have less access to markets and less ability to forge political connections. They have more difficulty claiming experience and bravery. (Tsing 1993:128)

The limits of the *kampung* are registered most clearly perhaps in the restrictions on the movement of women. There were many occasions when women of my neighbourhood travelled together outside of the *kampung*, for example, hospital visits. Often coordinated in conjunction with the local PKK sections, visits to ailing *kampung* dwellers, at home or in the hospital, were apparently a longstanding responsibility of adult female residents. For women to leave the *kampung*, was something of an endeavour, requiring not only that household work be completed or postponed and that children be consigned to someone's care but that transportation be arranged. Taxis were expensive and private cars, rare. Typically, women would gather to walk to the edges of the *kampung* and take the city bus together. On rare occasions they arranged to rent, at a reduced fare, a neighbour's van, usually kept for tourist use. Travelling in groups was one safe way for women to leave the *kampung* and cross the dangerous city.

On one particular late afternoon, a group of women gathered in the street in front of my neighbour's house for a trip to the public hospital on the other side of town. A young husband in the neighbourhood was quite ill, and the women gathered to make the obligatory visit. The sun was still bright, challenging the calm of the women who had bathed and changed to take this excursion. All the women who were gathered had on dresses, and all had the freshly powdered faces of those recently out of the *mandi* (bath) with the extra touch of lipstick for this special occasion. Most clutched a small purse and a handkerchief or package of tissues. More women arrived until the group numbered around six, including me.

When the full contingent had arrived, we walked slowly down one of the *gang* leading out of the *kampung*, greeting neighbours still sweeping the front of their houses or sitting on their porches and doorsteps. This part of the late afternoon in the *kampung*, after the sun has relented some of its fierceness, signals the slow transition into the *sore* (evening). In *Rumah Putri* the *sore* marked an increase in neighbourhood activity. Those people who worked outside the *kampung* were usually home, and having rested, were preparing to bathe. In this slow twilight, those waiting to bathe or those in charge of sweeping the alleyways in front of the house were outside. Neighbours caught up on news and shared gossip. People disappeared to eat and bathe before returning to chat (*ngobrol*) again. Devout Muslims could be seen heading to the mosque. Children were dragged in to bathe only to reappear with clean clothes, faces powdered white, and neatly combed, wet hair. This break between the workday and the night, which may also include lounging and visiting in the street but now also includes television watching, is characteristic of all Javanese towns I have been in, but its importance to creating a neighbourhood is clearest in the *kampung*.

So there were many witnesses that day to our slow walk down the street as we left the *kampung*. We were asked repeatedly *badhe tindak pundi* (Jv. where are you going?) or for my benefit, *mau ke mana* (Ind.). By this time, I was used to the evasions and half truths that answered this question and to the slow leisurely gait that Javanese use, especially freshly bathed women. Everyone we greeted and were greeted by were well known to the other women in the group. After all, the core of the group were members of a family with a long history in the *kampung*, the family that I found myself living among for nearly a year and half.

First, there was Bu Sae, my neighbour to the west and my mentor in the *kampung*. She was the fifty-year-old mother of four, who worked in the local PKK *warung* (food and/or dry goods stall) and whose husband worked in a pharmacy downtown. He was now a *pegawai negeri* (civil servant), as so many Javanese are. Although the wages for *pegawai negeri* are notoriously low, the positions are coveted because of the pensions that begin at an early age and are equivalent to something like half the original salary. Three of Bu Sae's children still lived at home. The oldest had already married and moved to a nearby town where she taught school while her husband worked as a lawyer. The second child worked alongside his father at the pharmacy. The two youngest had not yet found their livelihoods although both were out of high school. Apparently, there had only been enough money for the first daughter to attend university. The youngest daughter was taking computer classes while the second son whiled away his time gambling. It was Bu Sae who would take me under her wing, instructing me in housekeeping and the intricacies of *kampung* etiquette. Bu Sae was in many ways a model PKK *ibu* having been involved officially for many years.

Also in the group was Bu Apik. She was married to the one of the sons of the Cipto older house to our east, the parents of our landlord. The father of this family was related to Bu Sae as a cousin through their respective mothers, making Bu Sae and Bu Apik relatives. Bu Apik's husband was the fourth of ten children. He and Bu Apik lived with their three children in a small extension of the larger family house. Bu Apik sold *jamu*, traditional Javanese tonics and medicines, as did her mother. She, with the help of her husband, made the *jamu* early in the morning before selling it at the local *pasar* or market. Later in the afternoon, after the market closed, she would make more to be sold in the late evening at a stand that her mother had started outside the *kampung* near the closest entrance to the *kraton* (the sultan's palace). Her children, all still in school, helped with the small stall that was opened in front of their house in the afternoon from where Bu Apik sold treats and iced drinks. Bu Apik's husband had no form of employment, although he picked up odd jobs in the neighbourhood including washing the cars of a retired *jenderal* (general) who lived on the main street into the *kampung*. Bu Apik, like Bu Sae, was active in official community work, including PKK.

Bu Wit was also along. She was the wife of the sixth child of the Cipto's, making her Bu Apik's sister-in-law. Her husband had been raised by another member of the extended family, an example of the Javanese tradition of *anak angkat* (literally, lifted child) in which a child of a large and poor part of the family is raised by relatives who are childless or at least have fewer children and are perhaps better off. As in most cases, this son knew of the arrangement, and by moving between residences throughout his life, he had benefited from having two sets of parents. He worked as a *pegawai negeri* driving for a local hospital, a job arranged through the offices of the man who owned our house, a son-in-law of the main house. Like many lower level civil servants, this son only rarely reported for work and instead spent time pursuing side jobs through a puppet-maker in the neighbourhood.

Bu Wit worked as a seamstress inside her home. She had worked on a piecework basis for a Spanish woman who contracted for handbags and clothing from women in the neighbourhood, which she then sold overseas. Over the course of my time in the *kampung*, Bu Wit moved to sewing outfits for the wooden puppets of a puppet-maker in the *kampung*. She and her husband had three boys, all still in elementary school. They lived in a small brick house they had built in front of the main house. Not long before we arrived in the *kampung*, Pak Wit had been selected to serve as the new Pak RT, and so as his wife, Bu Wit reluctantly had become the new Bu RT. Neither Pak Wit nor Bu Wit felt comfortable with their new responsibilities.

The only remaining Cipto daughter living in the main house did not *ikut* (follow). She was the only married child living in the main house, and she and her husband and four girls made up a large part of this house, although there were three unmarried sons living in the house as well. Bu Tri was unemployed although she, too, had done piecework for the Spanish woman. Her children were still quite young, however, and she tended to follow the main family's pattern of underemployment and unemployment. Her husband was at the time of my fieldwork one of only two fully employed men in the main house. He worked as a *sopir* (driver). Bu Tri displayed a healthy disdain for PKK and the associated activities of women's community work. It was her resistance and resentment that gave me the clearest sense of the limits of official ideology.

Other women would follow as well, including the seamstress down the street, the former Bu RT who cooks small snacks out of her own kitchen, and the young mother who cooks for her husband's workers as they make fiberglass statues out of their home. This group of women typify the various lifestyles, occupations, and positions of the *kampung*. Although the most wealthy of the *kampung* were not represented, this group otherwise illustrated the various socioeconomic positions and relations typical of the neighbourhood.

This late afternoon trip to the hospital traversed the various meanings of *kampung*. The small group of related women and neighbours all belonged to the same RT and thus the same small section of PKK. They were used to cooperating both formally and informally because of and in spite of the administrative structure of the *kampung*. In their daily life, they encountered one another on the path to the market, in the street, sweeping, in the early morning hours or during the *sore*, and in thousands of exchanges of food, labour, and information. They were intimately involved in one another's lives, even when disputes separated them for years. It would be their interactions and their uses and misuses of PKK that would most deeply shape my understanding of *kampung* community, PKK and its programs, and the practise of the domestic in Java.

The movement of women inside and outside the *kampung* was one of the strongest indications of both its extent and its limits. What I saw in the *kampung* challenged my ideas about public and private and about any discrete single household. Following women, I found paths between and behind houses. I sat in kitchens and found out who helped whom and notably, who did not. It was in the paths between the houses that women's work and connections flowed, and so the community that in my reading was described for Java was real, but often not in its official capacity instead, through the informal work of women. Travelling through domestic spaces in the *kampung* with my neighbours as my guide I came to see the lived community and to understand its importance to domesticity and importantly, how it reformed community.

NOTES

1. The name given for the *kampung* here is not the actual one and so cannot be directly translated here. The flavor of the name is retained, however, in *Rumah Putri.*
2. Javanese language (Jv.) is comprised of registers that reflect the relative status of the speakers. *Ngoko* refers to the lowest register, and it is considered crude and suitable for intimates of roughly the same status. *Krama* is the higher register and is characterized by two forms, *madya* which is a mixture of *ngoko* and *krama* terms. *Krama inggil* is the highest register of Javanese and is associated with the refined patterns of speech that were used in the palaces of the Javanese sultans. The national language, Bahasa Indonesia (Ind.), based on Malay, was institutionalized in 1945 with Independence. In some contrast to Javanese, Bahasa Indonesia does not mark status, and consequently is often preferred by younger people. In *Kampung Rumah Putri*, however, Javanese is the language of daily conversation.
3. See Guiness (1986, 1991), J. (1980, 1986, 1992) and N. Sullivan (1983, 1994) for descriptions of some of the downtown *kampung* in Yogykarta. Seigel (1986) and Brenner (1998) offer descriptions of *kampung* neighborhoods in Solo. Murray (1991) describes prostitution in a Jakarta *kampung.*
4. The title of this section is a reference to Corrigan and Sayers 1985 book, *The Great Arch: English State Formation as Cultural Revolution,* and it is meant here as an homage but also to suggest the long making of *kampung* culture (Williams 1961).
5. See Graaf and Pigeaud (1984:172); Pires (1967[1512–1515]:173); Raffles (1978[1817]:83); Scidmore (1989[1899]:37).
6. Another argument about the changing nature of *kampung* is that, during the time of his reign, Sultan Hamengkubuwana IX, 1940–1988, desired a direct relationship to his people and thus cut off the retainers, ministers, and administrators who stood between him and local residents (Selosoemardjan 1962). The establishment of a one-to-one relationship between ruler and ruled is reminiscent of the establishment of the liberal state in Europe, the expansion

of the democratized middle class, and the foundation of a very "modern" form of political attachment (Moertono 1968; Ricklefs 1981; Selosoemardjan 1962).

7. See Alexander and Alexander (1982), Collier (1981a), Kano (1979), and Stoler (1977, 1981).

8. According to Adas, these intermediaries included the landowning *sikep*. Breman outlines a three-fold stratification present in the first half of the nineteenth century that is based on the distinction between those with rights to land and those without. The top stratum were village authorities and other notables, followed by the true peasantry or *sikep*, where the ownership of *sawah* was concentrated, and finally the *wuwungang*, the lowest stratum tied to landowners in a dependency relationship.

9. The economic downturn in the late 1990s and the political upheaval in Indonesia has made the development of this class seem more certain politically but less clear economically. Yet, in recent visits to the *kampung*, the changing fortunes of the rupiah and the economy were the talk of everyone, while appearances suggested that most people were in approximately the same class position as during my original time there. This is not to suggest that there has not been a real deterioration in the living standards in Java, particularly of the very poor.

10. The relationship of the *zakat* or obligatory charity of the third pillar of Islam and the mosque community could be read as parallel, in some sense, to the social fund of the *kampung* and the state directives that neighbours should be in *gotong royong* relationships. See Woodward (1989) and Bowen (1993) for a fuller treatment of the relationship between Islam and community.

Chapter Three

The House

At the centre of the whole Javanese religious system lies a simple, formal, undramatic, almost furtive, little ritual: the slametan (also sometimes called a kendurén). The slametan is the Javanese version of what is perhaps the world's most common religious ritual, the communal feast, and as almost everywhere, it symbolizes the mystic and social unity of those participating in it. Friends, neighbours, fellow workers, relatives, local spirits, dead ancestors, and near-forgotten gods all get bound, by virtue of their commensality, into a defined social group pledged to mutual support and cooperation. (C. Geertz 1960:11)

THE *SLAMETAN* AT MY HOUSE

Steve and I had joined a local Catholic prayer group early in our time in *Kampung Rumah Putri*. This group was predominantly made up of our older neighbours. We had found out early on that despite the Muslim majority in the *kampung*, a significant number of Catholics lived there as well, and indeed in our immediate neighbourhood, the Catholics were in the majority. The local prayer group met once a month at a member's house, the location rotating from month to month. In an effort to ingratiate ourselves as well as to bring our house into the exchange system, we offered to have the December prayer meeting at our house. We had no idea what we were getting into, nor could we foresee that our missing back door would be such an obstacle to hosting our neighbours at a *slametan*.

Clifford Geertz has written about the ubiquity of this ritual of commensality in Java (1960), and indeed he identifies it as a core ritual in the complex that is Javanese religion. The *slametan* has become a fixture of ethnographic analysis since Geertz's 1960 description. In this case, its centrality in Javanese social life is aptly mirrored by its importance in cultural analysis. The *slametan* is the condensed statement of several key Javanese values that are interrelated and mutually reinforcing. In its bare bones, the *slametan* includes a meal served to a group, typically of kin and neighbours, and prayers said over the food and to the spirits who may consume it as well. The desired effect of any *slametan*, whether a circumcision, wedding, or funeral, is the same: to produce what Geertz has called "the longed for state of *slamet*" in which nothing untoward happens

(1960:14; Pemberton 1994:4). The importance of *slametan* persists thirty
years later in *Kampung Rumah Putri*, but the *slametan* itself has changed.
Slametan continue to mark major life rites such as birth, marriage, death,
and circumcision, but they are also used, in attenuated form, in the routine administration of neighbourhoods and in the workings of PKK. In the
example at hand, this core ritual identified as Islamic by Geertz, was used
by local Catholics at monthly prayer meetings.

No attempt will be made here to locate the origins of the *slametan*, but
Bowen's emphasis on "transacting" with spirits is useful.[1] To hold a
slametan is to accomplish ritual work, in effect, to ask for and produce the
state of *slamet* through a particular kind of doing. The idea of ritual work
is literally captured in the Javanese phrase used for large *slametan* and
celebrations: *nduwe gawe* or to have work. Indeed, what is at the centre of
this work is the production of *pangestu* (Jv. prayers, blessings and good
wishes for all) by other people on behalf of the hosting family. Keeler
(1987) notes that in some cases the hosts of the *slametan* may absent
themselves from the proceedings, disappearing into the back of the house
and allowing their guests, guided by a local religious official, to conduct
the ritual work of praying and eating on their behalf.

The notion of transacting with spirits connotes an exchange: food for
blessings. And this exchange, food and prayer for *pangestu*, is also always
accompanied by the exchange of food and labour between houses. The
slametan is a ritual of commensality, but the act of eating together is neither common nor comfortable for many Javanese (Geertz 1960). My argument here is that, rather than eating together, it may be more appropriate,
because of the changes that I observed in *Kampung Rumah Putri*, to think
of the *slametan* instead as a ritual of communal feeding. People, kin and
neighbours, are fed along with spirits in exchange for *slamet*.

The *kampung* prayer meetings, occasionally called quite literally *sembahy-
angan* for prayer meeting, like various other religious and community
meetings, did not match entirely the classic *slametan*. Yet, whatever the
differences in form and context, commensal, communal meals remain
house-based rituals, and despite any differences, all these *kampung slametan*
require the labour of both women and men within and between houses.

For this *slametan* to be held at my house, Bu Sae and her daughter told
me early on that there was no way that I could cook out of my own kitchen.
Instead, the *slametan* would be held in my house but hosted out of Bu
Sae's kitchen. I did not fully understand why they did not want to use the
kitchen in our house, because it had running water and tiled counter and
floor space. Bu Sae's kitchen, in contrast, was a small dark, dirt-floored
annex to the main house, reached by a dirt path running along the east
side of her house and next to our own. There was very little room and no
clear space for food preparation. Yet, Bu Sae was insistent that we could
not know how many people would attend and thus we could not use my

house. What if we ran out of something, glasses, *piring* (plates), or tea? We had no back door to go get more. At some point, as so often happened during my time as a housewife in Java, the decision was made, with little input from me, that people would sit in our house while the food would be prepared and served from Bu Sae's house next door (see Figure 3.1).

Figure 3.1
The back door to Bu Sae's house appears on the right. (Photo by S. Ferzacca.)

Once again, my missing back door served as an entrance to see how *kampung* kitchens work, especially in the preparation and staging of community-level celebrations. By considering how this was accomplished between two houses and two kitchens, the elements of the Javanese house, architecturally and socially, can be identified as well as the role of gender in making houses within the community.

BU SAE'S KITCHEN

Bu Sae's kitchen was a roofed area on the east side of the back portion of her house. It was on the other side of the narrow path that ran from the side gate of her house, down the side of my house to her kitchen. My bedroom window, mercifully high and small in this regard, was a few feet from her kitchen which was open on two sides. I made Bu Sae laugh one day when I accused her of sending a chicken to spy on me, because one of the neighbourhood's free ranging chickens invariably flapped up to perch just outside my window and peer in.

Kampung kitchens are often dark, close, and low. The challenges to Western notions of hygiene, behaviour, and architectural structure are everywhere. Bu Sae's kitchen was no exception. There was a make-shift table, waist-high, that held salt, sugar, and the gear for making tea. There were two small kerosene stoves that were on the ground. The stoves were some 6–12 inches in circumference and stood about two feet high. I had the same kerosene stoves in my own kitchen, but up on a tiled, cement counter. Bu Sae also had a charcoal stove that she used for some special occasion cooking, such as my *slametan*.

The experience of helping to prepare food and watching it be prepared in Bu Sae's kitchen immediately defined for me what I thought important in a kitchen: the food should be kept up high, as far away from the dirt as possible; the counters and workspaces should be very clean and dry; and food waste and garbage should be put in covered containers and taken away quickly. These "rules" of mine emerged in my original struggle to understand cooking in *kampung* kitchens. The differences from my own sense of the appropriate went as far as the proper way to hold sharp knives while cutting or paring. I felt comfortable with the vegetable in my open palm and the knife being pulled back toward my thumb. I was remonstrated repeatedly by *kampung* women that I should hold the vegetable palm down and cut down and away from my hand. This bit of habitus was one I never grew comfortable with, but it, along with the other contra-examples of proper "kitchen-ness," demonstrated so clearly to me the importance of Bourdieu's concept of habitus as lived practice and embodiment in domestic spaces (Bourdieu 1977, 1984). Watching not only how women moved through kitchens, but who and what else moves through them, was some of the most important work I did.

The start of the day of my own *slametan* was not auspicious. I include here an extended part of my field notes.

> The portent about how nervous I was came when I awoke at 4:30 [am] and heard Bu [Sae] cooking [breakfast] and half-dazed with sleep thought I had better get next door and help cook gule [a coconut curry dish]. Cooking actually did begin early. After I bought the oranges, carrots & other items from Mbak [Tik, a market seller], Bu [Sae] and I immediately went home to cook.
>
> I have to backtrack and say that at some point this stopped being my sembahyangan & somehow or other became the responsibility of Bu [Sae]. It started becoming clear when she told me that she had already ordered the emping [bitter crackers] for me—because the prices would rise later in the Christmas season. Then she accompanied me to shop and bargain— hard-nosed she is. And a bit of surprise to the pasar [market] ibus who have come to expect me to be an easy mark. Later I told her that I hadn't yet seen the woman who sells pecel [vegetables with peanut sauce] so that I could order chickens. She told me that she had already sent Bu [Tri] to do that—and when I added a chicken she did the same. Later when I went to pick up the things ordered from Mbak [Tik], I found out that Bu [Sae] had already picked up half & asked [Tik] to write down the prices.

When cooking for the *slametan* did begin finally, it was only Bu Sae and me in the kitchen. The preparation for a *slametan* is accomplished largely through women related as family and as neighbours. In my own case, I had no basis for asking for help, that is, I was not in established exchange relationships with other women at that time (nor would I ever truly be). As I would come to learn later, there would be only a small number of people working on this fairly large *slametan*, made larger by the intense curiosity of my neighbours as to whether I could manage it or not. If I had known better and had established relationships with women in the neighbourhood, I could have asked them to come help; as it was I had to rely on Bu Sae's family network to supply the labour.

As the day wore on, different family members appeared to help. In addition to her sister, whom she had called from another *kampung* some distance away, Bu Sae conscripted her daughters to help too. Later, Bu Wit, Bu Tri and Bu Apik, all kin to Bu Sae through the Cipto house, made appearances as well. Each woman arrived independently, usually after having finished their own household chores and cooking. Not only must the woman hosting a *slametan* organize the labour, she must also feed those who come to help. So while Bu Sae made us lunch, her sister, who as it turned out was a specialist in *gule* (a Javanese curry) and who had brought some snacks for those helping cook, mixed the spices.

Like most *slametan* meals, the dishes are formulaic so that any woman who arrives to help knows what needs to be done. For very large *slametan* held over more than one day, such as those staged for *kampung* weddings, the woman of the house along with the wedding committee (*panitia*) mobilize the labor and organize the tasks. In this case, women may arrive with their own knives and dish towels. The female labor in a large *slametan* is immense, and it requires not only the well known conventions of work sharing and common recipes but often a committee of women close to the family. To stage such a big event means that a woman must be able to call on a large number of women outside her family to help, and such a call to help (Jv. *ngrewang*), is based on prior reciprocal exchange. N. Sullivan has described *rewang* (Jv.) networks in the downtown *kampung* where she did fieldwork: "All female members of a *rewang* network are related to each other because of each member's prior relationship with the *rewang* organizer, who is currently the focus of group activity" (1994:159).

On this particular day, some of the women helped me with the *acar*, a dish of pickled cucumber, shallots, and carrot. The cutting and washing of each ingredient seemed easy enough at the outset, but the precision of the cutting and the need for uniformity in size was hampered by the rough wooden table, not much higher than the stool I sat on, and the rough knife I was given to use. It looked less like a chopping block than a thin piece of discarded plywood with legs. And yet, it was after one of these sessions of communal cooking, that I saw Bu Sae, in a rare moment of reflection on her history in kitchens, fondly stroke the top of this small table as she rinsed it off and remember aloud that it had belonged to her mother.

It was at this moment that I remembered a bit of my own family history. I was sitting in a small cabin by a lake in the Ozark Mountains with cousins and an aunt or two. One of my female cousins wondered aloud why there was so little mention of women in the heroic, near epic, stories told about our family's history. My aunts couldn't really tell her why, but my sister suggested that perhaps we were looking in the wrong places. Perhaps the history of these women was in their recipes for biscuits, their patterns of moving through a kitchen, their unspoken but daily done domestic chores. And this is what I thought as I looked at Bu Sae looking at this small table. Perhaps it was no accident that my understanding of the importance of that moment came after struggling for months to "do life histories" of *kampung* women. The women I interviewed had real difficulty in producing a conventional "narrative" about their lives—a story about themselves with a beginning, middle, and an end (cf. Heilbrun 1989). Yet, here was Bu Sae making as poignant a point about women and their histories as I had seen, and I could not help but connect it to the women and histories in my own family. Although often overlooked as history making, the movements of women through kitchens is an embodied and lived history written in the space of the house.

Still, on this day, as I struggled to make the *acar*, my work felt less like a woman's work than a child's. Indeed, a child would occasionally stop and slice some of the cucumber and carrots, particularly if old enough and if sharply directed to do so by one of the older women in the area.

Yet, what seemed to me a job of chopping and roughly mixing was much more, and I was gently taken through the steps by one of my other neighbours, who couldn't help laughing a little at my incompetence. While the other dishes, the fried *emping*, a bitter cracker favored for the first course at many *slametan*s, and the main dish were well beyond my capabilities, I did get to watch women who were good at cooking do their work. Those who were not engaged in the cooking of the main dishes helped in many other ways (there was rice to cook, tea to prepare, dishes to wipe and stack, paper napkins to cut and fold). These same women would come back to help serve, after returning home to bathe in the late afternoon.

Late in the afternoon, Mei, my assistant and her sister came to help too. There was a minor rebellion when Mei insisted that the cake that was to be served as a first course along with the *emping* and tea should be served from my own kitchen. She was insistent and although she did not carry the day, I have come to understand that it was less her worry about the cake getting wet or the desire to have our kitchen used, than an attempt to control a part of the proceedings by controlling the food. As I said at that time:

> Mbak Mei and her younger sister arrived and promptly went on strike about Bu [Sae's] suggestion that we serve from there. There had been much talk during the planning about our lack of a back door—but I had persisted in thinking we would cook there and serve from here. But we—Steve & I— were finally made to understand that it was better from Bu [Sae's]. And I saw the wisdom in that. Not only could we add as needed—but Bu [Sae] has so much at her house (her store of kitchen items is unbelievable) but also she wouldn't have to leave the comfort of her own house.
>
> I decided to opt out of the potential fight & just tell them next door. They took it without comment, but I was really gratified later when they [Mei and her sister] moved to join us (fieldnotes).

The struggle over the staging area for this *slametan* was only possible because my house had no back door. Mei's claims to control were based on the idea that it was my *slametan* and should therefore be hosted out of my own kitchen. Bu Sae's claim to use her kitchen was based on a deeper principle of effortless hosting that my missing back door precluded.

When the guests began to arrive in the *sore* (early evening), both Steve and I were there to receive them. Earlier, I had returned to Bu Sae's house to help finish with cooking and serving, but instead, I had been sent back to my own house to be hostess. If I had been a Javanese *kampung* woman, it would have been more characteristic for me to have been absent and in the back working, but because of the arrangement for cooking at Bu Sae's and certainly because I was a foreigner, I was told to go and receive guests. I was not particularly pleased at this decision. Not only was I again shown not to be mistress of my own fate in matters *slametan*, but the formal *slametan* itself is a dreary affair.

The performance of the actual *slametan* marks the difference between those on-stage and those behind the curtain.[2] In C. Geertz's classic statement on the *slametan* (1960), only adult male heads of households attended. Geertz discusses the furtiveness of this ritual, the way that men came, ate very little, and then carried most of the food wrapped in banana leaves back home to share with their families. As Geertz describes them, no one would consider these occasions as festive or light-hearted.

In my experience, men *and* women of a certain age and background come to *kampung slametan*, unless it is a single sex event like a PKK meeting. People under 25 years of age or so typically do not come, but older couples and heads of households do. They enter quietly, then separate by sex to sit with their backs to the wall. This need to be separated by gender is deeply felt. I once witnessed a large woman scramble in a most un-Javanese way over the legs of a man to sit alongside the other women. I had not thought the spatial separation was that critical since inevitably one man and one woman sat side by side in places where the lines converged. Yet, men and women arrive and depart separately. Husbands do not accompany wives. Women travel in groups and men walk alone or in step with a friend.

At the door of the house in which the *slametan* is held, people shed their shoes and make their way to the male or female side of the room. Those who arrive after the first two or three guests drop to their knees to make their way across the room, marking the enduring importance of relative height in showing respect. Keeler (1984) notes that the position of highest status is that deepest in the room, facing the front door. This space is often reserved for high status male guests and for the hosts.[3]

Once seated, guests must sit in a very uncomfortable position, quietly, for what seems an eternity. Men seem to spend the time smoking, rocking in place, and staring at the ceiling. Women fan themselves with their handkerchiefs, apply eucalyptus balm to their wrists, and constantly re-adjust their position. They complain about the heat and how their legs hurt (I found that the women were no more comfortable than I was while seated at *slametan*[4]). Despite the changes from Geertz's description I was seeing, *kampung slametan* still lack any festive air. The people who attend seem stiff and uncomfortable. Conversation is desultory, and everyone seems strained and uncomfortable. In great contrast, on the other side of the curtain, women and children are eating, joking, and sitting however they please. I never experienced these ritual meals as fun—until I got to help on the back door side.

Something of my double position as both ethnographer and housewife in the *kampung* was represented by where I was posted during the *slametan*. If I had been accepted as the true host of my own *slametan*, I might have been allowed to stay in the back. In my experience, some women choose to join in with the formal, front door part of the ceremony, and others opt for the back door informality. In the main, as in the past, the female host's contribution to the *slametan* is the efficient organization and preparation of the food. Her management skills are made clear and her success is measured in this way. My own positioning reflected the degree of my integration into *kampung* life. During this early *slametan* of my own, I was forced to act as a foreigner, marked by my presence out front. I was delighted by my treatment on a recent return to the *kampung* when, after I dodged a formal visit in the front room by going to the back by the side door, I was rewarded by the gleeful smiles of the family, most of whom were in the back, snacking, and lounging.

My other experience on the other side of the curtain came when I was able to help Bu Sae with a *slametan* she was hosting herself. For this event, I sat in the back with the women of Bu Sae's network as we prepared plates and glasses of tea to be handed through the curtain that separated the interior of her house from the front room. The food had been carried from the kitchen to this interior room, and there it was put into the large flat bowls used for eating. The food and drink were then passed through the curtain as unobtrusively as possible to the waiting hands of whomever sat near the curtain. Then each glass or plate was handed around the room until each guest had received one. For my own *slametan*, tea was served from the front door, rather than the back, after having been prepared at Bu Sae's and then carried on a tray in the rain. For the actual serving, Bu Sae's younger daughter and some of the young boys and girls from the extended family came to help. During the final phases of cooking, young boys and girls were underfoot much of the time. Older males were nowhere to be seen, although often teen-aged and young adult males helped by carrying heavy serving trays. This same mixed group of youngsters got to eat the rice and curry in Bu Sae's kitchen after serving the guests.

For those of us who sat behind the back door side of the curtain at Bu Sae's *slametan* or who stayed in Bu Sae's kitchen for my own, the atmosphere was much more relaxed than it was on the front door side of the curtain. For Bu Sae's *slametan*, the women I was with tried to identify people by their voices and they peeked out through the curtain to see who had come—was it a good turnout? These women, and the young children who had the freedom to go between rooms, were festive. They told jokes, laughed, and smiled. And after the guests departed, they each ate a big plate of the food that had been served.

At my own *slametan*, once the tea and cake had been served, a prayer service was held. When the service itself was finished, the *gule* was served. While the food served before the service was yellow cake along with the bitter *emping* crackers, the second course was rice with *gule* sauce topped with shredded chicken and fried onions. The *gule* was accompanied by *krupuk* (shrimp crackers), the *acar* and *sambal* (hot pepper sauce or chutney), and of course, more tea. At most *kampung slametan* that I attended, men and women quietly ate the food given to them. The food was finished, and no more was given to be taken home. Both women and men might wrap up one of the sweets or easily handled parts of the meal to take home to small children, but there were no packaged foods to be carried home. And so it was at the *slametan* at my house.

The final phase of the *slametan* included the dispersion of the remaining food. Although ostensibly this was my decision, the actual negotiation with Bu Sae and her older daughter over whom would receive food was very instructive in terms of the relations of exchange in the *kampung*.

> First, food went to Bu [Apik], then Bu [Cipto] & Pak [Cipto]. And then a separate plate to Mbak [Tri] because as [Bu Sae's older daughter] said it was *lebih enak* [better] than one (an instructive message for me). Then Bu [Wit] got some food. When I suggested Bu [Sri] [another daughter of the natal house], she considered & then said that was too far & so "*tidak enak*" [not good]. That counted out Bu [Hartono] and Bu [Bambang] as well. Later when I mentioned Bu [Santoso], she too was ruled too far, altho [Bu Sae's daughter] did say 'do you want to send food to her?' & then quickly dismissed her as too far [although indeed she was quite close]. So the food broke down along the lines of family partially but Bu Sri was ruled out as too far. It was thus difficult to know if the determining fact was distance or family membership (fieldnotes).

I had mistakenly thought one of the motivations for the sharing was to help poorer neighbours, which was why I had mentioned Bu Santoso, a young mother living nearby in only one room with her husband and child. I have come to see instead that the food is used to repay those who help and those who are in established, consistent exchange relationships, including some family, poor relations especially. A poor neighbour must be in direct exchange relations to receive *slametan* food, but this would be extremely difficult in the first place simply because of their lack of resources. Otherwise, the only way to give food without setting up unreasonable expectations is to share food with poor family members who will help in whatever way they can.

So in essence, the existence of an exchange relationship based on shared experience of exchange or shared kinship was the way distribution was organized. The actual distribution was done out of the back door of the house using again the swift feet of young male and female helpers. The food had to be covered and given discreetly.

THE *SLAMETAN* AS A HOUSE-BASED RITUAL

The *slametan* brings *kampung* neighbours into the house through the front door. Food flows from the back of the house to the front to be eaten or taken home by those attending. In the past, men were responsible for the public face of the family or household represented at a *slametan* and responsible for bringing home the food to divide. Now, men and women both attend *slametan* and eat together, although on opposing sides of the room. The formal distribution of food is immediate, commensal, and public (that is, in front of others, particularly non-family members), which is quite a change. What has remained the same is the informal, but critical, flow of female labour into the house and the flow of food out of the house, through the back door to redistribute resources and maintain kin and exchange relationships.

The emphasis on feeding the community is clear when the *slametan* is viewed from the back door side of the curtain. While several scholars have discussed the importance of women's work in staging the *slametan* (Brenner 1998; Keeler 1987; N. Sullivan 1994), and the networks of exchange and social labor that are implied in helping, the focus on the *slametan* has consistently been on the work done on the front door side of the curtain.

In my own experience on both sides of the curtain, the *slametan* must been seen as implying both the social relations of community that are fed and reinforced through the front door and the social relations of kinship and shared exchange that are fed and reinforced through the back door. Carsten (1995) has suggested that for Malay culture, one might see the house as based on hierarchal relations of gender, while the community is based on a principle of equality between houses. This apparent paradox is resolved by seeing the house as part of a dynamic process in which the shared substance and undivided consumption of the family within the house, dominated by women, are matched by the balanced reciprocity between households (for Carsten, this is epitomized in marriage and relations between co-parents-in-law). Within the house, males and females are conceived as being like siblings (shared substance) while between houses they are seen as married couples (affinity). Importantly, the transformation between these apparently opposed principles is effected through cooking (Carsten 1995, 1997).

While issues of kinship, alliance and descent, and gender will be dealt with more thoroughly below, I would like to shift the focus slightly to the feeding of the community by households and social adults. Significantly, and for the focus of the rest of this chapter, the *slametan* is conceived as a house-based ritual of community feeding. As such, the *slametan* entails not only the domestic architecture of the house to organize the ritual but also the house as a social entity within the community, and so the house serves as a site for the combined labour of males and females to feed the community and as the focus of an extended cognatically related kin group.

In the following sections, the symbolic map of the Javanese house, the transformation of dualistic models of gender opposition within the house, the character of Javanese kinship and its relationship to houses and inheritance, and the role of the house as a social form in *kampung* community will be considered to suggest that, following Levi-Strauss (1987), the house is an important element of social structure in Indonesia. An analysis of the key role of the wedding as another house-based ritual precedes a concluding section on how the house and women's work on *slametan* have become part of a form of state instrumentality that extends directly into domestic space of the *kampung*.

THE HOUSE

> Much of what houses are and imply becomes something that goes without saying. (Carsten and Hugh-Jones 1995:4)

Houses are made of wood and cement, of bamboo and rattan, but they are also made of people. The structure of a house says as much about the cultural values of the society that produces it as it does the relations of those who dwell within it. The house, perhaps especially in Southeast Asia, has come to signify an anthropological concern not only with built form, but with its symbolic structure as a particular expression of kinship rules and as a schema for the meaningful structural oppositions in a society, such as male and female, public and private, formal and informal and so on. These different aspects of the house are not easily separable categories, practically or socially, and so before proceeding to descriptions of the Javanese house, and subsequently, domestic space within the *kampung* and the relevance of the house, the key elements of the recent reconsideration of the house are outlined briefly here.

The built form of houses in Southeast Asia has received renewed attention in recent years (Carsten and Hugh-Jones 1995; Fox et al. 1993; Mannikka 2000; Macdonald 1987; MacKinnon 1991; Waterson 1990). This is hardly surprising given some of the more spectacular house forms that occur in island Southeast Asia particularly. The house forms of the matrilineal Minangkabau of Sumatra, for example, include curving roof lines that mimic both the horns of the buffalo and the headdresses of Minangkabau women. In these forms as well as in the longhouses among the Dayak of Kalimantan and the soaring roofs of Tana Toraja, social organization and symbol are manifest in the actual architecture of the house. Although not as extraordinary as these examples, elements of Javanese house styles have also received attention, including the meaning of measurements and the key characteristics of house styles from simple to complex.[5]

The legacy of Levi-Strauss has been particularly important in recent reconsiderations of the house. Perhaps legacies would be the more appropriate word, because scholars analysing the house have followed two routes associated with the work of Levi-Strauss. The more general of the two approaches is that associated with symbolic oppositions manifest within the house. Levi-Strauss, is well known for emphasizing the productivity of oppositions for making cultural meaning. Scholars following Levi-Strauss, perhaps most famously Bourdieu (1977), have looked beyond the actual architecture of walls to see what cultural values are exemplified in house form. Given the emphasis on oppositions, symbolic maps of houses tend to schematize meaningful pairs such as male/female, high/low, sacred/profane, and so on. Bourdieu's innovation was to consider how symbolic values so mapped are made real when a person behaves as if they are important, when for example, a Javanese woman refuses to sit on the same side of the room as a man. As Carsten and Hugh-Jones (1995) suggest, it is when the body moves through ordered space and reads the house as a mnemonic for the embodied person that such maps are made real: "[t]hrough habit and inhabiting each person builds up a practical mastery of the fundamental schemes of their culture" (Carsten and Hugh-Jones 1995:2). Or as Bourdieu says of the Kabyle house, the symbolic content of the house is read and enacted when an honored guest is seated in front of the loom, when a bride sits in front of the loom wall, and when a sick person is put near "the wall of darkness" (1977:275). Or in the case at hand, when a Javanese person sheds their shoes and drops to their knees at the threshold, the house has in effect triggered a range of emotional and status registers that are only made real in the moment the threshold is crossed. The difference between ideal symbolic schema and the practice of gender and family roles remain an important part of the following consideration of the house and its role in gender and kinship.

Several authors have attempted to deal with the symbolic contours of the Javanese house specifically and in the course of that work have rendered schematics of the architecture of ideal, typical Javanese house styles in keeping with this kind of structuralist analysis (Keeler 1983; Koentjaraningrat 1989; Rassers 1960[1925]; Santosa 1996, 2000). For example, the Javanese house as described by Rassers (1960[1925]) shows the front of the house as dominated by an open pavilion known as the *pendapa*. This pavilion gives onto an open passageway that runs between it and the back part of the house, and interestingly enough, this area between the front and back sections of the house is designated as *kampung* by Rassers. In the back portion of the house, there is a large main room, but it includes along the back wall three rooms: the *sarong*, *boma* and *senthong*, although he notes other names as well (all terms in this section are Javanese).

Keeler's aristocratic home (1983; Figure 3.2) resembles Rassers's house plan. The front *pendapa* is separated from the main house by an open area. The back portion of the house includes an open verandah or *pringgitan*, and the inner part of the back house is divided into a main room with three *senthong* or rooms along the back wall and a *gandhok* along the side where household things are kept—"plates, kitchen utensils, some food supplies, lamps, etc." (Keeler 1983:2). The kitchen area is located, in a sense, outside the dwelling. Keeler's two simpler dwellings include the

Figure 3.2
Keeler's (1983) ideal Javanese houses: below, an aristocratic dwelling; following page, top, a simple home; and bottom, a more substantial dwelling. (Courtesy of Ward Keeler.)

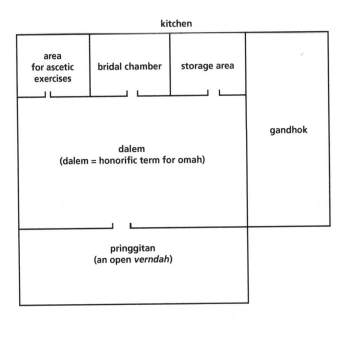

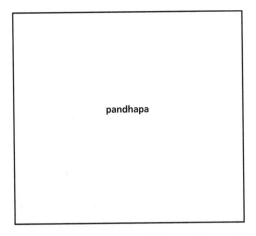

central room with a partitioned area or *jromah* (from *jero* for inside and *omah* for house) along the back wall, although the more substantial dwelling also includes a front room (*omah ngarep*; front house) and a *gandhok*.

Figure 3.2 (con't)

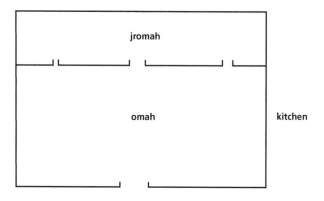

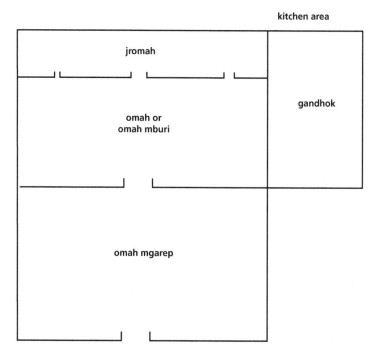

More recently, Santosa (1996, 2000) has detailed the architecture and use of four actual houses in Java, from a simpler *omah* to the Sultan's palace in Yogyakarta. He, too, identifies several common features in these house forms, including a central space, or *jogan*, within the main room of the house that is defined by four vertical beams, and three rooms at the back, which each house exhibits in varying degrees of complexity. According to Santosa, all of these houses emphasize the importance of the central interior of the house, marked by darkness and privacy, and the nested character of the house spaces which show varying degrees of openness; that is, as one moves toward the centre of the house, openness declines (Santosa 1996, 2000).

Both Rassers (1960[1925]) and Keeler (1983) deal specifically with the gendered character of the Javanese house. Rassers suggested that the open *pendapa* in front of the Javanese house is associated with male, phallic power which is public, while the back portion of the house is associated with the female, private, family space. Yet, Rassers also noted that the *keris* or *kris*, the sacred dagger that is the quintessential representation of Javanese male power, was stored in the back part of the house, which he had associated with female power.[6] This paradox actually opens up the reading of the ideal Javanese house to Keeler's emphasis on transformation and unity (quoted here at length):

> Rassers runs himself pretty ragged over the question of whether or not the *jromah*, or inner sanctum, is properly women's space, in contrast to the front, public area associated with males. Because the goddess of rice, Dewi Sri, is appealed to here, and because rice is stored in the *jromah*, Rassers is inclined to treat this area as women's. But then he feels puzzled by the occasions on which men take charge of activities in this area. I think he has complicated matters by omitting from his discussion the kitchen and *gandhok*. These are clearly women's space: they balance the men's sphere in front, and leave the *jromah* open to appropriation by both sides. In many ways—as Rassers eventually concludes—this area of the *omah mburi*, and the *jromah* especially, represent the unity and continuity of the family, as assured as both masculine and feminine roles. (Keeler 1983:5)

The openness of the interior house space to appropriation by both males and females is consistent with the use of the room as a staging area for *slametan*, as suggested above. Another example of this shared use occurred during a 2002 trip to the *kampung*, when I witnessed the amassing of some 200 plus boxes of cake to be distributed in honor of the 35-day birthday and naming of the son of Bu Sae's oldest son. The family was amused and perplexed by my contention that where I come from, the gifts for such an occasion come into the house, while I was equally amused and perplexed by all the gifts of food going out of the house. This difference highlights again the importance of feeding others in the transaction with spirits for blessings and good health and fortune.

For this occasion, males and females were working together making boxes, arranging to order and pick up the cake, and organizing their distribution. Indeed, male labour is critical for this kind of endeavour, and so all the men of the house as well as some male friends worked together to take cakes to friends and family outside the *kampung*. Bu Sae's second son and second son-in-law climbed on a motorcycle to carry cakes an hour east to relatives outside the city. The man on the back was loaded with two sets of two cakes, one on each hand, and these had to be held away from the motorcycle for the duration of the ride. This was work indeed, just as the Javanese describe such ritual happenings, and there is both tension and delight in the proceedings. The new father added and re-added how many boxes there were to make certain no one of any social or familial importance was left out. Names of recipients were gone over again and again. When I commented on all this work, Mas Didik said this was nothing compared to his wedding the year before when 400–500 people received such boxes. On this day of distributing boxes, a relatively subdued form of feeding others, there were still nieces called in to run cakes to neighbours and sisters to pack boxes, fold napkins, and insert the announcements, as well as all the men already mentioned.

All this ritual work accomplished through male and female labour within the house to share food with other houses challenges the easy opposition between male and female spaces, which typifies analysis of the ideal Javanese house. According to Santosa, for example, the Javanese house is broken into two parts, one "portion that is wider, brighter, more exposed, accessible, public and often predominantly male stands in front of the more narrow, dark, protected, enclosed, private, inaccessible part associated with the female" (1996:9). This opposition is reiterated in the contrast between the dark house and light *latar,* or yard, where communal activities occur, and Santosa notes that most ceremonies are held outside. Keeler reads the gendered symbolism of the house as evident in the association of the *jromah* or inner room with the womb: "[t]he links between the rice supply, a woman's chastity and the household finances suggest an analogy between the *jromah* and the womb" (1983:8). Javanese women are typically the family financial managers and are charged with conserving and distributing the family rice harvest in rural areas.

Even so, Keeler's resolution of Rassers' dilemma takes us beyond a simple structuralist reading of the house by focussing on the three rooms along the back of the inner house, or *dalem,* which he has distinguished as a room for ascetic practices, a central room identified as the bridal chamber, and a storage area (Figure 4.1; 1983). In Keeler's analysis, the room associated with asceticism is where the family *keris* is stored along with other *pusaka,* or family heirlooms. The storage area on the opposite side of the bridal chamber is used to keep food and household goods. In general then, these two rooms are associated with male and female, respectively. The central room of the three is a seldom-used room which effects the transformation of these apparent oppositions through marriage as is illustrated by the use of this room by the newly married couple and the performance of the wedding ceremony in front of the door to this room. It is in the middle room that apparent opposites are brought together. As will be clear in later sections of the chapter, although people are not necessarily married in front of a central interior room any longer, weddings are still significantly focussed on the inner room of the house.

All these ideal descriptions of the Javanese house focus less on actual houses than on the key symbolic values represented architecturally. For Keeler and Rassers particularly, the Javanese house can be "read" as a text for understanding gender oppositions and their meaning for the Javanese. Such a structuralist approach to gender is of limited use in Java, however. Java, like most of Indonesia, falls within Errington's Centrist Archipelago (1990), a place where cognatic kinship systems predominate, and males and females are conceived to be the same kinds of person.[7] Indeed, the lack of sharp opposition between males and females is taken to be the typical pattern across much of Southeast Asia, which is characterized by relatively high status for women and relatively little gender asymmetry (Reid 1988), although clearly there are differences in power and prestige between male and female across the region.[8]

It is, in fact, something of a cliché now to note that women in Java and much of Southeast Asia have significant financial and material power in some contexts, particularly as traders and managers of family wealth. Nonetheless, this instrumental or material power does not translate into the more prestigious potency or spiritual authority associated with males, or at least so it has been assumed.[9] Brenner's (1998) work on the successful *batik* makers and traders in a neighbourhood in the nearby town of Solo suggests that, on the contrary, women's effective power, especially in the context of the production of wealth in house-based enterprises, may domesticate such value and convert it into prestige in the name of the family. This analysis is particularly germane here, in a consideration of the house and house-based ritual. Despite the "official" ideology that women are ruled by their passion (*nafsu*) and men by their reason (*akal*), Brenner sees women domesticating value on behalf of their families in contrast to the dispersive threat to family fortunes posed by male passions of gambling and extramarital affairs.[10]

Brenner's idea of the fungibility of prestige is significant in this context. It is in the act of domestication or translation that male and female contributions to the house are rendered into prestige or status for the consumption of the family as a whole. The feeding of the community requires both contributions. Moreover, a strict focus on opposing gender values overlooks the key value of the social adult in Java and the *kampung*, and this is as a married adult, part of a couple. Brenner's analysis emphasizes again that men and women are not necessarily opposites or parts of a contrastive pair, but instead, male and female contributions to the family and the household are a part of a more complex set of transformations; transformations that effect the long term reproduction of houses and social groups, and houses as social groups. And in this we see again the dynamic process represented by the house, a process that is echoed in the role of the house in *kampung* kinship practices.

There is no question that males most often represent households to the larger community, and in some cases this means that an adult male sits in the front room during a *slametan*. Typically, an adult woman organizes and manages a *slametan* from the back of the house. And yet, the communal feeding and ritual work accomplished through the house is done by both males and females. Any putative distinction between male production and female reproduction is attenuated, muddled, or perhaps more to the point, shown to be incoherent for Java and Indonesia, and therefore its general usefulness is questionable.

The nested character of *kampung* houses is more relevant here, and it is related to the importance of thresholds as points of exchange between houses and the greater *kampung* community. In the staging of *slametan* and other rituals of sharing in the community, the house serves as an important node. Yet, it would be a mistake to see the walls as the house as solid and the division within to be dualistic. Instead, the space of the house is open to appropriation by both males and females, and the transformation of any symbolic oppositions within the house is keyed not only to the greater *kampung* community but to the practice of kinship within the *kampung*. The spatial implications of kinship practice will be made clear in the next section which considers patterns of inheritance and issues of public and private that are challenged in *kampung* living.

A FAMILY COMPOUND

Work on Javanese kinship too often tends to overemphasize ideal types to the detriment of actual kinship practices. Conventional descriptions of Javanese kinship (H. Geertz 1961; Jay 1969; Koentjaraningrat 1989) portray the nuclear family as the ideal in Javanese society along with bilateral descent and neo-local post-marital residence, perhaps following a brief period of matrilocal residence. Yet, as Koentjaraningrat points out, this model is not necessarily the statistical norm.[11] The majority in my immediate area of *Rumah Putri* was an extended family resembling the multiple nuclear family type described by Jay (12 of 41 households, or 29.3 per cent, contained a single nuclear family; 6 of 13 in *Langit Ayuh*, or 46.2 per cent.)[12] Although the nuclear family is indeed the ideal type, one that is supported in the programs and policies of the Indonesian government, many families do not fit the model. Indeed, the building of my own *kampung* house and its relationship to adjoining houses and the kin within them shows the limitations of the nuclear family model for *kampung* families.

The house I rented in *Kampung Rumah Putri* was a single node in a large compound of houses and related kin. Stretching between each house were lines of daily exchange through children, help, and resources that

illustrate both the relevance of extended kin networks in this working class
kampung and the challenges posed to them by changing socio-economic
conditions. Patterns of daily use and the fragmentation of land due to
inheritance and family development reveal that *kampung* space is in large
measure shared by extended families, and yet subject to redefinition based
on changing patterns of exchange, kinship, and rising incomes.

My first introduction to the house I lived in during fieldwork was before
it was completed, when my partner and I walked through the back of the
adjacent house, owned by the parents of our soon-to-be landlords to see
the unfinished back part of the house. This house was something of an
anomaly in what was a family compound of related houses, not just
because of its newness and its modern design, although it was certainly
different than the surrounding houses, but because it represented a break
in both the space of family relations and in their functioning.

Early on, Bu Sae herself had complained about the new house to me,
because before it was built, she was able to go to her cousin's house out
her own back door. She also complained that the new house with its long
cement walls had shut out the breeze that used to flow through her house.
Our new house blocked not only the flow of wind but of people and
things.[13] With the completion of the walled back portion of the house,
our new home effectively become one solid construction, from the narrow
street out front, all the way to the back wall of the property, which was the
boundary for the houses that faced the street behind. In effect, the new
house drove a wedge into what had been a more open family compound.

The blocking of wind and movement had significant effects for the
relationships between the related Cipto and Sae families; their daily, mundane exchanges were manifold. A typical exchange was the *jamu* herbal
health tonic that Bu Apik made every evening for Pak Sae, Bu Sae's husband. Bu Apik or a child would deliver it, and the glass would be returned
later. No money exchanged hands, but the *jamu* was one thing that Bu
Apik could offer to stay in Bu Sae's good graces, and to be able to call on
her for help when she needed it. Another exchange between the Cipto
and Sae households was in the form of a child of Bu Tri, the Cipto daughter who lived with her own four daughters in the main house. Bu Sae's
eldest daughter had not yet been able to have children, and so in an
exchange that gave her some experience as mother/elder sister and
relieved Bu Tri of one more mouth to feed, this daughter essentially lived
with the Sae family. She ate there, slept there and was supported in school
and clothing by Bu Sae's family. This pattern of child fostering or child
sharing is called *anak angkat*, as was mentioned previously. The key point
here is that *anak angkat* represents the sharing of child rearing among
related households, and in this case, the movement of the child between
houses exemplifies the exchange of resources between related families in
these houses as well. Young Tiwi frequently returned home for treats and

to escape the stricter rules of the Sae house. The construction of our house made all these daily exchanges more public, in a sense, because now the movement of the *jamu* and the child between the houses had to take place out in front, in the street, within sight of other neighbours.

My house represented more than the difficulty in moving between houses that formerly were joined by back doors, although this architectural change was significant in the *kampung*. It was clear that my house had been built by a segment of the family that was doing better, had chosen to build a house that they would not live in, and as a consequence, they cared little about the connection it would make to the rest of the *kampung*. Considering the importance of *kampung* kin and their relationships through proximity and exchange, it is quite dramatic that Bu Widodo sealed off the back of her parent's house from the house of another relative. It is unlikely that she would have done so if she had planned to live in the house herself. As it was, the house was a way to flaunt her lack of residence and her ability to build such a house.

Our landlord and another Cipto daughter had left the *kampung* when they married, but other members of the family had remained in the natal house or in the near vicinity. The Cipto house itself served as an anchor to a compound of houses for the remaining children. At the time of my original fieldwork, eleven people were living in the Cipto natal house. This large ramshackle house had a small, dark front room and then a corridor leading to the back, semi-enclosed area for the kitchen. Along the passageway, small sleeping rooms were indicated by the curtains covering their doors. It was unimaginable to me that so many people could inhabit such a small space, and indeed, it was not infrequent that the single males would sleep on the neighbour's porch, or in our house when it was vacant.

Extending to the east of the natal house was a small part of the larger building that belonged to Bu Apik and her husband, who is the fourth child of the Ciptos. Bapak and Ibu Apik had three children living at home at the time of my initial fieldwork. Their makeshift addition to the main house extended a few metres to the east, and it appeared to be one solid construction, although there was a space for a shared toilet between. Their living area comprised a small front room with two sleeping rooms hidden behind curtains.

The third child was Bu Rin who had been married and divorced. She and two of her three children had moved back to the *kampung*. During the first period of our fieldwork, she was living in half of a small house some two-hundred metres southeast of the natal house. The fifth child, Bu Sugeng, was widowed during our time in the field. She and her two children lived some one-hundred and fifty metres west in a house that was said to belong to her husband's family. Her husband, who passed away during our time in the *kampung*, was also a distant relative of the Cipto family.

The sixth child, Pak Min, was a civil servant working at the hospital. As a young child, he became an *anak angkat* to a member of the larger, extended Cipto family. Pak Min, because of greater resources in his job and his family connections, was able to build a small brick house in the front of the natal house compound, for his wife and three sons. This small house was less than five metres from the natal house. It contained a small front room, a kitchen area on one side of the back, and sleeping area on the other side.

The remaining four Cipto children all lived in the natal house. The seventh child was Mas Gus. At the time of our original fieldwork, Mas Gus was unmarried and one of the only family members still residing in the natal house who actually had steady employment as a clerk in an office. When we returned three years later, Mas Gus was married and he and his new pregnant wife were living together in the main house. Likewise, Bu Tri, who had four daughters in 1993, was still in the house in 1996 but with a new daughter. Her husband had gone to Jakarta to find a job. When we first lived in *Kampung Rumah Putri*, Pak Tri was employed, although not steadily, as a driver. His place in the natal family was a marginal one. As an adult male, it was unusual that he was still living with his parents-in-law after having four children, although there is a pattern in Java of a daughter, particularly the youngest, staying with her parents to take care of them in their old age and then subsequently inheriting the house. Pak Tri, however, had never been able to maintain steady employment and so seemed unlikely support for Bapak and Ibu Cipto in their old age.

The final two Cipto children, Mas Tono and Mas Ari, were unemployed and unmarried males. They both were high school graduates but remained unoccupied because, it was rumoured, they could not find anything that suited them. Although Mas Tono earned money occasionally by cutting hair, his brother did little or nothing to help his family. When we returned to the *kampung*, Mas Tono had moved out of the house and across town while Mas Ari remained, although he had managed to get a job.

The Cipto family compound alone should serve as a corrective to the notion of nuclear family residence, and in many respects, this is related to patterns of inheritance and socioeconomic standing. The older children were able to build on the plots of land that they were allotted (in some cases, sold to them) while their parents were still living. Clearly, there was not enough land for each of the ten children to receive a share, and those who came of age earlier were able to take advantage of their inheritance.

Beyond the complexity of the Cipto family compound, there are the extended kin relationships that connect the Cipto and Sae household with another series of nearby houses. Bu Sae and Pak Cipto are cousins, and so indeed, they are part of a larger set of linked houses. There were numerous other extended kin also living in the immediate area. Across the street from Bu Sae was her sister-in-law whose grown children lived in and around her house in another densely packed family compound. Behind Bu Sae was a sister-in-law of Pak Cipto. Several doors down was one of Pak Sae's aunts. Another member of Pak Cipto's extended family lived between his daughter Bu Sugeng's house and Pak Sae's sister. In short, this area of the *kampung* was filled with the kin, both far and near, of the Sae and Cipto families.

As I found little by little during my time in the *kampung*, the networks of kin in and around our house were dense and varied. The prevalence of extended kin and its importance in the day-to-day lives of my neighbours belied the emphasis on the nuclear family by scholars and the Indonesian government alike. Indeed, during my last visit, a young nephew of Bu Sae's was living in the house, having moved from Sulawesi to find work in Yogyakarta. The easy attachment of kin of all degrees of closeness was something I found repeatedly during my time in this working-class *kampung*.

My work in *Kampung Rumah Putri* suggests that while it is certainly true that descent is generally figured bilaterally and the nuclear family is the ideal, in practice, it is rare. The organization of *kampung* families in and through the built form of the house also showed that inheritance, while generally equal among male and female children, showed a tendency to favour female children, although this was not always the case. One dramatic example of the struggles over inheritance involved Bu Sae. Her father, Pak Parno, would not allow her to improve the house while he lived. Bu Parno had been dead for ten years, and so the house, in essence, belonged to Bu Sae, the daughter who had remained in the *kampung* and taken care of the family while her siblings had all moved. Her father's refusal to let her modify the house had become such a contentious issue that Bu Sae and Pak Parno no longer spoke. He lived in a small room in the house, with its own entrance, sharing walls but no doors with the main house; so while father and daughter actually shared the same dwelling, they were literally and figuratively cut off from one another. When I returned to the neighbourhood a few years later, the breach had been healed and Pak Parno had been reincorporated into the main house.

Like Bu Sae, Bu Tri will likely have her parent's home. The frequency with which daughters are called home to look after aging parents with the understanding that they will then inherit the house suggests a tendency for material goods to pass through women's hands. Nonetheless, there is still a marked pattern of ante-mortem dissemination of land and goods among all children, male and female. The clustering of successively smaller and smaller houses in around an original home is testament to this pattern. Pak Min's small house built literally in the front-yard of his parent's home is just one example.

Inheritance in Javanese society is governed by both *adat* or customary law and by Koranic law. While Koranic law in Indonesia dictates that female children receive only one half of the inheritance received by males,

Javanese custom usually works to give male and female children equal shares (H. Geertz 1961; Jay 1969:21; Koentjaraningrat 1989:155). My work in *Rumah Putri* suggests that family harmony is a motivating value in inheritance decisions, which is consistent with the "hard-headed *modus vivendi* reached through a process of give-and-take between self-interested people," Geertz describes (1961:48; cf. Koentjaraningrat 1989:155). The practice of *rukun*, or harmony, in my experience is combined with another Javanese ideal, that of giving more to those who need more. There seems to be a clear tension between wanting to make certain that all children are taken care of and the life cycle and socioeconomic differences within working-class families. So determining inheritance in the *kampung* is a matter of combining the generally equal inheritance between male and female children, in an attempt to maintain family harmony, but also making allowance for the occupation and life experience of each child.

The fragmentation of *kampung* land through inheritance is especially evident among the poorer families of *Rumah Putri*. In some contrast to the Cipto family is the Sastro family right across the street. Both Pak Sastro and Pak Cipto were in the military, although Pak Sastro achieved a higher rank. Both have large families; Pak Cipto has ten children and Pak Sastro has eleven. As already described, eight of the Cipto children live in the *kampung*, and six own or live on land that is, or was originally, part of the larger family lot. Only one of Pak Sastro's children lived at home at the time of my original fieldwork, and this was an unmarried daughter who had been "called home" from a job in another city to live with her parents. As a result, Pak Sastro's land has remained undivided.

The difference in inheritance patterns is surely related to socioeconomic status. Pak Sastro was able to send most of his children on to receive education past SMA, the equivalent of high school. Consequently, all of the Sastro children are employed, and indeed, several have moved quite far from the *kampung*, to Bandung in West Java, to Jakarta, and to Lombok, an island east of Bali.[14] The pattern of children moving away from their natal houses reflects the rising incomes and changing economy of Java and Indonesia at the time of my initial fieldwork. If the Cipto family had the resources, the children would have been better educated and more likely would have moved away from the Cipto compound. As it was, it was the older children who were successful enough to move on at all, while the younger children had even fewer resources as the family's fortunes dwindled.

The effect of the fragmentation of the larger piece of land held by the Cipto family is to produce a family compound of interconnected houses and households. Such compounds are typical of Javanese settlement in both rural and urban areas and have particular significance for the definition and use of houses and space in the *kampung* and the definition of family and household. The family compound is the first in a nested series of spaces that works to challenge any strict division between public and private. The growth of separate houses around the natal house defines an area within which family members move relatively freely, and in the case of the Cipto family, the houses ring an open area with a bamboo platform where family members meet when they are relaxing, watching children, and gossiping. Intimates of the family and other family members move easily though the compound, and neighbourhood children have the run of all the houses, yet less well known *kampung* members may not walk past the bamboo platform without compunction.

A more telling example of the nested character of these connected houses was the attempt to define the private within the compound even though the buildings are quite close and in fact may be physical extensions of one another. This was demonstrated to me by an exchange I witnessed between Bu Apik and her mother-in-law, Bu Cipto. As mentioned above, Bu Apik and her husband lived in an extension of the natal house. Indeed, Bu Apik could step out of her front door, look right and literally see into one of the bedrooms of the main house not five metres away. Despite their proximity, the two households worked to mark their separation, as was shown on this occasion when Bu Apik went to hail her mother-in-law. She walked to within two paces of the open door of the natal house, stopped and leaned forward from her waist as if there were a physical barrier, and only then did she call to her mother-in-law. This exchange took place deep within the family compound where the buildings were separated more in spirit than in fact, and the imaginary line drawn between the households was enacted in Bu Apik's leaning over it in her approach to the main house.

The flexibility of kinship and inheritance is evident in the impermanence of the dwellings and the fragmentation of land through inheritance in the *kampung.* Just as Carsten and Hugh-Jones emphasize, both the house and kinship are processual in nature: neither static nor permanent (1995:39). In fact, the extended family appears more as a practical unit of cooperation within a given space and time. The working class residents of *Kampung Rumah Putri* may indeed want for themselves nuclear families in separate houses, but in fact, they more often live in extended families and with other family members nearby. While a pattern of equal inheritance among males and females seems the norm, the individual family appears to adjust inheritance to the pragmatics of who can take care of aging parents, who can afford to make do without family resources, and what the life cycle development is of the natal family. The oldest children may get nothing if the family has nothing when they reach the age of marriage, or they may receive and use lands before younger family members. Those siblings who come later may benefit from living in the family home when parents are aged so that they receive the family house and lands upon their death. Often this goes to daughters who are more likely to stay home or move home to take care of parents. On the other hand, in a large family like the Cipto's the youngest members may find no land left to build on and only scraps to fight over. *Kampung* kinship (and inheritance) then, is a practical, adaptable grammar, whose emergent forms correspond to a given time, space, and class. And *kampung* houses are indeed works in progress. As the next section shows, Levi-Strauss's concept of the house society matches *kampung* kinship insofar as it captures this flexibility of kinship in practice.

THE HOUSE AS SOCIAL FORM

The second legacy of Levi-Strauss for understanding the house has been more restricted in its influence, being particularly relevant for Southeast Asia and Amazonia. In a series of Paris lectures, Levi-Strauss described the house or house society as a particular form of kinship that lies between unilineal societies, in which social relations are organized through kinship, and the complex societies, which are organized through property relations. The concept of the *sociétés à maison* prompted scholars to consider what this kinship type might look like in practice (Levi-Strauss 1983). The development of this provocative idea was left to those who followed Levi-Strauss (Carsten and High-Jones 1995; Fox 1993; Joyce and Gillespie 2000; Macdonald 1987; Waterson 1990), although the elaborations of this argument should not delay us here. The key issue is that the house society, conceived as an intermediate step between blood and soil, is organized around and through the reconciliation of competing social structural principles: identity through kinship and identity through property. The house as a form of kinship thus is hybrid and flexible: relations of kinship may be emphasized at some points and relations through the property, for example the house itself, may be emphasized at others. The mixed nature of this system and consequent flexibility may well be characteristic of all kin systems.[15]

Schrauwers provides a useful explication of one of the key features in Levi-Strauss's definition of the house, and that is its character as a corporate group, Levi-Strauss's *personne moral.* The house refers to a social group that holds possessions, both material and immaterial, together. Schrauwers notes the connection to Weiner's notion of inalienable possessions (Weiner 1992), those corporately held goods that have the ability to confer legitimacy and identity: crowns, crests, and palaces, for example. These immovable possessions serve to stand for the group itself, and so, like the house, they may serve as a fetish for the social group, or as Schrauwers puts it, such possessions or estates may provide an alternate metaphor for social body (2004:75).

There is some argument about whether the house society model holds for Java. Gibson suggests that "Levi-Strauss's concept of the 'house' cannot be applied in a straightforward way to the Indonesian societies characterized by Errington as 'centrist'" because "an idiom of siblingship, linked to an idiom of shared place, is far more important in organizing social life" (Gibson 1995:129; see note 18).[16] The character of bilateral descent is such that people are not unambiguously put into one group or another, so as Gibson notes, "all social relationships tend to be assimilated to kin relations, so that one is either a kinsman or a stranger, with no room left over for 'affines'" (1995:131). The house, in this sense, is understood as standing for something, the long term reproduction of the social group or the unstable union of competing social structural principles. It is useful here to remember that anthropologists tend to think of marriage as bringing together opposites, or at least very different kinds of social persons, while relationships of brother and sister are understood as being relationships of likeness and similarity.

For the purposes of the discussion here, the complexities of structuralism and kinship categories are put aside in order to focus on the role of the house as a master symbol and fetish (Gillespie 2000) for kinship practices and the kin group in the *kampung*. Here I emphasize Bourdieu's distinction between formal and practical kinship; the house is a focus of kinship practices in the *kampung*, but its importance is not the "result of obedience to fixed rules" (Bourdieu 1972:117). Rather, these house-based strategies of relationship are centrally concerned with social reproduction, a subject taken up in the next chapter. For the moment, an extended example of a wedding will be used to illustrate how the house works as a symbol of incorporation and transcendence of difference, not only differences between males and females, kin and non-kin, but also differences between houses within communities.

A JAVANESE WEDDING

In preceding sections, the important architectural features of the *kampung* house were shown to include a distinction between front and back as well as its nested character, with openness declining as one moves into the house. I suggested that any opposition between male and female space is dissolved by looking at the work of men and women in the feeding of the community. Moreover, a consideration of kin relations in and around *kampung* houses suggests that, like the house, kinship is processual, fluid and adaptable—in one family emphasizing continuity and consolidation and in another, disjuncture and dispersion.

Perhaps even more than the *slametan*, a *kampung* wedding demonstrates the key parts of the house as a built form and as the locus of kinship practice. Most *kampung* weddings, and indeed most Javanese weddings, take place in and around the bride's house. In addition to the legal and religious aspects of the union that may be carried out at the house, in the days leading up to the wedding, ritual preparations are focussed here. My own understandings of Javanese weddings (not to mention embodied culture) were significantly expanded by my participation in the wedding of

Bu Sae's niece, Mbak Ruci, who lived in one of the cities along the northern coast of Java. In the two days of celebrations and rituals, Mbak Ruci's
parents' house was the centre of much activity, bringing together relatives
from an extended bilateral kindred.

The large family contingent from Yogyakarta that included all of Bu
Sae's immediate family, their spouses and children, as well as Steve and
me, arrived on a Friday afternoon. There were many relatives already
packed into the relatively small space of Mbak Ruci's house. This house
was located in a relatively new development with better-off families, on the
average, than in *Kampung Rumah Putri*. In my experience, there is a lively
discourse about whether these new neighbourhoods work in the way older
kampung do, given competing visions of neighbourliness and the evolving
social relations that accompany changing socioeconomic conditions. None
of the houses in this new development resembled ideal architectural
forms. One thing is certain, these houses were built to share walls with
adjoining houses and had no back doors, although side garages could be
used for escape and the staging of *slametan*. To stage this wedding, for
example, two neighbouring houses across the alley and one on the side
provided their front porches as places for the buffet table, the emcee and
his equipment, and the caterer's supplies. While wedding guests would sit
in rows of rented chairs set up in the street, as is usual in places with no
extra room, the size of Mbak Ruci's parents' house meant that these other
critical functions had to take place at the houses of neighbours. The
majority of the wedding activities on the first day took place in the street
in front of the house, blocking it to traffic for the entire day. All of these
activities required not just the benign acceptance of the neighbours, but
their active involvement, and this was organized through the same ideas
of community and neighbourly cooperation that I saw practised in *Kampung Rumah Putri*.

On this Friday evening before the actual wedding ceremonies began, a
small *slametan* was held in the main, front room of Mbak Ruci's parent's
house. As with many traditional *kampung slametan*, a mountain of *gurih* rice
flavoured with coconut milk and turmeric formed the centerpiece, surrounded by small portions of many different foods, all offered along with
prayers for the couple and their wedding. This ceremony was relatively
informal and relaxed, and it accomplished the opening of the ritual activities that would take place across the next two days. Prayers were said by
a family friend. Only a few people were asked to take part in the prayers, so
that the ritual work was performed on behalf of the many others involved.

The only other activity I was involved in that evening was helping the
bride-to-be fashion the gifts of clothing from her prospective groom into
elaborate shapes of birds on trays, which were then covered with clear
plastic. We did this in the only other bedroom than her wedding chamber,
her parent's bedroom, which had been transformed with rented satin

finery (down to the covering for the wastebasket). These artfully wrapped gifts on their trays were returned to the groom, who would bring them back to his bride the following evening. There were also gifts from Mbak Ruci to her older sister, who should have married first by most reckonings. Many Javanese people still take seriously the idea that birth order should equal order of marriage. In fact, one part of the ceremony included Mbak Ruci formally asking permission to go first and ceremoniously cutting a ribbon across her sister's chest and giving her gifts.

The following morning, activities began in earnest. The caterers arrived to set up the street and to decorate the small, covered porch in front of the house. Palm fonds, bananas, and various forms of greenery were set up. The large bunch of bananas with its giant, bulbous, red, clearly phallic bud was a key decoration, as was a woven section of greenery that was hung with some ceremony by the bride's father over the threshold between the street and the family's property. A large tarp was stretched between the roofs of the opposing houses. Hildred Geertz refers to the *tarub*, or special extension to the house built to shelter the wedding guests (1961:67), and these decorations may be echoes of that tradition. In any event, the threshold so marked, along with that into the house proper, would be important sites for ceremonial transactions over the next two days, again indicating linkages across thresholds and the transformations effected through them.

The corner of the covered porch close to the house door was elabo- rately decorated for one of the first ceremonies on this day: the *siraman*, or ritual bathing of the bride. For this ceremony, the bride was dressed in batik *sarong* with a sleeveless *kemben* that left her arms uncovered. Around her neck was an elaborate necklace of jasmine blossoms. As she sat on a chair amid all the greenery, her mother, father, and her married aunts on both sides came forward to bathe her in scented water. Ladles of water were poured over her head and face, and hands were run down her arms and legs to spread the water over her entirely. She was kissed in turn by each (in the Javanese custom, her cheeks were sniffed). As this ceremony came to an end, the container that had held the water was broken by her mother and she was lifted in her father's arms and carried across the into the house. The symbolism of the washing of the bride plays on many notions. For example, a pregnant mother's body is washed by seven of her older female kin, and when a person dies, their body is likewise washed by close kin. Ideas about care and nurture of the young child by kin seem important here, especially as the end of childhood is marked quite dra- matically by breaking the jug which held the water. Still, the bride-to-be, after being bathed, was carried back into the house in her father's arms, just one in a series of associations between the bride and the interior of the house. This part of the ceremony was very powerful for those involved, and it is one that prompted tears on the part of the aunts who bathed the bride. There are not many guests for this part of the ceremony, and most were close friends of the family.

Not long after the end of the ceremony, the bride's parents emerged from the house to sell *es dawet*, a favorite drink of palm sugar and coconut milk. A jug with *es dawet* was carried by the mother of the bride, using a *slendang*, the cloth used to carry infants and children. To be carried in this fashion is *ngendhong* (Jv. the verb form). As Hildred Geertz (1961) notes, to be *gendhong* is a symbol of the total care of the child by the mother, and this symbol of the *gendhong* showed up again later in the ceremony. After the *es dawet* was delivered to the guests sitting in the chairs out front, they "bought" the drink with tokens they had been given. My questions about keeping a token as a souvenir prompted quite a discussion between the bride and her father about who got to keep the tokens and what they meant. Like many of the traditions of the wedding, the facts of meaning and usage can be fairly vague. Weddings of any size are run by a commit-tee, a *panitia*, charged with keeping things correct. As with the *slametan*, no time will be spent here on origins. The key thing is that people believe these to be important parts of the ceremony, and in the context of this discussion, the activities focused on the bride's house and her relationship to its reproduction.

These first ceremonies took place early in the day, and there was then a break until the evening's *midoreni* and prayer meeting. The *midoreni* is a party, again at the bride's house, that lasts until midnight when a fairy, the *widodari*, is said to descend to confer beauty on the new bride. On this evening, the bride was made up with an elaborate hair-do and make-up, although not nearly so elaborate as it would be for the following day. She stayed inside the house all evening while her friends and family came to see and talk to her. At one point in the evening, her groom approached the house on foot with his family behind him in a slow procession. They were announced by the emcee, who performed a running commentary throughout the house-based part of the ceremonies as he explained what was going on, often using flowery Javanese to describe the proceedings.

The groom after being introduced and having a family member speak on his behalf approached the threshold of the bride's parents' house property. There, under the plaited mat hung by the bride's father, he was given a drink of plain water by his mother-in-law and father-in-law-to-be who held the glass to his lips. He was then taken in all his finery, to sit on the porch outside the house proper, facing away to the street filled with guests. There he sat, denied all sustenance but water, while his bride, her family, and guests ate all they wanted. Hildred Geertz describes a dipper full of water being offered to both bride and groom, and she suggests that this is like the mother extending her breast, again a symbol of maternal care extended to both children (1961). Indeed, symbols of maternal care to both bride and groom, as if they both were children, moreover siblings, abounded in the wedding ceremonies. My own interpretation is no contradiction to Geertz's, but rather, it delays the shift toward treating the husband-to-be as brother and son, for it is striking that in the midst of abundant food, the groom is denied food, and he is also denied admittance into the interior of the house. It seems to me that this can be understood as marking his difference from the shared substance of kin within the house.

Eventually, the groom and his party left; it would only be after the rest of the wedding ceremony tomorrow that he would be allowed entrance, across the threshold, into the interior of the house. The evening ended earlier for some of us than others. Those of us in the wedding party had to get up at 4:30 a.m. in order to be dressed and made up at a salon. Javanese weddings are based on royal weddings, and the wedding party submits to drastic make-overs to achieve this effect.[17] As a female member of the wedding party, the front part of my hair was teased mercilessly and combed back to produce the high hump over the front part of the head. The back part of the hair is now typically a rented hairpiece that resembles the *konde*, which in the past, women could produce by wrapping their own long hair into this elaborate shape.

Thick make-up followed the hair styling—our eyebrows darkened and our lips painted a dramatic red. This was only the first stage of the process. We were then taken in turn to the back of the salon, where dressers helped us put on the *kain*, or the long piece of batik cloth that is wrapped tightly around the waist. This process was quite remarkable from my point of view. I was asked to put my legs together while the *kain* was pulled very tightly around my legs and waist. I had been forewarned to wear bloomers, but I hadn't realized until the women joked with me while I was being wrapped that my ability to go to the bathroom was now severely restricted. Wearing the *kain* and the *kebaya* (ornate blouse, usually made of lace for weddings) gave me a real taste of the difference in embodiment across cultures (cf. Sears 1996). It was clear that for me, this was about endurance of real discomfort for the length of the ceremonies, but for my friends, it was chance to dress as royalty. The lead-up to all the festivities had been marked by multiple trips to the fabric store and dressmaker. The delight in this out-of-the-ordinary consumption was very marked.

After both the females and males of the wedding party were dressed and fed again, we all departed for the church. When the couple arrived at the bottom of the steps outside the church, they were greeted by the priest who opened the ceremony by welcoming them to enter the church. In essence, he stood on the threshold of the church and invited them in, an action that echoed the importance of the threshold in the ritual activities conducted at the house.

The rest of the church ceremony followed a format that would be recognizable to most Catholics anywhere. The most clearly marked Javanese part of the ceremony was when the newly married couple approached each set of parents in turn to ask for their forgiveness. This is a standard part of a Javanese wedding ceremony. Often this is done in the bride's home, where the respected, new parents-in-law are seated on opposite sides of the interior room of the house. The newly married couple approaches them on their knees, in a posture of supplication, mimicking the approach that one makes to royalty. Each takes turns burying their head in the lap of the parent and asking in very hushed voices for their forgiveness for anything they have done wrong. In this case, the ceremony was done in front of the church, with the parents-in-law facing one another in front of the pulpit. Like the *siraman*, this portion of the ceremony was very affecting. Both bride and groom were clearly crying as they made their obeisance.

Following this most official part of the ceremony, the entire party returned to the bride's parents' house. In the wedding ceremonies of the *kampung* Muslims that I have witnessed, the formal, legal parts of the ceremony are conducted at the bride's home. In any case, the next part of the ceremony is invariant, in my experience. When we arrived at Mbak Ruci's house, the young couple approached the threshold of her parents' house together. There, each were given a bundle of *sirih*, the main ingredient of betel and an important medicinal and ritual plant. They then stepped a few paces away and attempted to throw and hit their spouse with the bundle. The story is that the one who is hit will be ruled by the other. As others have noted (see for example, Keeler 1987; Pemberton 1994), while this may have been a spirited contest in the past, now many brides put up only a token effort to win.

After the *sirih* is thrown, the groom breaks an egg under his foot at the threshold of the house. His bride washes his foot, and they enter the house. For this wedding, I saw for the first time the young couple being wrapped together in a cloth and brought over the threshold by the bride's father pulling the blanket into the house and the bride's mother pushing the couple from behind. As noted above, H. Geertz (1961) compares this action on the part of the bride's mother to the act of carrying children on the hip with a long piece of *batik*, and she suggests that the symbol of the *gendong*, used at the threshold of the house to incorporate the new son-in-law, signals his encompassment into the family.

I have included this extended description of a Javanese wedding to highlight the house-based character of the ceremony, something that has not received much attention in Java (Brenner 1998; Keeler 1987; Pemberton 1994; but see Waterson 1990). There is no question that weddings are important to Javanese people, almost as important as funerals. Their importance is marked in part by the elaborate preparations and high cost associated with them and by the gathering of large numbers of kin. What I saw among my *kampung* neighbours was that elaborate weddings are a mark of status. Having enough money to dress as a sultan for the day is desirable and prestigious, and these royal-style weddings are also moments for the self-conscious display of "high" Javanese culture.[18] Yet, for even my poorest neighbours, who could not afford the royal finery or the catered food, the house played a significant role, both as a structure and as a key symbol.

Given Rassers's reading of the house, it would be tempting to see the house as equivalent to the female and by extension the womb, and of course, Keeler considered this reading directly (1983). But the symbolic map of the Javanese house deserves a thicker reading. For example, the relationship of the wedding to the house may be seen in the opposite direction as well; that it is not the wedding that is like a house, but the house that is like a wedding. Indeed, Santosa cites a Javanese building treatise as saying, "erecting a house is like conducting a wedding celebration" (Santosa 1996:54). The association of the house with the wedding relates not only to gendered space, but its symbolic relationship to the self and the body.

One set of data that relates the body to the house fairly directly is the Javanese vocabulary used for the house, and concomitantly, for marriage. *Dalem*, the word used for the inner structure of the Javanese house, is also the *krama* (high register) word for "I". In Bahasa Indonesia, *dalem* or *dalam* means inner, deep, within (Echols and Shadily 1990). Similarly, the word *omah*, which is the *madya* word (or middle register in Javanese) for house is used as a verb to mean to be married, i.e., *diomah-omahake* (literally to be *house*-ed). Hildred Geertz uses the word *omah-omahan* (1961:55), while Robson and Wibisono (2002:521 define this as playing house. They go on to define *ngomahi* as meaning to provide for one's family, and *ngomahake* to domesticate or tame. Geertz also notes that *somahan*, which can mean household, is similar to *semah* for spouse. Interestingly enough, the word *krama*, meaning the high language register in Javanese, may be used to form a verb meaning fluent in Javanese and thus fully adult, which is also equivalent to being married. *Dikrama'ake*, means to be married, fully adult, and fully Javanese. Building on this even further, in the *Kawi* or older form of Javanese, *krama* means wife or husband. Whether the pairing of *omah* and *dalem* as the low and high forms of house or home is a transformation of, or a parallel form to, the pairing of the *krama* form *emah* and the *krama inggil* (the highest register) form *krama* meaning "to marry, set up housekeeping, to run one's home and household" (Horne 1974:411) is less important here than the concatenation of terms that are associated with the house: I, spouse, to marry, to be fluent in Javanese, to be fully Javanese, to be an adult. And it should be noted here that the gender asymmetry in these terms is relatively weak.

The relationship between being housed and being married seems clear. And although it is tempting to equate the house and the female, an emphasis instead on transformation and on feeding, as developed throughout this chapter, suggests other possible readings of the house. In the ceremonies described above, the threshold of the house figures prominently. The groom approaches the house but never crosses the threshold until the couple is finally married. Activities at the threshold emphasize the bride's attachment to her family even while they point to her changing status. She is washed as a baby, yet the container is broken to show that she cannot go back to being what she was before. Her parents both bathe her and feed the assembled group, selling them drinks on her behalf. The action of being carried as if still a child, is reiterated in the repeated reference to *gendhong* (to be carried in a cloth like a baby).

The groom's treatment prior to the completion of the wedding resonates with these meanings. He is denied all food and given only water to drink until he crosses the threshold of the house as husband. He is denied access not only to his bride-to-be, but also to her and her parents' power to feed and maintain him. When he does cross the threshold, he is wrapped like a baby in the cloth of his new *mertua*, or parents-in-law.

The ceremony of asking forgiveness is one of many that suggests the deep and important ties of family, and that the couple's happiness depends on maintaining relations of respect with their parents, and by extension, their parents-in-law. Notions of respect and hierarchy seem to be inherent in the ceremony of throwing the *sirih* and the bride's washing of the groom's feet. Nonetheless, there is also real emphasis on conjoining, on the release of fertility by crushing the egg, and even more importantly, in my view, in stepping across the threshold as a couple. The elaboration of this entry by wrapping the couple in a blanket to suggest a unity and the support for the entry, or perhaps even the pressure for it by the bride's parents, is significant. The young couple will stay in this house for some time. This may be a sort of weak bride service or matrilocal residence, but it may also suggest the centrality of the woman's family. According to Hildred Geertz (1961), this period with the bride's parents should be followed by some time with the groom's parents as well. Yet, given the slight preference for daughters as ultimate caretakers, it isn't surprising that the bride's family is emphasized.

In some cases, and perhaps more frequently in the past, newly married couples take up positions on an elaborate couch or a set of chairs at the back of the main room after crossing the threshold into the interior of the house. This seating in turn mimics Keeler's notion of the middle room in the back of the Javanese house that served as the bridal chamber and that he describes as representing the combination of male and female power in reproduction. The seating of the couple with their back to the interior wall does have the effect of emphasizing their association with house, and their stillness registers not only immobility and passivity (Geertz 1961), but also the expression of power and potency (Anderson 1990; Brenner 1995, 1998). Even in more recent weddings, with the *pesta berdiri*, or standing party, held at nearby reception hall, there is a point when the immobility of the couple is emphasized. For Mbak Ruci's reception, the couple stood before an elaborate backdrop on a small stage. Guests greeted them and had their photos taken alongside them, as would have happened inside the bride's house for a simpler wedding. In both the recent version and in the older practice of sitting passively on a couch, the bride and groom become set pieces themselves, enthroned and immobile before their guests who eat and watch them. Like the still kings of the exemplary centre, the couple impress with their nearness to perfection (C. Geertz 1980; Tambiah 1985; cf. Tooker 1996). In fact, Waterson relates immobility to gender complementarity:

> Immobility, then, represents a concentration of fertility, or of supernatural or political power. Dressing the wedding couple in royal finery suggests a symbolic parallel between reproductive and political power. Remarkable, too, is the fact that this immobility is always within a house, or else there is a particular association between a house and the person for whom immobility is enjoined. (1990:193)

For the Javanese case, immobility and interiority should not be understood as strictly female or male, nor as static or stationary. Instead, returning to Levi-Strauss's transformation of contrasting structural principles, it may be argued that the symbolic resolution and reconciliation of the opposition of male and female into the complementary and more stable unit of brother and sister is effected through the marriage ritual and bringing the male into the bride's house. It is much less useful to look at male and female parts of the house than it is to see the house as a place where hierarchy (sometimes figured in gendered terms) is resolved by the needs for cooperation between houses, and the wedding, like the *slametan*, is a perfect example of this. In the wedding itself, the in-marrying male, who might be understood as representing the tension-filled relationship of difference through marriage, is actually turned into a relationship of shared substance, like that of brother and sister. In a sense, the possible tension between consanguineal and affinal kin is resolved as all social relationships are assimilated to kin relations, so that, again following Gibson, "one is a kinsman or a stranger, with no room left over for 'affines'."

Remarkably, despite many transformations, the Javanese house still stands as a master symbol. In new suburban developments, and in fact most poorer *kampung*, houses do not match the ideal of a large interior room with three rooms along the back. Given the lack of architectural fit of *kampung* houses with ideal types, we might wonder about the relevance of this type of analysis for urban settings in Java. And yet, the staging of Mbak Ruci's wedding demonstrates clearly the significance of the house, not only to the celebration but to kin and to the greater community.

THE HOUSE AS COMMUNITY

Carsten has suggested that the "community is in one sense modelled on the house," and there is "a continuity between the house, the compound and the wider community" (Carsten 1995:120). And yet, while the community can be seen as an extension of the house, according to Carsten, they operate on two potentially contradictory principles: relations within the house, which she characterizes as hierarchical, and relations between houses, which are based on an idiom of reciprocity and sameness. While the principle of reciprocity does apply to relations between the house and the community, there is some difference between the more general exchange with the whole community effected through the front door of the house and the more specialized exchange with specific women that goes on out of the back door.

By looking at the centrality of the house and women in social life in Indonesia, Waterson argues against any opposition of public and private. Instead, the house is the centre of a chain of associations in social life: "metaphorical chains of association linking women, houses, kin groups, ancestors, the earth itself, and so on" (1990:196). So again, the idea of a separate private or domestic space is challenged in the *kampung*, where relations within the house are predicated on relations between (and vice versa).

For the people of *Kampung Rumah Putri*, the symbolic character of the house form is apparently minimal; at least, it does not conform to descriptions of traditional Javanese houses by Keeler and Rassers. It does resemble Carsten's description of houses in Langkawi, Malaysia, with their flat symbolism, unexceptional architecture, and impermanent construction (Carsten 1995:107). The symbolic character of the Javanese *kampung* house, I would argue, is realized not through its form alone but through its connection to other houses in the neighbourhood. Like the houses of Langkawi, it is the house as compound that is significant, defined less by the walls and rooms of the house, than by the paths, connections, and flows between houses. Carsten's description of Langkawi bears a striking resemblance to an urban Javanese *kampung*; houses tend to be built on a common piece of property, producing a family compound occupied by adult siblings and their spouses and children. This process of extension is "underlined by the fact that one term: *kampung*, is used for a compound consisting of one house, one of several houses, a neighbourhood of several adjacent compounds, and a village of several neighbourhoods" (1995:117–18). The "image of the community as an expanded house is lived out at communal feasts," which is also clear for Javanese *kampung* inhabitants and *slametan*. During a *slametan*, a single kitchen is used by many women to cook one meal that is distributed to many. The flow of women's labour into the back door and kitchen area and the flow of food out the front door through the work of men renders the idea of a discrete house form less appropriate for understanding Javanese houses and their symbolic lives. Gender relations are reproduced through this ritual feeding at the level of community as well as household, yet the unity of the married couple within the house is as significant as an gendered division of labour. Seeing the house as a conduit also moves our gaze away from the form itself to the spaces between the houses, to the pathways and open, common spaces.

The role of the house as a significant structure for cultural values, as well as for social organization, may ultimately bring us back to built form. The point where these two streams of theory inspired by Levi-Strauss concerning the house meet, lies, perhaps in the role of the house as a fetish. So in a sense, this is a yet a third way that Levi-Strauss has influenced thinking about the house. Fetish means here, a symbolically powerful representation of important social relations in a society, but the fetish also implies that meaning is displaced from the relationship to an object. The house in the *kampung* does stand for particular kinds of reproductive labour organized through gendered persons, defined in part because of their membership in the house as a locus for kinship and as a form of property. Yet, a close look at the house in the *kampung* shows is that it cannot be understood apart from the larger network of kin and community within which it functions. Domestic space is not confined within the walls of the house. The architecture of walls that separate rooms and the architecture of social relations that separate males and females, kin and non-kin, are less important than the paths between them and the movements of men and women within the larger context of *kampung* community.

NOTES

1. Since Geertz's description of the *slametan* as a core element in Javanese religion, some scholars have focussed on the origins of the *slametan*, whether in Islamic practices, in an pre-Islamic tradition of spirit and ancestor worship, or some combination of both (Woodward 1989; Beatty 1999; Hilmy 1999). Bowen (1993) locates in the Gayo practice of *kenduri*, in the highlands of the Aceh province of the Sumatra, a multi-vocal tension between reformist or modernist Islam and syncretic practices that include autochthonous elements of animism. See Keeler (1987) for an extended discussion of ritual work such as the *slametan* in central Java.

2. Keeler (1990) discusses Javanese women in terms of on-stage and off-stage performance, particularly in terms of language.

3. See Keeler (1984) for a discussion of the importance of the seating arrangements in Javanese visits. The host typically sits in the most interior position, with his or her back to the interior of the house.

4. The proper manner of seating for women is demanded by the *sarong*, but as more and more women have adopted Western dresses, style of seating has become more variable. And the discomfort of positions is now evident as women wiggle, shift, and generally try to find a position that is both polite and comfortable. Nonetheless, the soles of feet are never directed at others, and indeed, sitting with legs straight in front happens only at the end of the *slametan* and is typically done by older women whose leg pain has become more important than etiquette.

5. Prijatomo (1995) has also written on the meaningful measurements that are used in the construction of Javanese houses. See Koetjaraningrat (1989), as well, for detail on roof styles and variations in house styles.

6. Koentjaraningrat (1989) and Rassers (1960[1925]) both deal with the *keris* or *kris*. Briefly, Rassers refers to the kris as "an *organic* part of *Indonesian* culture.... We can observe the kris as a living cultural artifact in the Archipelago only" (1960[1925]:119). According to Koentjaraningrat, "[i]n Javanese culture, an extensive cult of *kris* daggers has developed ... the ceremonial system focuses on the recurrent elaborate ritual of cleaning it and the *slametan* sacred meals and offerings that go with it (1989:344). Kris are often a central element in a family's heirlooms or *pusaka*, although it is a rare *kampung* family that owns one.

7. Errington has made a contrast between the Centrist Archipelago and the Exchange Archipelago of island Southeast Asia (1990). This distinction is based primarily on Errington's idea of a fundamental split between those societies where male and female are viewed as basically the same sorts of beings, as in the Philippines, Sulawesi, Borneo, and Java, and those areas where marriage exchange is "predicated on the distinction between male and female, and the fact that women must leave their natal Houses (social groupings) in order to marry men who are not their 'brothers'" (1990:39).

8. See Brenner (1998), Errington and Atkinson (1990), Karim (1995), Keeler (1987, 1990), Ong and Peletz (1995), Peletz (1996), and Sears (1996).

9. This idea of potency has been associated with Anderson's (1990) idea of charismatic power that dims as one moves away from its source just as light dims when one moves away from a candle. Potency as a kind of power is also diminished by action in the world. Connections to Indic notions of the still center or the exemplary center seem clear (C. Geertz 1980; Tambiah 1985).

10. See Keeler (1987), Ong (1987), Ong and Peletz (1995), Peletz (1996), Wolf (1992).

11. Jay (1969) describes four types of families that compose rural, peasant households: the simple nuclear family; the augmented nuclear family which includes elderly retired parents; the multiple nuclear family which includes in addition to the original married couple, their own married children or includes married siblings in the case of a joint family household; and households made up of single adults. While Jay's data shows 74.4 per cent of households to be simple nuclear families, Koentjaraningrat finds the third type, the multiple nuclear or joint family, as the most dominant type. Norma Sullivan's work in 1979 shows that only 35 per cent of the families in the downtown Yogya *kampung* where she worked conformed to the ideal nuclear family (1994:118).

12. *Kampung Langit Ayuh* is something of an anomaly. It is a relatively recent settlement and most of the families in it have only recently moved to Yogyakarta, thus the higher number of nuclear families.

13. Ferzacca (1996) has documented the significance of "flows" and blockages in Javanese perceptions and practices related to the body and health. Anyone who has spent time in Java knows the dangers of *masuk angin* (wind that enters one), which seems to correspond to colds, flu, anxiety, and a variety of other complaints.

14. Pak Sastro's children tend to follow one another to new cities—another pattern of urban growth. In 1996 when we visited, Pak Sastro was making visits to his children in each of the cities where they have congregated. So despite their dispersion, Pak Sastro's children still exhibit the importance of extended family relations through a sort of chain migration.

15. Indeed, Schrauwers (2004) documents a tendency toward the development of "houses" even in unilateral systems in Central Sulawesi.

16. Grinker (1994) finds the idea of the house as successful for this very reason, that is, it provides a way to reconcile such opposition. Even Gibson (1995) himself comes to see that Levi-Strauss' formulation does work for the centrist archipelago, at least in the historic sense.

17. See Pemberton (1989) on the relatively recent advent of these "traditional" weddings.

18. It was during the same period of the wedding in Semarang that the first daughter of the Sultan of Yogyakarta (who had also married out of order) wed. The delight and attention to the details of this royal wedding were clear in the numbers of central Javanese who turned up for her royal turn around the perimeter of the Sultan's palace in a carriage (*kirap*). A documentary on this royal wedding was shown on television, detailing the ceremonies that were held away from the eyes of the public. Significantly, these ceremonies were interpreted by those charged with keeping and maintaining royal traditions.

Chapter Four

The Household: Making Do

Households are a problem for anthropologists for a number of reasons, historical, sociological and intellectual. (Wilk 1989:23)

The Cipto house and extended family compound formed the stage upon which many community dramas were performed. One particular incident, late in my fieldwork experience, had a powerful impact on how I viewed these shared houses. As Steve and I were getting ready to leave the field, we struggled with how to split our household goods. Although we did not have much, we had acquired enough in the way of household goods to be of interest to the neighbours. Long before our scheduled departure, various neighbours had expressed interest in specific items. We planned to give to those most in need, once various social obligations were met. As Reid notes, this kind of social debt as an obligation is a widespread component of Southeast Asian cultures (1988), and managing the ineffable but compulsory social debts was one of the most difficult tasks I faced as a household manager and *kampung* member. Our position as members of *kampung* community was honorary and somewhat superficial, but nonetheless, as rich *orang asing* (foreigners) we were expected to give something back. And of course, our goal in fieldwork was to become part of the community and inasmuch as we were successful, there were expectations from our neighbours that they would receive something.

Several lessons I had learned studying the lives of others, I only came to understand fully as they played out in my own life through the distribution of our household goods. In the *kampung*, much emphasis was placed on discretion in receiving and giving food to guests. The importance of the back door was partially that it allowed for the appearance of effortless hosting and hid the necessary work of exchange and consumption. In a similar way, the exchange between households must be covered, discrete, and effortless. I had an early taste of this when I gave an unwrapped t-shirt to young Yoto. He was the child of Bu Bambang, a woman in the neighbourhood who was rumoured to be a prostitute and the unacknowledged daughter of the widow down the street, Bu Hartono. The way *kampung* gossip went, Yoto had no acknowledged father, and indeed, the more vicious tongues in the *kampung* had suggested a lottery be done to choose one. Yoto's marginality in the neighbourhood was made evident in many ways, not the least of which was his poverty. At the time of our fieldwork, he was still young enough at ten to be acceptable in everyone's house, but that would change over time.

From my perspective, it was easier to gift him than other children, because his need was so much greater. Yet, for him, receiving an uncovered gift that he could not reciprocate was very hard. The *kampung* prohibition on uncovered exchange between two parties meant that by giving Yoto an unpackaged t-shirt I unwittingly had put him in the untenable position of not being able to carry it home. It was heartbreaking to watch him try to get his gift home, and ultimately, because I didn't initially understand his dilemma, he had to leave it behind to be collected the next day. For Yoto to receive something from me uncovered, something he could never reciprocate, was to mark him in the eyes of the neighbours as needy, undeserving, or avaricious. Having witnessed his distress, I was still unprepared for the trouble we would have in distributing our household goods.

Over our time in *kampung*, we had been most closely involved socially, economically, and personally with Bu Sae's family, whose house abutted ours on the west side. We had planned to give them several large items such as mattresses and curtains. Bu Sae had, in fact, requested these specific items months before we left. It wasn't until a few weeks before our departure that she made the unusual request that we bring the goods to her house after dark, when few people would be about. This kind of request reached absurd proportions when members of the related Cipto household, on our opposite side, asked that we pass the items we had promised them through the windows directly into their waiting hands. Clearly, neighbourhood exchanges take on a different aspect when publicly observed.

The culminating event in this chain revolved around our two kerosene stoves. I had already promised one of these small single-ring kerosene burners to my neighbour, Bu Tri, who was the married daughter still living within the Cipto household. I knew that Bu Tri's position in her house was not a good one. As mentioned before, her husband was the father of her four girls and worked only sporadically as a driver. As an in-marrying male, he had probably over-stayed his time in this house but was unable to establish his own house for several complicated reasons. Perhaps Bu Tri hoped to gain the Cipto house after her parents' death, because she was the last daughter in the house, or perhaps because she had married quite young, she did not want to leave her parents' home. She had little education and certainly had never earned much money on her own. My sympathy for Bu Tri and her family's tenuous position was often mitigated by Bu Tri's own brusque attitude. She and her husband did much in our early days in the *kampung* to make us feel uncomfortable. Still, I admired their unorthodox attitude at the same time; Bu Tri was the very antithesis of the PKK model woman in many ways.

At any rate, I had promised Bu Tri a stove less because of any outstanding obligation and more in the hopes of improving her position. In our final days as we cleaned and distributed items, Pak Cipto visited our house. As he was leaving, I asked Steve to give him the stove for his daughter, Bu Tri. It was with much alarm and surprise and no little dismay that we then witnessed, only a few moments later through our front windows, a scream-ing argument over the stove. Bu Tri attempted to claim the stove, while Pak Cipto, her father, claimed that it had been given to him. The yelling took place in the yard in front of the Cipto house, and it was extraordinary not only for its semi-public setting and the raised voices, both much against Javanese social etiquette, but for the nature of the discussion. Bu Tri and Pak Cipto lived in the same house and shared the same kitchen and hearth. We thus had witnessed before our very eyes a most vivid example of the difference between the house and the household.

THE GENDER OF HOUSEHOLD ECONOMICS

> Why then, given all we know about the variation in domestic arrangements is it so common to find the domestic domain treated as a universal, or at least very widespread institution? Even those who recognise that the co-resident nuclear family is a historically specific idea will in the next breath talk of 'the' family, 'the' household in a way that surreptitiously reintroduces an assumption of universalism. (Harris 1984)

The status of the household as a sociological object deserving of inquiry, a cross-cultural unit of analysis, and a lived reality was the subject of much scholarly debate in the 1980s (see for example, Moore 1988, 1994 and Wilk 1989 for overviews). The term *household* itself, in contrast to *house* and *home*, has come to connote an economic analysis of the domestic as a unit of production and consumption. Bartlett, for example, describes the dimen-sions of the household as including "four general categories of information: personnel and household composition; production activities and the division of labour; consumption activities and inter- and intra-household exchange; and patterns of power and authority" (Bartlett 1989:4).

The "discovery" of the household as worthy of scholarly reconsideration in the last two decades was prompted by a dissatisfaction with its theoret-ical autonomy from larger society and the presumption of its imperme-ability to larger economic and political processes (Moore 1994; Harris 1984; Hart 1993; Netting, Wilk, and Arnould 1984; Wolf 1992). Ironically, many of the attempts to redefine the household have recreated the very obstacles leading to its study in the first place, and simultaneously reiter-ated the struggles many of us experience personally around issues of the domestic: are resources pooled, decisions joint, and economic investments the same? What has been produced in this struggle over defining the household is not only more finely grained portraits of production and consumption but the establishment of household as an enduring unit of economic analysis. More to the point here, the perpetuation of this argument ultimately still fails to grasp the critical importance of social reproduction in the constitution of households.

Two critical questions in the early consideration of household, or domestic production and consumption, addressed, first, the existence of pooling within the household and second, boundaries between the presumably altruistic and moral regime of the domestic unit, and the self-interest that governs the economy. Pooling of resources within the household is based on a historically specific idea about family form and gender relations, one that has roots in the modern West and the emergence of the liberal state and the modern family.[1] Pooling assumes that those within the household share collective resources and make collective decisions. The presumption of pooling comes from the naturalization of the household as the proper site of unified production and consumption by a genealogical family bound by ties of love and sentiment.

In some contrast, the houses of *Rumah Putri* often contained more than one family and more than one *kepala keluarga* (head of the family). N. Sullivan (1994) notes that within a nearby downtown *kampung*, residents made a distinction between *keluarga* (family), *somahan* (hearthhold), and *rumah tangga* (household), and these distinctions corresponded to a genealogical unit, a corporate unit, and an official, formal taxable unit, respectively (1994:115–6). The hearthhold is the "locus of household food preparation" and thus falls within women's responsibility, while the household as official unit of representation is the responsibility of men, although these are two aspects of the same unit. In my early census-taking in the neighbourhood, the inhabitants of *Kampung Rumah Putri* readily would mark distinct families within houses by identifying separate *kepala keluarga* (family heads) within a single dwelling. Even so, there was often an implicit acceptance of a senior couple as the head of the entire household, and in some cases, this head of the family or household was understood to be the senior woman.

Such differentiation within the household has been used by feminist scholars to challenge the model of the household as governed by altruism and pooling, and to look instead to the differences within households (Folbre 1988; Harris 1984; Rosaldo 1980; Yanagisako and Collier 1987). Marxists and feminists alike argued for analysis of the inner workings of the household, putting aside the affective, sentimental attachments presumed to pertain there. There has consequently been a move away from seeing the household as anti-social, isolated and undifferentiated (Moore 1994) and towards seeing it as a site of bargaining and negotiation, between men and women particularly, with boundaries open to the influence of a world capitalist system.[2] It is useful to remember, too, that all women do not have the same bargaining power within the household. Indeed, the recent sociological attention to multiple subjectivity should have us looking instead at the differences *within* genders in terms of production, reproduction, and exchange. Can we really assume that a mother's position inside a household is equivalent to that of a daughter's, a mother-in-law's, a sister's? Intra-household bargaining has been one avenue for looking at differentiation within and between gendered persons in households (Holloway 1984; Moore 1994), providing a powerful critique of any presumed joint utility by household or by gender.[3]

Nonetheless, despite years of analysis questioning the divide between the domestic and the public, it is this very separation that continues to guide research. Analysis of exchange within the household typically describes it as centripetal, altruistic, cooperative and juxtaposes it with the centrifugal, selfish, individualistic exchange characteristic of the extra-household exchange. As Folbre notes, "there is a delicious political paradox in the juxtaposition of naked self-interest, which presumably motivates efficient allocation of resources through the market, with a fully clothed altruism that presumably motivates efficient allocation of resources within the family (Folbre 1988:252). As old as Adam Smith, Folbre notes, this definition of the modern economy is based on a boundary between market and private sphere.

These various arguments appear to be a search for the site of unified action; all actions within the household are unified, or all actions by women within the household are the same, or based on the same set of interests. The evolution of analyses of the household illustrates a successive peeling away of layers as scholars try to penetrate the core of the household. What quickly becomes evident is that there is no core. There is no single individual, function, or resource that is the household. Instead, there is a nested series of social forms, the result of complex and competing claims and investments, none isolated from the larger workings of capital and society. For Java, this nesting reiterates the spatial organization suggested in the previous chapter: the house is just one in a series of nested spaces associated with increasing intimacy, and the linkages within the house and between houses are simultaneously building blocks for and the replication in miniature of the larger community.

For now, I put aside ideas about pooling within households; there certainly is some pooling in the *kampung*. I will also leave aside the idea of separate spheres; there are certainly separate spheres in the *kampung*, because the government of Indonesia insists there should be (a subject treated in more depth in the next chapter). Rather than beginning to address the character of the "household" and its economics by accepting its existence, I choose to think ecologically, as Wilk suggests, and look instead to systems of reproduction and how they shape social life into "households."[4] For the rest of this chapter, the term household will refer the co-residential provisioning unit, that is people living together within the same house and providing for the direct support of members, occasionally under a single head. This social group may also include separate families, figured here as equivalent to hearthholds.

The question of terminology is particularly important, and substituting family as a smaller unified whole runs the risk of merely repeating the problem of assuming that people so described all share the same goals, resources, and power. In part, family is used here because of its relevance for *kampung* members and Indonesian government practice. That is, the willingness to identify family heads (*kepala keluarga*) follows as much from the naturalization of this unit through government counting and surveillance as from its reality as a natural group. It was striking how readily people grasped the "household" census information I was after during my initial interviewing. Indeed, each house in the *kampung* bears the markings of the official numbering system near the front door (related to the RT/RW system described earlier in Chapter Three). This "legibility" (Scott 1998) of the household is an artifact of the Republic of Indonesia's policies of neighbourhood and household control, and it is an apt example of governmentality. The concept of governmentality has been used to describe this susceptibility to being counted and accounted for by the modern state in its management of society and economy (Barry et al. 1996; Burchell et al. 1991; Dean 1999; Foucault 1979; Rose and Miller 1992; O'Malley et al. 1997). PKK and the RT/RW system are some of the primary forms of governmentality experienced by kampung residents, and it is no coincidence that these forms of state accounting have had an effect on how they see the household and family.

WITHIN AND BETWEEN

The fight over the kerosene stove had shown that any presumption of pooling within *kampung* households was questionable. There was also evidence that there was as much exchange between families in other households as there was between a family or families within the same household. In the case of the Cipto family, for example, the retired couple at the centre of the household received help from several other families and households in the *kampung*. Bu Sri, the divorced mother of two, regularly gave money to her parents, as did Bu Sugeng. These daughters did not live in their parents' household, although they did live nearby in the *kampung*. Their monetary help was only one form of aid that they shared with the natal house.

Yet, such sharing is not unchallenged in the *kampung*. The strained relationship between Bu Sae and her father, Pak Mongo, which resulted in their literally sharing the same roof but having no other contact, illustrates clearly the lack of pooling *within* houses. There was no exchange of help, money, or food between their sections of the house until the breach was healed and Pak Mongo was re-incorporated into the main house. Moreover, the flows of goods and people across the thresholds of Bu Sae's house to other related houses in the Cipto compound showed that pooling takes place between houses as much as within.

In the last chapter the networks of exchange between women in different houses for *slametan* and ritual celebrations was described, and perhaps the most consistent example of pooling between households in the *kampung* was the movement of women's work along these networks to help in the staging of family and community celebrations. These exchanges were constituted by more than labour and included, as well foodstuffs, small services, and even children and childcare. The phenomenon of *anak angkat* is just one example of exchange between houses related to the care of children.[5] In this way, the costs of raising a child, as well as the benefits of their future income are shared between households. Moreover, the child herself works as a carrier of goods and services between households, literally, in the sense of consumable goods and figuratively, in the sense of improved circumstances that are shared in their own children and the greater potential income generation for both sides of the fosterage relationship. *Anak angkat*, like women's exchange networks, define pathways between households and families and their movements across their lifetime show how reproduction can be shared between households (cf. Stack 1983).

My work in the *kampung* suggested that exchange went on through houses and between houses. The vivid example of intra-house division around the kerosene stove was matched by the flows and connections between houses. Not only was there more than one family or hearthhold within single households, but a single family could support more than one household. A closer consideration of the kinds of work that women do in the *kampung* suggests the permeability of boundaries and their linkages to *kampung* and beyond. Before considering the broader issues of the Indonesian economy and its position in the international political economy, a walk through the work lives of *kampung* women is provided to put flesh on work and labour statistics.

WOMEN'S WORK

A walk down my street in the *kampung*, with visits to its many houses and households, shows the different forms of women's work inside and outside the house. Out of my front door, and a very few steps to the right, is the path to Bu Sae's back door. It was in her kitchen that I saw most clearly the extra-household linkages through food and people. Within her house, there were her husband and eldest son, who both brought in income from the pharmacy. Her eldest, a daughter, returned with her husband most weekends, bringing money but taking food and lodging. Her other two children were unemployed. The younger daughter was pursuing courses sporadically; the younger son gambling and playing. Young Sita was the *anak angkat* from the Cipto house on the other side of me. Bu Sae helped support this large family by earning wages each morning and some evenings at the PKK stall in the *kampung* market. This work was her only "formal" employment. She was responsible not only for running the counter but also for buying, stocking, and managing the *warung* counter. Bu Sae also sold the ice made in her refrigerator and cooked and sold peanuts out of her own kitchen to earn additional income.

The Cipto compound on the other side of my house included Bu Apik, who made and sold *jamu*, the health tonic, at the local market during the day and just outside the *kampung* in the evening. She also ran a food stall out of the front of her house. Bu Wit worked as a seamstress out of her home, after attending some training sessions sponsored by PKK. Bu Tri did occasional piecework, always out of her own home.

Across the street from the Cipto compound was Bu Sastro who was one of the rare *kampung* women who identified herself as a housewife and reported that this was the only work she had ever done. Her husband was a very respected man in the *kampung*, a former army officer. She had raised their twelve children, who had since spread to all parts of Indonesia. At the time of my first fieldwork, one of her youngest, a daughter, had been called home by her parents from her work as a lab tech in a neighbouring city to keep them company. Pak Sastro, a pensioner, left the *kampung* early every afternoon to pickup his grandson, who stayed with his grandparents until his parents returned from work.

Bu Budi, a widow, lived in a single rented room within a larger building just east of the large Sastro house. She supported herself by cooking for others when they required extra help. Bu Dinar, who lived in the larger part of the same building, cooked cakes and meat pies in her home and sold them on commission out of a store in downtown Yogya. She was helped in this work by her children living at home. She also was full-time care giver to two grandchildren who were brought to her home each morning and picked up each evening. Bu Dinar had moved when we returned to the *kampung* after three years, and in the meantime, two of her daughters had become involved in a cottage industry making quilt covers, purses, and pillowcases out of a house within the larger area of *Kampung Rumah Putri*. This business was the project of one of her daughters who had been unable to finish college due to illness.

Bu Purnama and her family lived in a small house in front of Bu Dinar's building. She was educated and had become a school teacher in a nearby town. Her husband was a labourer. Although Bu Purnama had no other employment when I first met her, by the time of my second fieldwork stay, she had opened a *warung*, selling matches, sugar, mosquito coils and other small dry goods, out of her home. Room for the *warung* in her small house was only available after the death of her mother, who had lived with the family providing full time childcare for her four children.

The complex of apartment-like divisions that housed both Bu Budi and Bu Dinar also contained the household of Bu Tini. Bu Tini's husband ran a small fibreglass trophy factory out of a shed next to their home, where he employed two workers. Bu Tini cooked the noon meal that the workers received as part of their wages. She had no other employment, although she had become Bu RT by the time we returned to the *kampung*.

The alleyway in front of her door ran all the way to a ramshackle house in the back that belonged to Bu Bambang. She, in turn, had rented half of the building to Bu Sri, daughter of the Cipto house. Bu Bambang, the mother of young Yoto, had no visible means of support, but as described above, ugly *kampung* gossip suggested that she earned her money through prostitution. About halfway through our time in the *kampung*, Bu Bambang started selling iced drinks in the afternoon and snacks out of small roofed platform erected for the night watch.[6] It was not much of a business and attracted mostly those sympathetic to her plight. Those less sympathetic described her drinks as *kotor* or dirty and shunned her. Bu Sri, her renter, had the more enviable job of working at a large tourist hotel in downtown Yogya. She supported her two children from a marriage that had ended.

One of the astonishing discoveries of my fieldwork was finding out that the woman who lived in the large house in front of Bu Bambang was in fact her mother. When I initially interviewed her, Bu Hartono claimed to have only one daughter who lived in Jakarta. She never admitted her relationship to Bu Bambang to me, but others eventually let me in on this secret. Bu Hartono's working life was a good illustration of the multiple strategies used by *kampung* folks to support themselves. She was herself a long-time widow who received her late husband's pension, but she also had the most extensive *warung* stall on the short block near my house. It was a separate small building in front of her house with sufficient supplies to supplement any last-minute cooking needs, in contrast to most *warung*. She was also a neighbourhood fixture, sitting on a bench in front of her *warung*, calling out to everyone that passed, keeping tabs on *kampung* movements. She made extra income by renting out parts of her house. During the first period of our fieldwork, she eventually rented out two sections, reserving only one for herself. Upon our return, we found her living across the street, with the older widow of a wealthier family, after having rented out the entire house. This widow was the mother of one of the few older single women I met in the *kampung*; she was a school teacher whose family wealth provided her with a nicer home and lifestyle than most *kampung* families. In fact, she had a niece and nephew living in her large house as they attended university in Yogya, illustrating again how extended families are used to distribute resources and spread burdens.

Other women in the neighbourhood included the young wife of a law student who worked as middle person in a variety of industries. She lived in the rental house on the east side of the Cipto compound. Although her main work was in supplying plastic products to shops and *warung*, at least one time during our stay, she had temporary piecework that she farmed out to her neighbours in the Cipto household. One of these enterprises was stuffing pillows with kapok, and her nearby female neighbours provided the labour. Such ephemeral cash-earning jobs bloomed and disappeared throughout the *kampung* on a regular basis, providing opportunities for the very unskilled and poor such as Bu Tri to earn cash.

Down the street, on the corner farthest from my own house, was the house of Bu Min. She, her husband and school-aged children lived in small cement block house. Her husband worked as a labourer in the wood industry and was gone from the *kampung* for long hours every day. She herself was a seamstress, working out of her house, often with the help of one of her children. This family struggled to keep all their children in school at the same time due to the fees.[7] Her next-door neighbour to the west was Bu Wicaksono whose husband had a job at a bank. Although she was doing better financially, Bu Wicaksono also earned money by selling used clothing out of her home. She would buy the clothes, store them at home, and then sell them again in various locations. This kind of work was also pursued by a couple who lived in a tiny apartment in the back of the single school teacher's home. In the large dilapidated house next door to them was an older woman, Bu Lestari, who claimed no employment but then admitted in an embarrassed way to me that she loaned money in the *kampung* to help support herself. It was clear from her manner that this occupation is not a highly respected one, although it is prevalent in the *kampung* and among women.[8]

Bu Lestari's household illustrates an interesting aspect of Javanese reproduction. Not only did she support an adult son who appeared to be mentally disabled, but amazingly, she likewise supported an aged and ailing husband who had years before left her for another woman. When he became sick, he returned to Bu Lestari's house and she took him in. Polygamy is still practised in Java but not widely. Serial monogamy is better used to describe the pattern of multiple marriages in Indonesia among the lower classes (in contrast to the tradition of plural marriage in elite and court culture). Divorce and separation are not uncommon in Java. Official divorce is rarer than separation that is followed by other unofficial marriages, and the experience of Bu Lestari shows that often partners move back and forth between marriages and houses across their lifetimes.

All of the women I interviewed in RT Barat[9] work to earn money, with the exception of Bu Sastro. The households of RT Timur will not be presented in detail, but some aspects of female labour activity there should be mentioned. RT Timur appeared to have more women in professional and clerical positions. One extended family compound had three sisters, all nurses, living with their families. Their husbands did some of the child-care in addition to pursuing a variety of informal sector activities, such as a short-lived enterprise raising chickens.

In the eastern part of this RT there was also a pocket of poverty that included some of the poorest households I encountered in the *kampung*. The varieties of income-generating activities in this area of dense settle-ment included laundry services, batik piecework, cooking, and day labour. There were eight households/families in eleven structures in this part of the RT, while in the comparable area across the alley on the north side there are only three structures with three families.

This RT, perhaps more than RT Barat, illustrates the extremes of house-hold circumstance in the *kampung*. RT Barat exhibits less differentiation, and the majority of the households can be classified as working class. RT Timur includes households with no electricity and families who cannot afford to cook rice everyday (an index of poverty immediately understood in the *kampung*), and these households exist cheek-by-jowl with well-to-do, solidly middle class households. Perhaps the best example of the well-to-do end of the spectrum was the woman whose husband was a judge and who worked herself as a teacher in the morning and then as a very suc-cessful seller of spices at the large downtown Yogya market, Beringharjo. This couple had no biological children of their own, but were raising the daughter of another family member. Their household included servants, and they were financially able to own two automobiles.

In several households, grandparents provided primary childcare to grandchildren during the day. In these cases, parents put their children in schools in their own parents' neighbourhoods so that children could leave from and return to their grandparents' homes each day. A similar arrangement was the attachment to a younger family's household of parents or more typically a widowed mother as primary childcare provider and housekeeper, allowing the daughter to work outside the home. The attach-ment of a younger sibling or niece is equivalent, although in this case, the female will probably only be in the house temporarily until she marries, while a widowed mother will typically stay until she passes away.

The contribution of men, particularly grandfathers, to this kind of reproductive labour is considerable and should not be ignored. Because of the early retirement age in civil service and the army, many men find themselves without formal sector work at a relatively young age (55). Men in this situation in the *kampung* often help with the grandchildren as much as their wives.

In general, there were three categories of male employment within the *kampung*. There were a number of small-scale industries run by men with the help of their families. They included a *wayang* puppet and tourist business, two fibreglass statuary factories, and a fried noodle (*mei goreng*) stall. Bu Sae's youngest son, by the time we returned to the *kampung*, had begun a small name card business in her house. There were men employed in the formal waged sector as civil servants, including the army and the police, while the remaining number typically worked as private sector clerks. A number of these men were retired, as mentioned above, and often these retired men did not take up other work but collected their small pensions and pursued occasional waged labour or informal *kampung*-based work. Poorer *kampung* men worked as low-waged occasional labour in the informal sector, often as day-labourers. Bu Apik's husband made occasional money by washing the cars of a well-to-do ex-army man on a neighbouring street. There was a pedicab driver in the neighbourhood, and Bu Tri's husband had on-again, off-again employment as a driver. The puppet-maker at the western end of my street, on the opposite side of Bu Sae's house, often hired the unemployed men of the *kampung* to do odd jobs. Pak Wit occasionally worked as a driver for him, despite his own formal sector job at the hospital.

What is most striking about my brief survey of patterns of employment in the *kampung* is the concurrence of particular female patterns alongside specifically male types of employment. The spouses of unemployed and underemployed males were often involved in a complex suite of income-generating activities, typically in the informal sector. It was most common among poorer segments of this part of the *kampung* for both male and female labour to be underpaid, unstable, and manual. Still, another pattern was a female in a professional or civil service job whose spouse had stable but underpaid manual labour in the formal sector.

Official statistics may not capture all categories of women's work, even as more women are working (Grijns and van Velzen 1993). Birth and work histories I collected from the women of *Kampung Rumah Putri* and from *Kampung Langit Ayuh* where I did some comparative interviewing, show that women move in and out of formal and informal sector work, changing work as the structure of their families and houses change. Women may work without wages in a family enterprise, such as Bu Wit's job making clothing for *wayang* puppets and the various piecework jobs subcontracted through the young wife living just east of the Cipto compound. There are also the very poorly paid service jobs such as selling out of a *warung*, cooking and selling food, and sewing. The tendency to combine several occupations, perhaps including both formal and informal labour, surely reflects the lack of opportunities for employment, plus the need to supplement incomes and work around the changing demands of family.

This brief look at the actual situations of *kampung* women immediately demonstrates several key characteristics of urban female employment, and by extension, male employment. First, it is a rare adult woman who does not or who has not worked for wages or cash during her lifetime, whether in the formal sector as teacher, nurse or clerk, or in the informal sector as seamstress, *warung* operator, masseuse, or cook. Many of these women are also involved in the reproductive labour for the extended family, whether as primary care giver during the day to grandchildren whose parents both work outside of the home, as attached care giver in a child's family, or as younger sibling and niece attached as housekeeper and child-care provider.

Grijins and van Velzen (1993) offer a summary sketch of a typical labour history for a woman by life cycle, demonstrating a pattern of Javanese women's active economic involvement remarkably consistent with women's work in *Rumah Putri*. Young girls start as family workers, helping with domestic work and with family-level production. They may be wage workers from a very young age in family enterprise. Bigger factories hire girls in their teens and early twenties, and entrepreneurialism is rare among young, unmarried women. Home industries require space and so, are typically associated with older women who have children and have access to house space. Women in this stage of life may also work in nearby small-scale, residentially based enterprises that attract young mothers who need the flexibility to go home and check on their children. Women with more than two children are less flexible, and so often look for sub-contracting work to do out of their home or engage in family labour instead. Women with older, school-age children tend to become entrepreneurs and often have larger enterprises. Single elderly women are often forced to become small home-based entrepreneurs selling their own goods, or handicraft workers of traditional goods.

Although it was a rare *kampung* woman who did not acknowledge some wage earning activity, such work experience may not be officially reported because of prevailing gender ideologies. In the downtown kampung described by Norma Sullivan, many of the women known as "housekeepers" worked to generate income. "Yet they would deny that their paid extra-domestic activities were 'proper' work, because popular and official gender ideologies persuaded them that proper work was done by those working outside the home and community, ideally by men" (Sullivan 1994:33).

The diversity of occupations for *kampung* women is indicative of the surplus labour in Java, but it is also a product of long-standing patterns of female work outside the home. Despite the effects of the gender ideologies represented in PKK ideology, women in Java have always been economically active (Carey and Houben 1987; Dewey 1962; Reid 1988; Stoler 1977). What has changed is the character of their work. Some patterns of informal labour have intensified, at least partially because of programs such as PKK and the development of Indonesian economy within the larger international political economy. Before turning to those issues, some more attention to issues of terminology is necessary.

The distinction between productive and reproductive labour refers to the commonly accepted distinction between work outside the home that creates new value, and work inside the home that maintains people and society. Reproductive labour is used to refer to the domestic activities that include having and raising children and housework. The implication that productive work is creative and value-adding while reproductive work is repetitive and value-conserving has had dramatic effects on how the domestic work typically performed by women is valued. The term house-keeping, with its emphasis on keeping, signifies the conservative value attributed to domestic work.

To walk through the work worlds of Javanese *kampung* women illustrates immediately how difficult it is to draw lines between formal and informal work or between productive and reproductive labour. In fact, the distinction between formal and informal sector labour maps all too neatly onto the opposition between productive and reproductive labour. The formal sector typically refers to work that is counted and controlled formally; that is, statistics are kept, and wages and work conditions follow industry and government standards. As with many under-developed economies, defining formal sector employment is problematic because such standards have not been fully institutionalized. The informal sector includes not only illegal and black market activities but the many home-based, small industries that escape both government protection, and control. Most of the work of *kampung* women falls within the informal sector, giving them, on one hand, the freedom to pursue flexible work arrangements, and on the other, leaving them vulnerable to wages, hours, and conditions that are not monitored. Even so, this sector has, at least since the New Order government, been used to attract and employ women, because although it is not controlled by the government, this sector has proven to be very useful for the larger Indonesian economy, as will be discussed in a later section.

Like the corresponding notions of the family and the household, this distinction between productive and reproductive labour may tell us more about development of the modern Western societies that invoke it, than it does about cross-cultural labour and work arrangements. It is important to note that to make a distinction between formal and informal work, just as that between female and male work, raises more questions than it answers (Rosaldo 1988), for it is a moving target whose definition is extremely sensitive to macroeconomic performance and national economic policy. The distinction between productive and reproductive labour is even more susceptible to manipulation by national governments and may conceal linkages between work marked as productive, public, and within the purview of males, and that marked as reproductive, private, and female. The subject of reproduction and the constitutive role it plays in production is taken up more fully after a consideration of the broad outlines of the Indonesian economy and the role of female labour within it.

THE INDONESIAN ECONOMY: STABILITIES AND DEPENDENCIES

How are we to understand the small-scale industries, home-based piece-work, and marginal income-generating activities pursued by women in the *kampung* in terms of the structure of the Indonesian economy? A lynchpin, is domestic policy, which is manifest in the programs of PKK, and which is domestic in the double sense of the private sphere of the household and the public sphere of the nation's internal affairs. In Indonesia, domestic policy includes not only the policies of PKK aimed at encouraging women to be good housewives, but also economic policy aimed at absorbing excess labour supply and encouraging export-oriented growth based on labour-intensive, low-skilled and low-waged manufacturing. All of these policies and practices have had significant effects on the female workforce and women's work in Indonesia.

A thumbnail sketch of Indonesia today would include its designation as a low-income, lesser developed country or LDC. (Annual per capita income is low at US$810 (World Bank July 2004; World Development Indicators Database). Real income was growing at an impressive 4 per cent annually (World Health Organization 1989) until the turmoil surrounding the end of Suharto's regime in the late 1990s and the subsequent re-shuffling of Indonesia's government. The percentage of the labour force employed in agriculture has decreased over the last 30 years. Although each decade since 1970 has seen a drop in the percentage of Indonesians living below subsistence levels, early predictions of its future as a solidly middle-income country, with an annual per capita income of around $1000 have not yet been borne out. These rosy predictions had to be revised in face of the crash in Asian markets, the end of the Suharto regime, and the continuing troubles in Indonesia's political and economic fortunes.[10] Although punctuated by a series of crises, the Asian economic crisis of the 1990s being only the latest, Indonesia's economic performance has been consistent. It is this stability across the near 60 years of economic performance that is of interest here.

Two broad trends are identified as having particular effects on women and their economic contribution: the release of large numbers of female workers in the Javanese countryside due to technological change, and the effects of excess labour for a national comparative advantage in low-wage manufacturing. The introduction of Green Revolution technologies of hybrid seeds with the accompanying changes in fertilizer, pesticide, and farming practices in the late 1960s and early 1970s produced dramatic changes in the Javanese countryside. Perhaps most problematic was the rapid disenfranchisement of labour in the agricultural sector, especially female labour. Several technological innovations had adverse effects on women and poor rural households. The change from the traditional *ani-ani* knife used by women to harvest rice to the sickle wielded by men is "perhaps the most often cited example of female economic displacement in the literature on women and development" (Wolf 1992:48–49). The introduction of rotary weeders replaced hand weeding, "another source of income for women from poor households" (Wolf 1992:49; Husken and White 1989:182). Another technological change with particular effects on women was the introduction of the mechanized rice huller. According to estimates, this change translated into an estimated loss of $50 million in annual income for women (Papanek 1983), and "[e]stimates of jobs lost ranged as high as 1.2 million in Java alone and as high as 7.7 million in all of Indonesia" (Cain 1981:134). Collier et al. (1973) estimated losses to agricultural labourers of earnings approaching US $50 million annually for Java, which represented 125 million woman days of labour.

This series of technological changes was particularly significant for women from poor rural households and had the effect of releasing large numbers of women from agricultural labour. The disenfranchisement of labour only compounded Indonesia's population problem which had its roots not just in the colonial era, but even before (see Oey-Gardiner 1993:203). The magnitude of changes in agriculture, despite declines in fertility, caused a large increase in redundant labour. In the decade 1980–90, the male population increased faster than the labour force, and the increase in female labour participation was even more marked (Wolf 1992:46). Much of the labour released in agriculture was not absorbed into manufacturing, which has grown slowly, but instead was absorbed in the informal and low-waged sectors of the economy (Jones 1987). Between 1971 and 1985, the number of rural women employed in the non-farm sector almost doubled. As Oey-Gardiner notes, the effect of increased labour force participation was the "feminising of the overall labour force"(1993:204).[11]

Gerke has argued that women have been more flexible in adapting to changes in employment because "women have always been involved in a greater variety of income earning activities in the small-scale trade sector and in food production" (Gerke 1992:96; see also Stoler 1977). Thus for many rural women, what had been side jobs in trading or small-scale home industries became their primary means to earn a living. Older rural women tended to be left in the stagnating traditional handicraft industries, while younger women took advantage of the available manufacturing jobs (Grijns and van Velzen 1993; Wolf 1992). These patterns of adaptation to the loss of agricultural jobs depended in part on a tradition of economic activity by Javanese women, but they also became a resource for state policy directed at the support of the under and unemployed.

Throughout the Southeast Asia cultural region, women are economically active, especially in trading. While rural women have long dominated the trading sector in Java (Dewey 1962), urban women are often traders as well. My own interviewing in the *Rumah Putri* market showed that only eight of the sixty-seven women who regularly worked there actually lived in *Rumah Putri* (see Figure 4.1). The typical profile of the market woman was a rural woman whose children were school aged at least. There were some unmarried women, but many fewer than the older middle aged to elderly trader. For the most part, the women at the *Rumah Putri* market were referred to as *bakul* (market seller), which has connotations of poverty and low status, and most, but not all, were indeed poor rural women. These patterns of active engagement in wage earning are belied in the ideology of PKK which works to mask the superfluity of the female work force, as well as the large numbers of unemployed and underemployed males. High levels of unemployment in the general workforce have been compounded by high levels of under-employment. "The 1990 Population Census showed that around 38.7 per cent of people work less than 35 hours a week" (Wolf 1992:49). Despite the clear evidence for the redundancy of female labour, particularly in rural areas, some have concluded that the long time spent by youths looking for employment is the more salient feature of the Indonesian labour market profile (Oey-Gardiner 1993:204). A structural fact of life according to Jones (1987), most of these unemployed youths are supported by family and friends, and they are more likely than the older unemployed to live in a household with at least one working member (Oey-Gardiner 1993).

Figure 4.1
The market in *Kampung Rumah Putri*. (Photo by S. Ferzacca.)

Yet, this feature of the Indonesian labour force is not unrelated to female unemployment. The ability to support young unemployed males and females is related to the unpaid family labour as well as to the informal sector labour of females, the very kind of work promoted by the programs of PKK, which offers training and support for home-based industries. Consequently, patterns of female labour are intimately connected with patterns of male employment or unemployment. It is impossible to neatly oppose female strategies to male strategies in a one-to-one relationship, and this is consistent with the larger argument about households made here. Rather than considering inside versus outside work, or formal versus informal work, or male versus female work, the question must be what are the linkages between these various economic activities, linkages that illustrate how unpaid household labour is directly influenced by what is taken to be formal sector work. This connection between women's "proper" household work and formal sector employment becomes even clearer when export-oriented manufacturing in Indonesia is considered.

The connection between female labour and export-oriented, labour-intensive manufacture is now well-known (Ong 1987; Wolf 1992; Zavella 1991). It should come as no surprise then that the posture toward foreign direct investment and the employment of women might be linked. A review of foreign direct investment (Hill 1991; Newberry 1997) illustrates the successive policy shifts that have led to a relatively open disposition by the Indonesian government toward direct investment by foreign concerns. The result has been significant growth in foreign manufacturing that takes advantage of the cheap labour available in Indonesia. "[U]nlike its neighbours, Indonesia has not been attracted to the concept of export processing zones (EPZ)," although there has been much growth in labour-intensive, export-oriented industry, particularly in West Java (Hill 1991; cf. Robison 1986).[12] It is not surprising that part of the attraction that Indonesia has for international capital is its low-wage labour force. Export-oriented industrialization likewise requires higher levels of state involvement in disciplining the labour force than other forms of manufacture (Wolf 1992; Robison 1986). In an effort to lure foreign investors, the Indonesian government advertises one of the lowest average wage rates in Asia, for workers are forbidden to strike by the state. The argument that docile female labour is particularly effective or attractive for labour-intensive, export-oriented industry is not a new one (see Ong 1987). That the reproduction of this labour force is tied up with state-sponsored reproduction is not typically acknowledged or understood. The programs and premises of PKK do more than support the prosperous family through women's low-cost social welfare work, they also support a large number of unemployed and underemployed family members. The domestic work advocated for women through the ideology of PKK also has the happy advantage for the Indonesian government of encouraging women to stay out of formal sector employment even while they pursue cottage-based, informal sector work from inside their home to provide support for what is in essence a large reserve army of labour. These large numbers of unemployed and under-employed men and youths are sustained by both the make-shift and domestic work of women, and are thus readily available for work, but just as easily dismissed, with their subsistence costs covered by the informal sector work of women.

The labour redundancy that characterized employment in the Republic of Indonesia at the time of my fieldwork, and which continues until the present, is due to a variety of factors, including high numbers of unskilled labourers and an underdeveloped industrial sector. As in many countries of the global South, this situation has produced a continuing dependence on the low-skilled informal sector for the absorption of labour and for producing Indonesia's comparative advantage in export-oriented manufacturing. The motivation for the government's interest in programs such as PKK that instruct women to stay at home and care for their families but also earn monies out of their homes should be understood not only in terms of the patterns of *kampung* employment, but also in terms of larger issues of national labour superfluity. The informal sector work of women subsidizes under-employed and unemployed family members, but such state-sponsored reproduction of the labour force also serves to keep labour unrest low, people fed, and overall wages low as well. Indeed, PKK and domestic community programs appear to be motivated in part by the simultaneous needs for low-wage labour for export-oriented manufacturing, absorption of excess labour, and low-cost infrastructural improvement and social development.

The release of millions of female labourers from agricultural work through Green Revolution technological change and consequent changes in the social relations of production include: the rising feminization of the work force, and the rising education of the whole labour force; the introduction of the domestic and community programs of PKK; and the Republic of Indonesia's disposition toward foreign investment and its apparent reliance on low-waged, labour intensive, export-oriented manufacture as a comparative advantage, even post-crisis. These ingredients are a powerful mix of motivations for the Indonesian government to purse a particular set of domestic policies. Ultimately, these policies mean the reproduction of a large number of low-skilled, low-aged labourers but also the reproduction of *kampung* community and the housewives who support them.

REPRODUCING THE DOMESTIC COMMUNITY

Reproduction assumes central importance in the case of Indonesia and its state-sponsored programs of domesticity included under the umbrella of PKK. This is reproduction in its expanded sense, including not only the making of babies, but the making of the labour force and particular social forms, such as the *kampung*.[13] PKK, when considered in conjunction with shifting patterns of labour employment and utilization in Indonesia, provides the government with a means to reproduce a large reserve army of labour, as Marx would describe it.

How is this so? Not only are PKK housewives exhorted to stay at home and raise good citizens, they are also urged to develop craft and small business skills so that they may help support their families. As a result, the national housewives organization supports the reproduction of large numbers of labourers who can be employed sporadically. PKK is not just about the reproduction of dutiful citizens, it is also about the reproduction of cheap, available labour and the absorption of surplus labour, perhaps particularly male labour. And, wittingly or not, it also reproduces the *kampung* as particular type of social formation. For these reasons, analysis of the role of reproduction in linking the "domestic" with market exchange is critical.

Social reproduction has been theorized from many perspectives, not the least of which are marxist and feminist anthropology. Interestingly enough, Claude Meillassoux wrote one of the most famous analyses of the connection of domestic reproduction to larger scale economic and political institutions in his *Maidens, Meal and Money* (1981, French edition, 1975), and his work was central to the debate on the domestic mode of production that was current in Marxist-feminist circles in the 1970s. Meillassoux's description of how the reproduction of migrant workers in France was accomplished through their home communities in Africa served to show the critical importance of reproduction and the domestic community to capitalist production. It was Meillassoux's thesis that the reproduction of the labour force was supported by the unpaid domestic work of the household and that, in fact, capital was subsidized by the domestic mode of production. Moreover, his analysis suggested that the effect of production on the organization of social reproduction can extend across international boundaries.

In essence, Meillassoux is arguing that a domestic economy, or an entire domestic community, exists to support capitalist production, even when that production is spatially and culturally distant. Meillassoux's argument is a powerful one that begins to provide a way to think about the state-sponsored reproduction in urban Javanese *kampung*. The work of women in the informal sector and in the domestic sphere, as well as in the *kampung* community itself, supports the reconstitution, maintenance, and replacement of a ready low-waged labour force (Polanyi 1944), as well the reproduction of the *kampung* itself as a particular kind of social formation.

Maxine Molyneux (1979) famously added an important addendum to Meillassoux's argument. Arguing that housework cannot be seen as separate from the larger economic system, Molyneux critiqued the failure to problematize the status of women and the family (see also Moore 1994). What requires explanation are "the specific political, historical and economic reasons which result in 'family' wages being paid to members of some classes and strata and not to others, to men and not to women, and by some capitalists and not others" (1979:13). Again, the relationship between the domestic economy and the capitalist economy becomes a question, not a given. The key point of Molyneux's argument for the discussion of housewives in *Kampung Rumah Putri*, is the identification of the connection between the creation of housewives and the needs of the state and economy.

> [T]he 'family wage' and the'housewife syndrome' help to conceal high unemployment—specifically high female unemployment, and in certain ways to legitimise it. Women can be seen as constituting a specific stratum of the reserve army, called upon in times of war or rapid accumulation, but returned to their 'place' in the family if these jobs contract or the men return to them. Because this 'place' exists and because of women's supposed 'natural' pre-disposition towards it, women's unemployment is potentially less politically and socially problematic. (Molyneux 1979:26)

This argument is strikingly similar to the pattern described here: that, partially through the programs of PKK, Javanese women have been encouraged to take roles in the informal sector with the effect of reducing pressure on the formal sector and of supporting and reproducing the large numbers of unemployed and under-employed men and young people. High levels of female unemployment are masked, costs of social reproduction are kept low, and labour unrest is averted. Meillassoux's conceptualization of reproduction and how the domestic community is created in response to the organization of production, when combined with Molyneux's corrective focus on how housewives may be produced in the process, begin to shape an idea of the role of the household, the housewife, and *kampung* community in *Kampung Rumah Putri*.

The chronology of the development of PKK as a government program is of some interest to the argument here that the Republic of Indonesia gains in multiple ways from the movement of active female labour out of formal sector productive work and into informal sector, home-based productive and reproductive labour. Through its programs of support for healthy children and families, PKK is of course very involved in reproduction of human beings. Its emphasis on the proper nationalist education of children by their stay-at-home mothers also suggests involvement with reproduction of socially and politically appropriate citizens. And yet there is more to PKK than this. In its literacy, credit, and education programs, PKK works to produce a particular kind of gendered working experience along with the social form most appropriate to its continuation: the *kampung* community.

The original home economics seminar that is conventionally taken to be the basis for PKK in Indonesia was hosted in 1957. Yet, the institution and promulgation of PKK programs did not occur until much later. It is perhaps not surprising that the series of technological and labour changes that occurred in the countryside during the 1970s was followed closely by the period when programs of PKK were intensified and extended throughout Indonesia. PKK was institutionalized in 1973, and it was during the second five-year plan (1974–79) that the focus on women was intensified (Gerke 1992).

The increase in state intervention in the agricultural sector, which led to the disenfranchisement of female labour through changing technological and social relations, at the same time that PKK programs appeared aimed at encouraging women to stay home and support their families, appears more than coincidental. The scale of PKK once it was nationalized in the early 1970s suggests its importance to the government: "when one considers that there is a PKK in each one of the nearly 700,000 villages in Indonesia, and that two-thirds of government funds for women in Indonesia are allotted to PKK, the implications are great" (Suryakusuma 1991:55). One can, however, argue that the government's desire for national development of human and productive resources could logically lead to these outcomes as well, and indeed, no hypothesis of a governmental conspiracy is offered here. Instead, the near simultaneous release of female labour and the institution of programs aimed at domesticity has many causes and multiple effects. Yet, it is clear that the government of Indonesia does see PKK as having economic implications. As Suryakusuma writes:

> While PKK is associated with women, it is ultimately directed at families. The family supports society and the state in three ways: *first, as an economic unit, a place for reproduction, formation of a work force and also as an arena for consumption*; secondly, as 'bi-social' unit, namely where the biological relationship of mother-father-children are given a social construction; thirdly, it provides the venue for the formation of an ideological unit—a system of values, beliefs, religion, social traditions, culture and conservatism inculcated since childhood. (1991:58; emphasis added)

Yet the connection between PKK and its economic uses for the Indonesian government's management of the economy lies not just in the direct propaganda about the family and women's role in supporting it. It also concerns the aspect of PKK activities that has received less attention: those government programs and monies directed at informal sector enterprises. Part of the very mixed message of PKK is that not only should women be good stay-at-home mothers dedicated to raising good citizens and helping to manage their local communities, they should also earn extra money to add to the family's fortunes. Of course, this work must be done out of the home if the other admonitions of the PKK program are to work. So how are women to manage this? The government of Indonesia has in effect encouraged women to pursue informal sector work out of their own homes. This encouragement comes in the form of PKK literature but also in the form of skills training and small amounts of money to support such small home-based industries. For example, the PKK *warung* begun by Bu Sae and her friends was initially funded by the government, and while not a home-based operation, this small store was in the immediate community and served their neighbours (see Figure 4.2). There were numerous other small handicraft businesses that had received small seed monies and training through PKK, such as those devoted to making leather goods and handbags, handmade pillows and bed covers, and sewing.

Figure 4.2
The PKK *warung* started by Bu Sae. (Photo by S. Ferzacca.)

One example I witnessed in another area of the *kampung* was a small handicraft enterprise dedicated to making shoes and handbags out of banana or palm leaf. The woman who started this cottage industry had received both credit and training through PKK to begin her business. She employed some eight to ten women who worked on her front porch, making the uppers by hand. She then subcontracted the leather trim and sole work out to a nearby leather industry, another small-scale and *kampung*-based enterprise just down the alleyway. She managed the business out of the front room of her house which also served as the shop where shoes could be purchased, although the majority of her shoes were sold on consignment outside the *kampung*.

This small-scaled operation is an example of the best in PKK-supported *kampung* industry. Not only did this woman become an entrepreneur who supported other small, local businesses, but the women who worked for her were mostly young married mothers who could bring their youngest children to work and who could also easily return home to see to older school-aged children as needed. In this way, these small-scale, informal sector, cottage industries provide a means to support *kampung* families and allow mothers to remain close to home. On the other hand, it is worth noting that women so engaged are not competing directly with men in the formal sector labour market. Indeed, these small industries serve to support *kampung* families by allowing women to earn some wages without leaving their communities and while still working in the home to cook and clean for other household members engaged in formal sector work, or as was often the case, not working at all.

The positives of PKK-sponsored small enterprise for stay-at-home mothers can easily obscure the history of active wage-earning on the part of Javanese women. The pun on the name *Perempuan Kurang Kerja* or PKK as "women without enough work" is more than incidental; it signifies the local sense that PKK activities are make-work and no real substitute for gainful employment. The contradiction at the heart of PKK rhetoric—that women should stay at home, but also work—exemplifies the other contradictions in the program, that is, women decry PKK and make fun of it, but they still use it, a theme picked up in the following chapter.

What is clear from my experience in *Kampung Rumah Putri* is that women are involved in various wage earning activities. In this way, households are able to support themselves in the face of low male employment and male under-employment. And this tendency for *kampung* women to pursue multiple jobs and informal sector work out of their homes is encouraged through the programs of PKK which emphasize *ketrampilan* (skills) and *pengetahuan* (knowledge), not to mention the provisions of actual support through credit and classes for beginning cottage or small-scale industries.

This pattern of part-time, informal work and a multiplicity of occupations is not new, but in a mimicry of Clifford Geertz's agricultural involution (1963), this sector has come to absorb infinite amounts of labour in urban settings. The benefits for the Indonesian government seem clear. In a situation of surplus labour and a bottleneck in the employment of the young and better educated, the informal sector labour of women serves to keep households afloat while it removes women from the active search for employment, which might put them in competition with the male unemployed. While the official stance towards women in formal sector employment appears positive, the practices of the government work to encourage women to stay home and work in cottage-based informal sector businesses. And up to this point, the informal sector appears to be infinitely absorptive.

In a fascinating continuation of the patterns described above, the Indonesian government and the *post-Reformasi* (era of reform) NGO-sector recently have aimed significant efforts towards developing the small and medium enterprise (SME) sector in Indonesia. For example, my experience as a volunteer with a local NGO based in Yogya demonstrated that a portion of its programs were aimed at the development and support of small businesses (*kerajinan kecil*) in the informal sector. As one worker described to me, these are often businesses that are *super-kecil* (or super small), and these are dominated by women. In an explicit acceptance of the large percentage of businesses that are quite small in Indonesia, programs have been developed to support and nurture these small enterprises. This pattern of poor and lower class women beginning small-scale enterprises out of their homes thus appears consistent across political and economic regimes in Indonesia, based perhaps in part on long-standing patterns of multiple employment, but just as importantly, on patterns of policy by the Indonesian government.

Beyond this long-standing pattern of female work in the informal sector, the ease with which PKK has been insinuated into the lives of working class *kampung* women is explained not in its rhetoric, which so many *kampung* women deny, but in its compatibility with local patterns of exchange and reproduction, part of a larger pattern of making do in *kampung* community.

THE LOGIC OF MAKING DO

The men, women, and families I lived and worked among in *Kampung Rumah Putri* were making do: spreading burdens between houses, cobbling together formal and informal labour, and using both the offices of PKK and local patterns of sharing to look after one another. The logic of their making do is intimately tied up with reproduction in all its senses, and it is also linked to state programs. In a sense, this logic of making do returns us to the household as an economic unit. Only this time, exchange between households is the key to their reproduction.

Making do is used here to refer to the suites of activities that are engaged in by *kampung* members, both male and female, to support their families. The patchwork of formal and informal sector work, makeshift jobs, local exchange of goods and services, and reproductive tasks are combined in a pattern that is shifting and fluid. This making-do-to-get-by can be understood as an example of the often overlooked fourth form of exchange described by Polanyi, and that is householding (1944). Rhoda Halperin (1994) provides an updated consideration of householding in her ethnography of the residents of Kentucky's Appalachia. Poor, working-class rural Kentuckians share many similarities with patterns of employment and sharing in the *kampung* in that they mix economic forms among parts of dispersed extended families. Both groups make use of informal credit mechanisms, services exchanged between households for goods and services rather than cash, small-scale industry, childcare and housekeeping services performed by family members, periodic labour in the informal sector, as well as a range of formal sector employments. As in rural Kentucky, these economic practices vary in their level of integration into formal sector production monitored by the state, and the mix of activities varies by gender and life stage.

A key component in Halperin's interpretation of householding is that the primary focus of economic activities is the *provisioning* of the family network in the 'Kentucky way,' a pattern of "multiple and interconnected livelihood strategies" that integrates nuclear families that are spatially separate because kin are expected to help one another as needed (Halperin 1994:152). Householding does not imply or require actual households. It may involve individuals, pairs, or groups or households. "The model of householding allows us to understand the limits of households as provisioning units" (Halperin 1994:149).

Indeed, this is much like what I saw in *Kampung Rumah Putri*, especially the mix of formal and informal activities and the tendency for goods and services to move between the households and hearthholds. The "*kampung* way" then is a householding strategy that integrates households in exchange networks that are based on the practical need for getting by. References by residents to *hidup kampung* (*kampung* life) and the ways of the *wong kampung* (*kampung* people) are likewise indicative of a sense of integration with neighbours in patterns of cooperation and sharing perceived to be different than social relations outside the *kampung*. The strategies of *kampung* residents and the rural poor of Kentucky both appear to be aimed at making do within a constraining capitalist system, all the while maintaining labour and productive flexibility and movement.

This adaptation to the evolving economic system in Indonesia is particularly successful for urban *kampung* residents (and likely for rural dwellers as well) who can move between informal sector work and temporary work always bolstered by family exchange. Indeed, evidence that urban workers returned home to rural areas during the recent economic crisis supports this idea (Jones 2000). In many ways this strategy might be seen as a holding action, providing poor Kentuckians and *kampung* dwellers alike with a means to get by. Yet, the multiple livelihood strategy of *kampung* dwellers cannot simply be understood as a temporizing action by those caught between full capitalist employment and an agrarian past. As was suggested in the discussion regarding employment and labour practices in Java, the Republic of Indonesia is not a passive player in this; indeed, it cannot afford to be. Any real distinction between capitalist and non-capitalist sectors becomes artificial when the state's role in organizing reproduction is revealed.

PKK literature promotes the view of the single family unit: two parents and two children living in a single dwelling. Yet, the literature also advocates that women's work extend beyond the boundaries of the household to support the local community and those within it that need help. Further, the programs of PKK are aimed at teaching skills or *ketrampilan* so that women can earn *tambahan suami*, or supplemental income (literally, in addition to husband), which has the undeniable effect of absorbing excess female labour and of supporting large numbers of under-employed males and teens as well. That the *kampung* represents a large army of reserve labour seems clear. And it is PKK that provides the ideological vocabulary for producing and sustaining a domestic community—the *kampung*—and for organizing support for the reproduction of the reserve army of labour it represents through a bio-social group—the household—focussed centrally around unpaid work of some—the housewife.

HOUSE-HOLD AND HOUSE-KEEPING

Hold: to keep fast, or from getting away, with the grasp of the hand or by any means; prevent or control the motion of movement of by grasping or by means of detention or constraint; to keep or maintain a grasp on something; keep hold; adhere or cling as if by grasping; maintain connection, or remain fast; keep from be coming loose or giving way; also, to remain attached, faithful, or steadfast; the act or an act of holding fast by a grasp of the hand or by some other physical means (as, to catch, lay or take hold: to release one's hold); grasp; grip; hence a non-physical grasp, control, controlling force, or dominating influence; also, confinement or imprisonment; also, possession or occupation as of the land; also a thing that holds fast or supports something else; a receptacle for something; a prison or prison-cell; also, something grasped for support; a dwelling or habitation; a place of refuge or shelter.

Keeping: the act of one who or that which keeps; observance; guarding, custody, or care; maintenance or keep; holding, reserving, or retaining; also just conformity in things or elements associated together; agreement, congruity, or harmony. (The New Century Dictionary, 1948)

The shouting match over a kerosene stove should lead us to question not just how much pooling goes on within a single house, but to questions about the constitution of units known as households and the making of housewives as their central pivot. The boundedness of the household as an economic unit does not survive close inspection in Java. The reproduction of male and female as different kinds of economic persons is guaranteed by PKK, because as women are told to stay home, they are relegated to the make-shift, make-work sector that supports the formal sector work of men and the large numbers of unemployed and underemployed who live in *kampung*. And this differs by life-cycle. The adult women of the *kampung* are not only supporting the patchy employment of husbands, they are also supporting sons and daughters, and sometimes nieces, nephews, mothers-in-law, and so on.

Yet, the constitution of households and housewives is not just a passive making through the domestic policies of the Republic of Indonesia as a response to employment dislocations and the needs for foreign direct investment. Neither can the constitution of households through the logic of making do be understood only as the resistance of the working class and poor to the deepening incursion of global capitalism. Just as the definition of hold includes both the idea of refuge and of prison, and to keep means both to maintain and to guard, the household in *Kampung Rumah Putri* has both faces, and the housewife is doubly made: to keep families afloat and to organize reproduction for the needs of the state.

What seems equally clear is that Indonesia can provide community support for basic welfare measures—child and elder care, for example—without paying directly the price for this support. In this fashion, the Republic of Indonesia not only absorbs and supports large numbers of under-employed adults and young people, it also improves its infrastructure, human and otherwise.

NOTES

1. See Boris and Bardaglio (1983), Donzelot (1979), Harris (1984), Harrison and Mort (1980), Matthews (1987), Scott and Tilly (1975), and Tilly (1993).
2. See Rosaldo (1974, 1980) for reviews of some of the foundational issues in analyses of the domestic sphere within anthropology.
3. Becker's "new household economics" (1981) represented a break with previous analyses of the altruistic, peasant household by extending neo-classical microeconomic analysis to within the household. Yet as Wolf describes, "the peasant, formerly the bumbling idiot of modernization theory enslaved by tradition," was than "transformed into a hyper-rational strategist, playing the social game according to optimal strategies"; the domestic group formerly viewed as passive and "lacking in rationality suddenly had its qualities reversed" (1992:13). Becker's work represents an advance on the conventional view that the household/ family are somehow isolated from market forces, yet his use of a joint utility function for the household suggests an internal homogeneity that is problematic, especially for those interested in gender asymmetry within the household.
4. Wilk suggests an ecological perspective, treating households as systems analogous to ecosystems. "Ecosystems are not naturally bounded units either.... Closure can never be assumed, though degrees of permeability can be defined" (Wilk 1989:31).
5. This relationship is described here as fosterage because typically the child in question is aware of his or her biological parents and may move between their natal house and that of their foster parents during their youth. But there is quite a lot of variation in this relationship. Children may be fostered by people who are not kin, and some children never know that they are not the biological child of the people who raised them. This fosterage is used not just to spread

out the costs of reproduction but also to provide childless relatives with an infant and to give very young, unwed mothers a chance to avoid motherhood at too young an age (H. Geertz 1961).

6. The *Pos Kamling* (from *Pos Keamanan Lingkungan*, or neighbourhood safety post) is one of the remnants of the WWII neighbourhood system instituted by the Japanese. Small shelters are built in every neighbourhood for the nightly neighbourhood patrols that are staffed on a rotating basis by the adult men of the area. In many neighbourhoods, although the open-fronted bamboo shelter remains with the large hollow log for sounding the alarm, no one actually sits the night watch, although this varies by area.

7. Compulsory schooling is required for all children through the elementary grades, but all schools, public and private alike, charge fees. The burden of school fees is the universal complaint of all *kampung* families, and the difficulty in paying them twice a year is likely a significant factor in the dropping birth rate.

8. My experience in the *kampung* suggests that in addition to the rotating credit associations associated with various *kampung* organizations, there are many opportunities to obtain credit. Moreover, credit serves an important function in supporting working class families who have no surplus cash and no cushion for emergencies. It likewise is an important link in *kampung* networks that define and support community.

9. RT divisions are referred to by numbers. I have designated the two RT where I did my work as *barat* (west) and *timur* (east) for convenience and the purposes of anonymity.

10. Although the predictions of disaster for Indonesia's poor as a result of the crisis have not proven to be true (Jones 2000), there is no question that the downturn in the economy since 1997 has increased poverty and disproportionately affected the working poor. Comprehensive analysis of the Indonesian economy post-crisis is necessarily preliminary at this point.

11. Before the economic crisis in the late 1990s, there was general agreement that the major problem facing the Republic of Indonesia was excess labour (Cain 1981; Jones 1987; Oey-Gardiner 1993; Wolf 1992). Most scholars agreed that over the twenty-five years prior to the 1990s, the increase of the female labour force has been greater than that of the male labour force. High levels of unemployment in the general workforce were compounded by high levels of under-employment. "The 1990 Population Census showed that around 38.7 per cent of people work less than 35 hours a week, while around 34.3 per cent work more than 45 hours a week" (Wolf 1992:49).

12. According to Hill, the Indonesian government, since 1986, "has operated an especially effective duty drawback scheme for exporters which has been so successful that it has obviated the need for such zones" (Hill 1991:5). Although manufacturing has had a low percentage share in Indonesia's gross domestic product (GDP), it has increased consistently: "from 1973 to 1984 Indonesia's manufacturing output grew faster than that of all the Asian countries listed" (Wolf 1992:37).

13. See Moore (1994), Harris (1984), Harris and Young (1981).

Chapter Five

The Home

The government will support PKK which we hope will be a spearhead for the development of society from below, 'motored' by women. I ask that the various activities programmed at the national level be channeled through PKK. We can have many programs for women to enhance the role of women in development. But it should not be forgotten that these programs are aimed and to be implemented by women in the villages, whether in the urban or rural areas. If there are too many organizations, it is not in accordance with their simple desires and way of thinking, and will only serve to confuse them. (Presidential meeting Suharto, Indonesia's second president, on the occasion of the National Working Meeting of P2W-KSS, 2 March 1981, cited in Suryakusuma 1991:57.)

Sesudah bertjakap-tjakap seperlunja, kami bertiga permisi pulang. Kami mengambil djalan melalui kedai-kedai, dan pasar pula. Tapi pikiran saja terus melajang. Melajang memikiran satu soal,—soal wanita. Kemerdekaan! Bilakah semua Sarinah-Sarinah mendapat kemerdekaan? Tetapi, ja—kemerdekaan jang bagaimana? Kemerdekaan seperti jang dikehendaki oleh pergerakan feminismekah, jang hendak menjamaratakan perempuan dalam segala hal dengan laki-laki? Kemerdekaan a la Kartini?

After we had discussed what had brought us there, the three of us excused ourselves and left. We took the road home through shops and markets. But my thoughts continued to wander. Wandering into thinking about a particular problem—the problem of women. Freedom! When will all the Sarinahs attain their freedom? But, yes—what kind of freedom. Freedom like that desired in the feminist movement, that desires to equalize women in all the rights of men? The freedom of Kartini? (Soekarno, Indonesia's first president; from his book Sarinah: Women's Duty in the Struggle for the Republic of Indonesia, 1951:8)

SEPARATE SPHERES

Perhaps foolishly, I had offered my house as the meeting place for the local PKK (*Pembinaan Kesejahateraan Keluarga*) meeting. Little did I know that this seemingly ordinary meeting of housewives, just one of countless neighbourhood meetings I had attended, would figure so prominently in my understanding of the shifting political alliances in the neighbourhood. Because while I was attending to my guests, fractures in the fragile bedrock of community were being attended to as well.

The PKK meeting held at my house illustrates the multi-vocality of "community" in one urban, working class neighbourhood and how it is experienced by one woman, my neighbour, Bu Sae. This particular meeting, as I came to understand much later, differed from a typical neighbourhood PKK meeting in several important ways. First, of course, was the locale. Before using my house, meetings had been held jointly with the adjoining neighbourhood association to the east, despite government directives that each section meet individually. But since my arrival in the *kampung*, the two sections had split unhappily over money and shared goods. Each RT typically owns mats, glasses, dishes, and other items necessary for holding ceremonial dinners or *slametan*, and women in the *kampung* repeatedly told me that this kind of cooperation is fundamental to community life and well-being. The difficulties in this kind of sharing were illustrated vividly in the messy break-up of the sections after one group refused to divide the goods equally with the other.

So at this first individual meeting for the unit in which I lived, a smaller group of women met under the leadership of Bu Wit, the wife of our new local section chief or RT. As his wife she was expected to serve as the head of all the women's activities within the RT. Another apparent difference at this meeting was the introduction of a new, richer credit lottery (*arisan*) requiring a contribution of 5000 *rupiah*, (US$2.50 in 1992). *Arisan* are a fundamental part of PKK meetings, and for many women, the main reason they attend. Like the sharing of plates and glasses, the circulation of money and credit are not part of any government program but a persistent element in community life. Still, this new 5000 rp *arisan* was a little out of the ordinary, just one indication of the emergence of more "middle"-class incomes and lifestyles in the *kampung* and their contradictory effects for community. The usual *kampung*-variety *arisan* contribution is 500 or 1000 rp. While 5000 rp was not beyond the reach of most of the women at this meeting, it was clearly easier for some than for others to contribute that amount to the credit lottery once a month.

But it was not until my close neighbour, Bu Sae, came slowly toward the door and perched on the threshold, halfway in and halfway out, that one of the biggest changes in this meeting was made manifest. Her attendance touched on issues of kinship and family enmity, economic and social jealousy, and finally the formation of the *kampung* as a moral community. And although I did not fully realize it at the time, her presence sent shock waves through the room.

The effect of Bu Sae's presence, and some of her experiences in the *kampung*, have much do with local understandings of community in the *kampung*. Her experience as a Bu RT herself, her involvement in *Dharma Wanita* (The Duty of Women, the national organization for the wives of civil servants), and her position as one of the managers of the local PKK *warung* all marked her as a woman who made successful use of the resources of the Family Welfare Movement (another common translation of PKK). Her experiences illustrate the meaning of community in one urban, working-class neighbourhood and the continuous reconfiguration of community by state and citizen alike in the ongoing process of state formation. But to truly understand Bu Sae's position in *kampung*, it is critical to place her within a moral universe of family, home, and community, and in so doing, reveal how the organization of PKK provides both limitations and opportunities to the working-class women of Indonesia.

THE HOME

In previous chapters, the "house" was considered as a summarizing term for anthropology's analysis of the role of kinship and built form in making the domestic. The "household" underwent an equivalent analysis of its character as a summation of the domestic as a particular kind of economy with distinct forms of reproductive labour and exchange. "Home" is the final term in this triptych of approaches to the domestic. As it happens, home and the ideal of home life gloss the emotional and moral dimensions of the household in common speech and in academic parlance alike. Like house and household, the home appears to us as a natural, bounded unit, in this case associated with the emotions, sentiments, and morality of the domestic sphere. Upon further inspection, the location of the good woman as the domestic angel within the domestic sphere is revealed as an historical project, one with dramatic effects for propriety as a feminine project as well as for limiting and directing the political power of this moral project. As with house and household, the boundary between the domestic and the public raises a question, a question about the relationship of the moral power of the domestic to larger issues of race, sexuality, women's education, and their roles in conserving tradition, in nationalist revolution, and in social reform.

The literature on the emergence of the ideology of home as the domestic haven, seat of filial piety, of sentiment, of family values, and the habitat of the domestic angel has been analyzed predominantly by social historians and feminist historians as the peculiar result of the emergence of the bourgeois nation-state in England and parts of Europe.[1] The haven in the heartless world with its domestic angel is not just a Victorian image that weighs like a nightmare on the minds of the living, it has inspired volumes of scholarly work on the ideological construction of the bourgeois home and family and its realization or lack thereof in the lives of colonists and the colonized alike.[2]

The "Victorian debate on women" and their proper place emerged during the age of empire in nineteenth-century Europe, when evolutionary histories, social Darwinism, and laissez-faire liberalism were at their height.

Middle- and upper-class women were being consigned to the domestic sphere
as distinct from the public, a feat made possible by the simultaneous
consignment of lower class women to the domestic sphere of elite women's
kitchens, not to mention the public, industrial sector. The emergence of
the housewife in the First World was the "result of a protracted historical
process comparable with and closely related to that of proletarianization,"
a process Bennholdt-Thomsen calls 'domestication' or 'housewifization'
(1988:159). Although it was the experience of middle- and upper-class
women that would inform bourgeois ideology, as Maria Mies, who coined
the term housewifization (1986), suggests, it would result in all women
being socially defined as housewives, dependent on their husbands,
whether they were or not. In this way, the class specific outlines of the
domestic sphere were extended to all women. The separation of women
away from the world and within their homes became the dominant model
even for those women who had to leave the countryside to live in the city
and work in the factories and for those women who earned their wages
inside the domestic haven reserved for others (Tilly and Scott 1975).

The creature at the centre of the home, the domestic angel, has turned
out to be remarkably resilient across cultures in every succeeding generation, despite the fact that she was the product of a very particular phase
of industrial capitalism in one part of the world. Part of the resiliency of
the "housewife" and "good mother" is her association with what are often
taken to be essentially feminine qualities such as nurturance, care, loving
sacrifice, all of which were understood to be manifestations of her biolog-
ically determined role as mother. The emergence of two spheres, one
associated with the public power of the state and market and one associated with the private, intimate power of love and motherhood defined
woman's authoritative action as based on her "natural" role. The naturalization of the mother's placement within the home has created the dura-
bility of this idea of separate spheres despite many years of critique about
the elisions and particularities in its historical making. The opposition of
the domestic to the public, like that of nature to culture, has been considered extensively within anthropology (Collier and Yanagisako 1989;
Ortner 1974; Rosaldo 1978, 1980; Yanagisako and Collier 1987). Like the
house and the household, the boundaries of the home are susceptible to
social relations, and in this case political projects, that extend well beyond
any boundary around the domestic sphere.

The social process of naturalizing women's place within the home was
mirrored by the simultaneous naturalization of racial categories as defining appropriate social space. The physical enclosure of the middle-class
European woman in the single family home flowed from her capture
within an ideological space that served to exclude not only the dirty world
of money and manufacture but the poor, the racially degenerate, and by

extension to the colonies, the native. The physical space of the home became wedded with the moral space associated with appropriate sexuality, proper child rearing, and appropriate social behaviour to such an extent that in European colonial experience the building of square homes and straight paths was presumed to be an effective way to induce right thinking and Christian behaviour in the colonized (Comaroff and Comaroff 1992.)

For Java, purity of race and questions of racial degeneracy were a powerful means to control social distance in the colonies that was intimately connected to presumptions of appropriate home life, marriage, and family. In the early stages of colonialism in the Dutch East Indies, for example, domestic reproductive work, including sexual intercourse, was performed by the native *nyai*, who served as a housekeeper and bedmate to the lonely Dutch man (and here we see again how reproductive labour is defined not by nature but by the demands of particular productive systems, in this case, colonial extraction). The VOC (*Verenigde Oost-Indische Compagnie* or United East Indies Company) would not allow women to join their husbands without special dispensation (Gouda 1995; Stoler 1985a), although after 1652, "general practice was to allow men above the ranks of soldier and assistant in the civilian hierarchy to bring out their families" (Taylor 1983:29). In the early years of colonialism then, social and sexual relationships were relatively fluid. Children born of Dutch-Javanese unions were recognized as Dutch, and the society in the Dutch Indies included many Eurasians. Over time, as the colonial presence deepened, Dutch women were allowed to emigrate and what had previously been a situation of fluid social arrangements between colonials and the indigenes became rigid (Stoler 1989a, 1989b, 1996).

The policing of this social distance often fell to women, whose position as reproducers of Empire's children and culture obscured their commonalities with other, subordinate women. Colonial discourse on both race and gender concealed the issues of stratification within the empire, both at home and in the colonies. *Nyais* were replaced by proper Dutch wives whose children still may have been raised by native "baboes," but whose parents were purely Dutch. The separation of Dutch families from polluting indigenous influence was assured by time away at "hill stations." Even so, threats to the purity of Dutch femininity provided more reason to be strict with the potential sexual competitor that was the indigenous male, the so-called Black Peril, "the superior fecundity and deep-rooted sexual intemperance of the native world" (Gouda 1995:184). Yet, this image of the ideal good woman in need of sexual protection had a way of flipping over to reveal the dangers of unbridled sexuality for the moral order as well. Very little separated the domestic angel from the "primitive" women living in a brutish state of nature, but this very little bit would come to represent the dividing line between nature and culture, anarchy and civilization in the colonial boundary-making project (Tiffany and Adams 1985).[3]

Stoler has written most extensively on the effects of colonial domesticity
for race and gender (1995, 2002; Cooper and Stoler 1997; see also
Pramoedya 1991). In effect, the consignment of European women to the
domestic sphere was used as a mandate to preserve them and their children from the dangerous and dirty world of the native, but it was also used
as the moral charter for confining native peoples to particular social
spaces. Consequently, there is some irony in the acceptance of native
Javanese women as domestics within the most intimate of spaces, despite
the increasing social distance based on race.[4]

Domesticity and the notion of the ideal home also served to position
women as guardians of tradition. Removing women and the home from
the expanding world of commerce and industry, implied that the domestic
sphere was associated with the conservation of tradition. The connection
between women's domestic roles and the preservation of tradition and
authentic culture in the First World had the effect of associating women
with the purest symbol of Western civilization, and this white woman's
burden had profound effects on the colonies as well. Not only were the
domestic angels charged with keeping a good house but they were also
critical to policing the boundaries of appropriate sexuality and probity,
and importantly maintaining the purity of their culture. The white woman
as a trope for civilized culture eventually would be replaced by the native
woman as the symbol of tradition during nationalist revolutions.

In Java, women came to be seen as mediators between the world of *adat*
(customary law and usage) and Dutch middle-class values, such as those
promoting housewives. The importance of women's domestic routines as
a measure of culture was identified early on. "Women's rituals and routines
in daily life, in turn, constituted a yardstick with which to measure the
meaning and 'authenticity' of tradition" (Gouda 1995:81). As Princess
Kartini's sister Kardinah said in 1914, the strength of a culture resided in
"the preservation of women's purity" and women should function as
"guardian angels" of the best spiritual and cultural value of Javanese tradition (quoted in Gouda 1995:80–81).

Nowhere are the contradictions and ambiguity of the ideal woman and
home clearer than in their use as justification for nationalist revolution,
just as they had been used earlier for colonial conservation. Caught
between the desire to modernize their countries along the lines of European technologic and economic excellence and the desire to assert their
independence, nationalist discourse in the Third World often made use
of an invented tradition that privileged women as a sign of distant and
glorious past civilization (Chatterjee 1989; Jayawardena 1986; Said 1979).[5]
Women's active roles in nationalist revolution often resulted in a reduction
of their freedom as the success of their role as symbol of indigenous
tradition served to remove them from public and political life.

Paradoxically, the restriction of women to the domestic sphere granted them the moral authority to address social reform. The term "cult of domesticity" actually was used specifically for changes in early to mid-nineteenth century Anglo-America. By 1850, "[t]he home was so much the centre of the culture that historians speak of a 'cult' of domesticity.... Women in their homes were the locus of moral authority in the society" (Matthews 1987:6). The welter of books on domesticity and proper house-keeping that appeared in nineteenth-century America included Catharine Beecher's 1841 *A Treatise on the Domestic Economy* with its discussion of de Tocqueville and republicanism along with a series of laundry lists (Matthews 1987:7).[6] The work of Harriet Beecher Stowe also identified the political potential of domesticity. "Stowe used the moral authority of the housewife to justify speaking out against slavery," and consequently, the apparently neutral domain of the homes assumed "an expressly political function" (Mattews 1987:34).

Moreover, the location of the "mother" within the home, and therefore, beyond the reach of politics has, in fact, great symbolic and practical political power itself. This power may be used for progressive aims; for example, in recent years the Mothers of the Plaza in Argentina proved to be such a powerful protest against the ruling junta as they marched day after day holding the pictures of their disappeared children because they were just mothers, and because they brought the private pain of a mother's love into the public domain of the Plaza (cf. Hayden 1003). Yet the symbolic power of the mother and her practical work may be captured for less happy social causes. Claudia Koonz (1987) documents the role of Nazi women in a regime that sought to end women's electoral privileges as it sanctified their roles as reproducers of the master race. De Grazia considers similar maternal politics under Italy's fascism (1992). As Young (1997) notes, the idea of home is available both for conservative uses and for reinterpretation. bell hooks (1990) for example, locates within the African-American home, the power to resist the domination of other social structures.

The ambivalent political power of the mother, or the *ibu*, is evident in Indonesia as well. Madelon Djajadiningrat-Nieuwenhuis coined the term *ibuism* to refer to the combination of elite *priyayi* values with those of the Dutch petit-bourgeois to produce an ideology that sanctions any action taken by a mother on the part of family, class, or country without asking for anything in return (1987:44). The middle-class connotations of house-wife in Indonesia, and its association with the Dutch colonial household have been extended to all Indonesian women through the state-sponsorship of domesticity. *State ibuism* has been used by Suryakusuma (1991) to suggest the New Order government's role in promoting such self sacrifice for its own ends through programs such as *Dharma Wanita* and PKK (see Figure 5.1).

Figure 5.1
A billboard in downtown Yogyakarta. Note both the juxtaposition of tradition
and modernity and the centrality of the ibu (mother) in traditional dress. (Photo by
S. Ferzacca.)

The reduction of women's roles to those defined by the domestic did
not mean a lack of political power, and as it turns out, the home was an ideal
platform for particular forms of political power. Yet, the avenues so defined
limited the forms of women's advancement. Women's education is one
example of this, although ultimately, like the nationalist and reactionary
politics that called upon women's domestic and moral power as the foundation for larger political projects, women's domestic education became
the reason for the extension of their private, domestic work to the rational
management of communities.

Home economics antedates the cult of domesticity slightly, appearing
at the end of the nineteenth century (Matthews 1987), and it springs from
a slightly different logic.[7] Associated with the science of managing the
household, home economics developed as an academic discipline in part
as the only avenue for scientifically minded female scholars in an age
before they were accepted in other established disciplines. Thus, women
such as Ellen Swallow Richards graduated from Vassar and attended MIT
to teach in newly created departments of domestic science where they put
their abilities to use in making management of the household a rational
science devoted to efficiency and health (Matthews 1987; Hayden
1981:306). The founders of the field "defined home economics (or domestic
science) as a comprehensive social and physical science encompassing

sociology, economics, nutrition, sanitation, and architecture" (Hayden 1981:306). The early era of home economics saw an emphasis on the scientific analysis of food and on technological, measuring, and time-saving innovations that would improve the welfare of all by improving the efficiency of kitchens everywhere (Matthews 1987; Shapiro 1986). While the cult of domesticity had emphasized the status-enhancing work of the home-bound wife who cooked sumptuous food in part to elevate the prestige of her husband and family, home economics emphasized the importance of counting pennies and time in the production of healthy meals.

Despite their different logics, the domestic cult like domestic science defined the appropriate means for women to be useful to their societies as well as giving them a space, albeit restricted, for advancement. For example, the development of home economics and the idea of women's special domestic roles were an early justification for the education of women. In Java, there is evidence for an early emphasis on domestic education in the example of Raden Ayu Kartini, or Princess Kartini, the Javanese noblewoman whose letters to a Dutch sponsor are a famous example of the plight of royal women in Java (Kartini 1920). Kartini was an early advocate for the training of young girls in useful, that is to say domestic, skills. "The powerful legacy of Kartini, the refined and well-informed daughter of a prominent aristocratic family in Java, exerted an indelible impact on colonial definitions of educated womanhood in a self-consciously 'modern' guise" (Gouda 1995:82). In fact, there is a "cult" of Kartini that equals the cult of domesticity in the metropole. Her advocacy for the need to train young girls, based on her own isolation from the world of learning she desired, led to the establishment of the Kartini schools which along with the Van Deventer schools sought to provide an education for "native" girls. These schools, however, were aimed at elite *priyayi* girls and based on the notion that in training these young women, there would be a trickle down effect to the poorer, humbler classes. Young girls so educated were expected to share their knowledge with those less well off than themselves. They were "encouraged them to roll up their dainty sleeves, so to speak, and to descend into the village and use their ingenuity in trying to teach better housekeeping and culinary skills to uneducated or overburdened subalterns." (Gouda 1995:106)

The implicit class stratification in elite *priyayi* women's new duties was made explicit in the creation of second class, *istri* (literally wife) schools for poor women to learn home economics so that indigenous girls could prepare for their future as housewives (Gouda 1995:86). Central to the curriculum of both sets of schools was the importance of women's place in keeping good house and thus keeping good society. Diminished welfare, or *mindere welvaart* (Dutch), was understood not to be the result of colonial racial hierarchy but the "inevitable result of their economic rationality or inferior housekeeping skills" (Gouda 1995:81). Although Gouda describes

the invisibility of poor rural women and plantation labourers in the rhetoric on girls education in colonial Java, the connection of domesticity to
both morality and the preservation of class implicated all women in its
logic. She goes on to note the general contradiction in the call for education to raise women's status with its use to tie them more closely to
tradition and housewifery (particularly when it could be argued that Javanese women had higher legal status under *adat* than did European
women in the colonial era).

It was yet another irony then that the designation of a separate domestic
sphere associated with good mothers also served as the springboard for
women's social reform movements. As with the role of the home in colonial society and newly independent nations, women's community associations were taken to be based on women's natural domain for authoritative
action, the home, being extended to the larger community. For example,
the women's club movement in early twentieth century America was a
manifestation of this urge to reform based on women's natural duties. In
1915, Mary Beard argued that "women, traditionally responsible for children, naturally sought to improve schools. Their housekeeping responsibilities led them to a concern with the cleanliness of community streets;
their responsibility for the family's food led them to support the pure food
movement" (Steinschneider 1994:10). Using terms like domestic feminism and social feminism, some scholars have sought to reframe women's
contribution to community through domesticity as progressive (Hayden
1981). Indeed, women's roles in the domestic sphere granted them the
"right and a duty to enter civic affairs" (Steinschneider 1994:13). The club
movement was yet another example of how women's "empire" was fully
political and how the prerogatives inside the home could lead to the
impetus for social change outside the home. Moreover, there is an implicit
acceptance that the home and the community are parallel structures. Fox-
Genovese has strongly made the point that women have an ancient tendency to form communities (1991). In seeking to pursue western individual rights, she contends, feminists have forsaken their age-old connection
to community. Fox-Genovese's work runs the risk of a retrograde naturalism
when she makes connections to ancient tendencies. Yet, it is clear that "social
housekeeping" based on an extension of women's defined domestic roles
has been the effect of the creation of the domestic sphere in many places.

Indeed, this notion of women's social housekeeping appears to be the
basis for the state-sponsored domesticity of the Republic of Indonesia
represented by *Dharma Wanita* and PKK. As a government publication puts
it, PKK is "aimed at establishing a healthy prospering family in order to
create a welfaring community" (Department of Information 1984:31). As
suggested in Chapter Four, PKK has served in some sense to consign
women's labour to informal sector household-based work with particular
effects for wages and the reproduction of the larger labour force. At the

same time, PKK and *Dharma Wanita* position women as pillars of the community, responsible for the moral upbringing of children and good citizens as well as the management of moral communities. Although the emergence of PKK was described earlier, it is useful here to consider how the mandate of good mother and wife evident in the programs of PKK and *Dharma Wanita* was produced.

Dharma Wanita developed in a fashion quite similar to PKK yet its membership is based on being the wife of a civil servant rather than on being an adult, married woman. *Dharma Wanita* (The Duty of Woman) is often punned as Drama Wanita, and it is associated with charitable works by middle-class women organized through their husbands' places of work on behalf of the poor. PKK, in some contrast, is based on local residential groupings whose activities are directed at local needs. Julia Surykusuma (1996) and Sylvia Tiwon (1996) have both considered the emergence of the mother at the expense of the wife in Indonesia's social programs. *Dharma Wanita* calls on women based on their position as wives, while PKK seems more clearly aimed at the mother. Surykusuma has argued that the New Order's family principle, or *azas kekeluargaan*, suggests that the "Indonesian government has settled on the primary category of 'wife' as the most convenient means by which to contain women" (1996:99). Quoting from an official description of *Dharma Wanita*, Suryakusuma says that the main duty of the wife as faithful companion is "to support the official duties of her husband by creating a harmonious atmosphere, avoiding anti-Pancasila [state ideology] behavior, in order to create a state official who is authoritative and clean" (ibid.). The use of the word clean glosses not just hygiene but appropriate social conduct, including sexual conduct.

Tiwon (1996) also notes an interesting elision in the representation of Kartini herself. Although Princess Kartini, has come to be known as Ibu Kartini, she did not long for that role. Indeed, despite her prominent role in representing the dreams of young Indonesian women for an education, Kartini herself knew a very circumscribed life within the walls of her father's palace. She was married at a very young age and died at 25 giving birth to her first child. Tiwon lists the various ironies of her life: that she would long for a democratic education as a member of a noble family and that she would be assigned the honorary title of "mother" despite her own wishes to be a single woman.[8] Today, *Hari Ibu Kartini*, or Mother Karini Day, is celebrated throughout Indonesia as a kind of mother's day. Kartini has been transformed from a young woman rebelling against the conventions of marriage and motherhood into "the officially sanctioned model" of *ibu* that occurs "simultaneously with the rearticulation of the word *ibu* itself" (Tiwon 1996:57). This "rearticulation of the word *ibu* itself" is meant to suggest that the use of the term mother for adult women is a relatively recent phenomenon. Tiwon, for example, quotes an early

19th century Javanese chronicle (*Serat Chentini*) as portraying women's primary roles as wives not mothers (1996:57); the use of the term *ibu rumah tangga* for housewife is probably of European ancestry, a translation of the Dutch word *huisvrouw*.

Tiwon also identifies the elisions and transformations in another important New Order myth which is clearly linked to fears of the uncontrolled sexuality of women not properly located as wives and mothers within the home. The alleged role of communist women in the mutilation of the six generals killed in the 1965 "coup" that brought Suharto to power is the stuff of popular legend. As the story goes, the generals who were killed were first kidnapped and taken to *Lubang Buaya* (literally crocodile hole), where they were made "a vile plaything by the women" who were dancing naked, under the direction of the Communist party leader, D.N. Aidit. "The women were given penknives and razors and they proceeded to taunt the generals, to strip them of their clothes and to slowly torture them, gouging out their eyes, slashing their bodies and stabbing their genitals" (Tiwon 1996:64). Orgies with the young soldiers were said to follow. Witnesses were brought forward to testify to the use of aphrodisiacs for the women at the training ground so that they could service the men there. The women were said to have been trained in sexually arousing dances. Indeed, in the diorama depicting the confrontation of the generals by members of PKI on the night of their deaths, women are shown with their hair down, their arms raised aggressively, eyes wild.

In fact, there is no good evidence that these highly sexualized accounts are true (Anderson 1987). Still, this imagery of wild female sexuality as a threat to political stability was useful as the Suharto government moved to strip the active women's organizations associated with GERWANI of any revolutionary political content.[9] What would emerge in its place were the officially sanctioned roles for women defined in PKK and *Dharma Wanita*. In other words, the vital women's movement of the Independence era was de-legitimised through such stories and replaced by the quasi-public organizations of women as wives and mothers who work on behalf of their families (Branson and Miller 1988; Wieringa 1993). This association of women with *state ibuism* has meant inevitably that they are associated with clean living and normal sex, and women who do not conform are labelled as dangerous and outside the norm (Buchori and Soenarto 2000; Sunindyo 1996; Suryakusuma 1996). Murray sees in the development of *Dharma Wanita* the merging of a pseudo-traditionalism with Western models of sexuality in an elite-controlled "regime of truth" (1991:7; see also Sears 1996b).

Women's newly defined position as moral arbiters placed them at the forefront of national development and campaigns of moral suasion (Garon 1993, 1997). Yet, PKK ideology especially is aimed not only at the development and support of the family, but as suggested above, at the community too. Indeed, there is no need to search for subtle connections between the government's positioning of women as housewives and their use in the development and maintenance of community.

> Nevertheless, the essence of the execution of the program and goal of PKK has never changed, that is, it continues in order to increase the prosperity of family throughout Indonesian society. Within the context of prosperity, among other things, it embraces desire and hopes for guiding the family that is healthy and the community that is healthy. (report from PKK Tim Penggerak Pusat, Central Movement Team, 1987; author's translation)

The report cited above is entitled "*Pernan Ibu Rumah Tangga Dalam Penyehatan Lingkungan*" (or the Role of the Housewife in a Healthy Community), and it was prepared for the national PKK organization. The report outlines the needs for improvement in community health, particularly as regards trash, waste water and the yard. The role of women as housewives is crucial to this effort.

> PKK as the one movement whose basis is in the neighbourhood with housewives as the agents, indeed has a large potential for playing a role as the vanguard in moving the participation of society in various sectors of development. (report from PKK Tim Penggerak Pusat, Central Movement Team, 1987; author's translation)

The location of women's work and moral authority within a separate domestic sphere has been the result of a particular historical process in the First World, yet the good housewife and mother has been reproduced in the colonies as well. The domestic sphere, with its relationship to racial and sexual boundaries has served both to confine women as a symbol of tradition, purity, and nation even as it has been used as the mandate for their education in domestic skills and their attention to necessary social housekeeping on behalf of their communities. The paradoxes and ironies of the creation of the good housewife are evident in the emergence of the PKK *ibu* as well as the *Dharma Wanita* wife. Yet, the moral contours of official ideology do not entirely match those of the *kampung*.

THE MORAL UNIVERSE OF THE *KAMPUNG*

To understand the particular effects of PKK for Javanese women, community, and political culture, the practice of *kampung* morality must be considered. The daily dramas of *kampung* life illustrate not only the value and salience of community for *kampung* inhabitants, but the key role of women in its functioning. In this process, the programs, practices, and propaganda of PKK have become resources to be used in the negotiation of community and morality by *kampung* dwellers. Changes in lifestyle and *ekonomi* (economic status) are registered in these dramas, as the scripts for ideal community are invoked as a means of social control and adaptation.

When Bu Sae approached my house and perched on the threshold so that she could attend the PKK meeting at my house, it seemed a happy thing to me. I was pleased that she felt comfortable enough to come. After all, I had never seen her attend a PKK meeting in this RT, even though she clearly lived within its bounds. I imagined that I had somehow managed to bring together the women of the RT. But in fact this apparently mundane change in Bu Sae's behaviour called into question old boundary lines, past transgressions, and current jealousies and so, reverberated along many fragile *kampung* fault lines. As with many of these apparently small-scale, minor events that in fact indexed larger *kampung* political and social structures, I did not understand what was happening at first. It was obvious when she arrived that the atmosphere in the room changed. Voices dropped, pitches rose, bodies hunched in. Only Bu Apik laughed and noted her attendance. Yet, the reasons for these reactions were not clear to me at the time.

As it turns out, Bu Sae was a lightning rod for *kampung* morality. She represented not only the generation of working-class families whose children were doing better, she personally was an example of a successful PKK *ibu*. Her success in raising her family and in serving the *kampung* were part of the reason for the jealousy she evoked, but her personal demeanor was also a factor. In her income-generating activities, Bu Sae fit the PKK ideal. Not only had she and the other women of the PKK *warung* pursued government funds to open the *warung*, she further added to her family's income by cooking peanuts to order and by selling the ice from her refrigerator. Bu Sae was an active member of PKK and one of the few women in the *kampung* who professed to have been a member of *Dharma Wanita*. Although she said she was too old to attend anymore, she remained an automatic member of *Dharma Wanita* because her husband's job at the pharmacy had been classified as civil service. The back room of her house had a large cupboard that was still filled with the plates, cutlery, and glasses necessary for hosting *arisan* and *slametan* from the time when she served as Bu RT.

It was not just her PKK activities that earned her local enmity but the fact that her loyalties seemed to lie away from her closest neighbours and the relatives who lived around her, although she had kin throughout the immediate area of the *kampung*. During their time as Bapak and Ibu RT, Bu Sae and her husband actually served in an RT to the west of the one where they resided. In part, this was related to the number of relatives they had in that area. Although the Cipto household lay within her own RT, many of her husband's relatives lived in the RT to the west. Bu Sae had further commented that PKK in the other RT was more *actif* (active) and modern than the one in which they resided. It was clear from local sentiment that Bu Sae did not go unpunished for her defection to another

RT. Even more, Bu Sae's "modern" attitude and openness to the lessons and opportunities of PKK did not always fit well with the *kampung*'s general distrust of government and the pretensions of the upper class.

Ultimately, Bu Sae proved to be so formidable in *kampung* morality because she had definite ideas about appropriate behaviour. Her troubled relations with the Cipto household had as much to do with her disapproval of their profligate ways as it did with her relative prosperity in comparison to that household. There was a certain righteousness about Bu Sae that rubbed some people the wrong way. Her ambivalent position in the neighbourhood was illuminated from several different perspectives over the course of my fieldwork. The different shadows mark the various boundaries in *kampung* community.

For example, in taking in one of Bu Tri's young daughters, Bu Sae was following the longstanding tradition of *anak angkat* in the *kampung*. Bu Tri did not have the resources to raise her four girls (five upon our return in 1996), so the clothing and schooling of one by Bu Sae's family were a boon. This young daughter, Tiwi, was fed at Bu Sae's house where she also slept, although she would take advantage of the opportunity to do either of these things at her natal house on occasion. Her presence in Bu Sae's house was partially due to Bu Sae's oldest daughter who was childless. On her weekend visits to her mother's house, this daughter became the primary care giver for Tiwi.

Despite what appeared to be a happy solution to the problem of Bu Sae's lack of grandchildren and her abundance of resources in contrast to Bu Tri's abundance of children and lack of money, the sharing of the upbringing of young Tiwi caused some tension between the branches of the family. This tension was most evident in the evenings when Tiwi could often be found playing with her sisters at the Cipto compound. She knew that she would not be compelled to study or eat properly in her natal home, and she took advantage of that freedom. This frequently meant that she had to be called back to Bu Sae's house where she was certain to be fed, bathed, and made to do her homework. It was always evident in these exchanges that Bu Sae and her daughter thought little of the way the Cipto side of the family raised their children. For her part, Tiwi's mother thought little of the high and mighty ways of her *Bu Lik* (from *ibu cilik*, literally small mother, a term used for an aunt younger than related parent and referring here to the younger age of Bu Sae in relation to Bu Tri's father). The interactions around the upbringing of young Tiwi illustrate not only that reproduction in the *kampung* is often spread between "discrete" households, it suggests again the moral character attached to issues of reproduction. Raising good children and keeping good house are often used as barometers of social character in the *kampung*, and so it was with the wife of the puppet maker.

Pak Cerma and his wife lived just to the west of Bu Sae, where they had moved just after our own arrival in the *kampung*. We were pleased by the arrival of Pak Cerma and his home-based business because he served to distract attention from us. His business of making *wayang* puppets attracted tourists and so also the attention of our neighbours. His daily workers made the leather puppets in a covered area in the front of the house, so that tourists could watch the process. Pak Cerma's other enterprises, tourist transport in vans he owned, and truck hauling, provided some make-shift employment for *kampung* men. For example, Pak Wit, the new Pak RT, began to work as a *sopir* (driver) for Pak Cerma in addition to his job as a driver for the local government hospital. His younger unemployed brothers took to sitting with Pak Cerma's workers and sometimes running errands when the occasion arose.

Pak Cerma appeared to be a good addition to the neighbourhood at first, at least to the Cipto family who never turned down a good time. At nights, the men would gather to play *keroncong* music in the open area in front of his house that earlier had been filled with workers (*keroncong* music is the Javanese equivalent to country-western music and is derived from Portuguese fado music). The men would typically sit up until late in the night drinking *jamu*, although in this case the health tonic was often bolstered with beer or wine. These late night gatherings often led to card games as well.

Over time, in a fashion so subtle that I almost missed it, local *kampung* sentiment begin to shift against Pak Cerma and his family. What began as whispered conversations among women as they swept their front steps and the narrow street in front of their houses each day, soon became a full-fledged lobbying effort on the part of women to do something about the situation at Pak Cerma's. Apparently the gambling had become a problem. Bu Apik's ne'er-do-well husband was taking money from her purse to gamble and was losing. Other men were losing money too. The fact that women typically control family finances made neighbourhood wives immediately aware of the peril posed by this new problem. To make matters worse for Bu Sae, who practically lived next door to Pak Cerma, her unemployed, younger son had taken to spending his nights there as well.

I began to hear stories about the troubles at Pak Cerma's. His wife, who was never given to much involvement in *kampung* affairs anyway, was described as being a bad housekeeper. This whispered campaign emanated from Bu Sae and Bu Apik, the two women most unhappy about what was happening. In *kampung* cases such as this, the plaintiffs typically seek out the Pak RT to ask for his counsel and intervention in what is perceived as a threat to *kampung* security. Unfortunately, the Pak RT had become one of the cohort of regular gamblers at Pak Cerma's. As a result, the women sought the help of one of the local neighbourhood's other moral bulwarks, Pak Sastro. While the impetus for change was the product of the lobbying of women who felt the threat first, they looked to a male patron to take direct action. Their choice of Pak Sastro illustrates that official *kampung* leadership does not always match official community leadership. Pak Wit was a reluctant RT head, and his youth and inexperience provided him with no status. His job as a civil servant, his mild manner, and his family's long-term residence in the *kampung* explained his choice as RT, but it was an honour he did not want. In contrast, Pak Sastro did not hold an official position, but he was considered by most to have high status because of his war record, his relative affluence, and his successful family. He served as a moral arbiter in the *kampung* but not overtly so. In the case of Pak Cerma's deviance from *kampung* norms, Pak Sastro was apparently asked to approach him. Not long after, the gambling stopped.

This example of moral control in the *kampung* illustrates many things. First, it suggests that neighbours, especially women, monitor one another's behaviour. After all, the first reports I heard were about Bu Cerma's poor housekeeping skills. It also illustrates the indirect power of women in mobilizing support, while leaving direct action to a male. The role of all *kampung* dwellers in watching one another's behaviour is a key component in *kampung* life. *Kampung* folk feel responsible for watching over one another and in fact entitled to know what is going on in their immediate neighbourhood. The episode with Pak Cerma also shows that official leadership is not enough in the *kampung* when it is not backed by other types of local status and power. Further it shows the importance of long-term residence in the *kampung* with the attendant involvement in relationships with others. During the troubles with Pak Cerma, Bu Sae told us that Pak Cerma had not lived in the *kampung* long enough to behave in such a way. This comment is also directly related to Bu Cerma's lack of involvement in *kampung* exchange relationships. If she had been more involved in patterns of exchange with her neighbours she would not have been so open to the criticisms being made. Finally, it shows that the official boundaries of RT/RW are only partially salient. The street that separated Pak Cerma's house from Bu Sae's was also the dividing line between the two RT, yet the action to correct the situation crossed that boundary and had more to do with kinship, proximity, and local prestige structures than it did with official administrative boundaries. Nonetheless, the sentiment behind the action was directly in line with PKK sentiments: it is up to the women of the community to safeguard the *lingkungan* (surrounding area) and protect cooperation and harmony there.

Yet another example of community morality mobilized for what might conventionally be considered a private concern actually happened a year or so before I arrived in the *kampung*, although based on what residents said, it remained fresh in people's memories. The fullest telling of the incident came from Bu Apik herself, who was at the centre of the events. According to Bu Apik, her husband was bewitched by a woman who lived at the other end of our street, in the far eastern section of the adjoining RT. Her bewitchment led him to begin an affair with her. It had to be magic, according to Bu Apik, because the woman in question was blessed neither in looks nor temperament. This affair between a man and a woman at opposite ends of the street that stretched between the two extreme ends of the adjoining RT apparently became a cause for public scandal, because a community meeting was convened in an attempt to solve the problem. At the meeting, Bu Apik's husband was asked to choose between the two women—publicly. This meeting was a painful event in Bu Apik's life, because her handsome, troublesome husband chose to stay with his lover at that time. When we arrived in the *kampung*, Bu and Pak Apik had been reunited, and although I never heard how that happened, I heard repeatedly about their earlier troubles.

It is inconceivable to a North American audience that a neighbourhood meeting would be called to settle an instance of marital infidelity, but different codes of behaviour and community conduct were at play in the *kampung*. And the tacit agreement to play by the rules is part of the responsibility of living in such a close and closed community. This agreement is made clear daily in the *kampung* especially as new challenges to its logic arise.

Bu Apik and her continuing troubles provide a counterpart to her relative Bu Sae's life and role in the family and *kampung*. Bu Apik, like Bu Sae, was an active member of PKK.[10] She also served as an officer in the larger RW administration, with duties that included keeping track of local women's use of birth control. Although she was even more active in *kampung* offices than Bu Sae during the time I was in field, in almost every other way she was the opposite of Bu Sae. Physically, she was tall, loose-gaited with a open and ready smile and laugh. Bu Sae was small, compact, and maddeningly difficult to read when she chose to be. While Bu Sae was living with her children and husband in her parents' house, Bu Apik was living in a small extension of her in-laws' house. Bu Sae was comfortably established with a husband and a grown son working in addition to her own wages and anything added by her schoolteacher daughter living in a nearby city. Bu Apik was the only visible support for her family, and although her husband often helped her prepare her *jamu* health tonic for sale, more often than not he took money from her purse to pursue his own pleasures. More than once in my presence Bu Apik found money missing from her purse and wondered out loud if *Setan* (Satan) had gotten into it.

Bu Sae and her family were all Catholic, and while they did not partic-ipate in the local prayer group, her children were active in the church. Bu Apik and her husband apparently did not agree about religion. Pak Apik's parents were practicing Catholics, but he claimed to be a Muslim. Yet, when we were first in the field, Bu Apik made a monthly trip along with other Catholic women to a set of graves north of Yogyakarta thought to be particularly powerful in answering prayers. Then when I returned to the *kampung* after three years, bringing Bu Apik a rosary as a gift, she admitted with chagrin that she was now a Muslim.

There were a variety of reasons why Bu Apik's family, although well liked, did not have the same status as her kinswoman, Bu Sae. There was the way Bu Apik made her living. *Jamu*, the ever-present health tonic of Java and most of Indonesia, is sold in numerous ways: in restaurants, from small stalls, in powdered and liquid form at the grocery stores, and often from the bottles carried from house-to-house on the back of a female *jamu*-seller. *Jamu* itself comes in a variety of flavours with various herbal ingredients with associated healing properties. The vast majority of *jamu* drunk by *kampung* dwellers is of the generic variety. For women, *kunir asem* (predominantly tumeric and tamarind) is said to keep one slender. For men, *beras kencur* (including rice and a variety of ginger) is to keep them strong and virile. Not only do the effects tend to be sexual in character, but *jamu* sellers themselves, particularly the women who walk door-to-door, are popularly thought to be loose women. This stereotype undoubtedly stems from the fact that *jamu* women travel so much, and in general women who travel freely are thought to be equally free sexually (cf. Tsing 1993). Bu Apik did not sell her *jamu* door-to-door, but after selling to women in the market each morning, she did sell *jamu* each night, typically to young adults and men, from a stand near a busy intersection within walking distance of, but significantly outside, the boundaries of the *kampung*. Thus, Bu Apik, despite her work with PKK and her various religious practices, was suspect in some ways because of her movements outside the *kampung*—after dark.

Bu Apik's experiences illustrate several issues in the *kampung* moral order. Dissension and troubles within a family are central to daily *kampung* gossip, so that most of the women in the RT knew of the troubles Bu Apik had with her husband and children (although Bu Apik was never shy in telling willing listeners about her problems). Bu Apik's status in the neighbourhood shows that being a good PKK woman is not enough. Bu Apik did not have the wherewithal to be a Bu RT because her husband could never be elected as the Pak RT (in fact, it was his *younger* brother who was selected for the job), nor did they have the space or the money to host any of the necessary meetings. Still, Bu Apik did try to recuperate some of the status lost through her family's behaviour by being active in the officially sanctioned activities of PKK. To be fair, her efforts to that end were not unrewarded. Bu Apik was well known and well liked in the area, but she did not have the stature of Bu Sae, who despite her status, was a more problematic figure.

Kampung morality hinges on more than the behaviour of women, although women are, just as the PKK cant would have it, a critical point of articulation between individual households and the community. A central concern of *kampung* residents, repeated endlessly and without much variation, was the value of community life, of *hidup kampung* (or *kehidupan kampung*, or *kampung* life). Here are the words of Bu Soetomo, a *kampung* official mentioned earlier, comparing her life in the *kampung* with that in other areas of the city.

> *Di Kota Baru sudah jalan lagi. Ada tetangga yang meninggal, Pak RT memberi undangan. 'O, ibu itu meninggal, nanti ibu-ibu perlu [garbled], diam. Kasih undangan. Kalau di sini, ndak. 'O, di sana ada yang meninggal.' Semua datang, ya toh? Kita bantu. Itu enaknya tinggal di kampung. Kota orang [garbled] itu lebih akrab, lebih baik daripada di komplek-komplek orang kaya-kaya itu. Ya? Karena di sana ndak membetulkan bantuan. Ya? di situ kan masih tolong-menolong.*
>
> In Kota Baru it's yet again different. There if a neighbour dies, the Pak RT sends out announcements. "Oh, *Ibu* So-and-So has died, later women will be needed [to help]." There is only silence. And they are given announcements [literally invitations]. But here, not so. "Oh, there is someone over there who died." Everyone comes, you know? We help. It's good to live in the *kampung*. City people [garbled] are more intimate, are nicer than rich people who live in complexes. Right? Because there it's not necessary to help. Right? Here we still help one another.

The importance of help and community support was repeatedly discussed in *kampung* conversations during my fieldwork. These patterns of cooperation in the community were being challenged, particularly by new behaviours in the *kampung* that were noted with some ambivalence by my neighbours. The first, most apparently mundane situation was that of street cleaning in evening. It was usual at this time in the neighbourhood for the streets and alleyways to be filled with playing children, adults both male and female sweeping, and groups of neighbours chatting in-between sweeping, smoking or watching children. This period also corresponded to a shift from daytime productive activities to nighttime family activities for many. This time for seeing and talking to neighbours was also considered crucial to the community and its maintenance. To come out and *bergaul* (mix) and *ngomong-omong* (talk) or *ndobos* (bullshit) was considered to be crucial to good and harmonious neighbourship. The *kampung* had several media for communication; there was a loudspeaker that announced meetings and deaths, there were the newspapers posted on public boards, there was the kitchen path network between women, and there was the afternoon exchange.

Unfortunately, changes in workday rhythms and in the numbers of televisions, among other things, have led to changes in this neighbourly exchange. There was talk along the street about those who shut their doors and did not come out to *bergaul*. These were the same people who had stopped coming to communal work sessions and to community life cycle events such as weddings and funerals and who merely sent an envelope of money instead. The option of sending money had long existed in both the countryside and the *kampung*, but only the very well-to-do had taken advantage of it until recently. For the elites it was not unexpected to send money rather than labour, but as incomes rise in the *kampung*, more and more people choose to send money rather than come themselves.

The use of *kerja bekti* or community work groups to take care of roads, wells, and drainage is also in decline. According to many *kampung* members, community labour has apparently always been stronger in rural areas, where its early model may have been corvee labour for the Dutch. Yet, there is still evidence of such group work projects in the *kampung*. The most recognized use of this labour is to beautify the neighbourhood for the August 17 Independence Day celebrations, which typically last for most of the month. Fences are painted, trees trimmed, houses prettied so that *kampung* will look its best. Other types of community work projects are the maintenance of the local *balai* or meeting hall, which is used for events such as the various RW meetings and for some of the baby weighing meetings. Local groups may also combine to improve their street, with the wealthy contributing money and the less well-off contributing labour to refinish streets. These types of projects may also provide extra income to poorer neighbours who make their living doing manual labour.

These examples of *gotong-royong* or mutual self-help were described proudly to us, but were less evident in practice than in conversation. In one of the most poignant examples of the anthropologist taking what his informants tell him at face value, Steve arose early one morning because we had understood that it was a day for *kerja bekti* in our RT. He decided to tackle the dense growth along the fence line of the empty lot across from our house. It made for a vivid scene: Steve red-faced and sweating as he tugged at tough tropical plants intent on staying put while all the neighbours walked by or sat and smoked. Only the Bu RT, Bu Wit, looked chagrined at the effort Steve was putting into mutual self-help all by himself.

Despite the very real gap between *gotong royong* rhetoric and practice, there was clearly evidence of communal cooperation in the *kampung*. Funerals still provoked the strongest support from neighbours, and sickness and hard times also lead to aid. Yet, some forms of community cooperation were disappearing in the face of changing urban life. That the older forms still had some meaning was clear in the report of a neighbour putting up a satellite dish, and to the disappointment of his neighbours, not sharing the signal.

The ethic of community can be marshalled as a powerful form of local control. That there is an important morality attached to *kampung* life was clear in all our dealings with neighbours. *Kampung* dwellers refer constantly to the difference between life in the *kampung* and life outside. It is safer in the *kampung*, people are *lebih akrab* (closer, more intimate), there is a *tolong-menolong* (mutual help) at work in the *kampung*. Those who do not abide by the general ethics of *kampung* life are subject to various types of reaction to bring them in line with local values. There are unexpected results in this community morality, however. While Pak Cerma's nightly card games were stopped, the gambling at the local *gali*'s (gangster) house on the next street over was on-going. His presence in the *kampung* was actually viewed as beneficial because *kampung* inhabitants believed that he warned other gangsters to stay away from the *kampung* and thus kept it safe.

THE GOOD PKK WOMAN
AND *KAMPUNG* ACCOUNTABILITY

The relative power and status of women in Southeast Asia has been the source of much scholarly attention, as mentioned previously.[11] The conventional treatment of women's power in Indonesia has long been tempered by Anderson's discussion of male potency (1990), according to which, culturally valued forms of power are more available to males who are able to increase their power and potency through attention to ascetic practices or *prihatin*. Women, on the other hand, while clearly associated with the instrumental power of the material world of household finance and market trading, are denigrated within this particular system of cultural values. Women are taken to be incapable of denying their passions or *nafsu*, and therefore unable to attain potency (cf. Peletz 1996).

Brenner's compelling answer to this theory has already been described (1995, 1998). She locates women's power in their ability to transform the potentially dangerous desires of men and the morally ambiguous world of money and trading into family status. Through their domestic work, women are able to accrue status, despite the fact that they are denied, ideologically, the means to attain potency and power. Brenner offers a theory of circulation, in essence, that locates women's effective power in the world as an avenue to the increase and conservation of family status through the circulation of money through the domestic. This reading of Javanese women's "domestication of desire" (1998) is consistent with the themes developed in the previous two chapters and elaborated here: it is circulation and linkages between houses, households, and homes that is more important than any dualistic opposition between spheres. The foregoing consideration of women's sources of moral authority should have demonstrated that the sources of women's roles are various and contradictory. The Republic of Indonesia has figured women rhetorically as both models and maniacs, as Tiwon (1996) argues. Still, the nature of their power and status must be understood not only in the context of nationalist and colonialist projects, but in the lived practice of family and community.

When the moral contours of the PKK woman and her community work are considered alongside local issues of moral conduct, it is clear that *kampung* morality is not disconnected from the state-sponsored forms of appropriate domesticity and citizenry. Values circulate both through local systems of exchange, reciprocity, and neighbourly support, as well as through official rhetoric about *gotong-royong* and the welfaring community.

This is not to say that everyone subscribes to these beliefs wholeheartedly. As already demonstrated, many women and *kampung* folk have a very developed sense of irony about some of the contortions required in state rhetoric. Still, every time an official transgression is noted and acted upon and every time a woman or family seeks status through official service, they are indexing these different ethics, making them real, and in effect bringing them into closer alignment. Moreover, whether women agree with PKK or not, it is often true that to give a credible account of oneself within *kampung* community may mean making use of the resources of PKK.

The question of accountability is associated with ethnomethodology (Garfinkel 1967; Giddens 1995; Goffman 1959). This approach to daily interaction considers the interplay between standards of action and judgment that reveals tacit or taken-for-granted understandings. Garfinkel describes the attention to these interactions as,

> paying to the most commonplace activities of daily life the attention usually accorded extraordinary events, ... activities whereby members produce and manage settings of organized everyday affairs are identical with member's procedures for making those settings 'account-able.' (1967:1)

Daily interactions in the kampung then includes such ongoing, contingent accomplishments. "[T]hey are carried on under the auspices of, and are made to happen as events in, the same ordinary affairs that in organizing they describe" (Garfinkel 1967:1). Taking the ethnomethodologist's emphasis on accountability, and on giving credible accounts through daily practices of living and telling, the moral universe of the kampung and its reproduction become significant for understanding women's power and status and for the circulation between two regimes of value. *Kampung* housewives when giving credible accounts of themselves as good women, mothers and citizens tap both local and state level ideas. As Moore notes, in a situation of a diverse number of discourses, certain discourses may be used at one level in one context, and yet, "they will affect claim procedures at other levels and in other contexts" (1994:99).

In the observable and reportable events between neighbours, the regimes of moral value (Appadurai 1986) that circulate between *kampung* and state standards are brought to bear on daily lives and issues. And in this process, the fungibility of these registers is clear. When Bu Cerma's husband is critiqued indirectly through the denigration of his wife's housework, the morality of the good home and mother enshrined in PKK becomes part of *kampung* accountability. When Bu Apik attempts to improve her tattered social status through good works organized by PKK, local notions of accountability incorporate state values too.

Passing as a good PKK housewife means, necessarily, the reproduction of a particular gendered experience. When *kampung* women attempt to fit themselves around PKK directives, an international division of labour, a national developmentalist regime, and a local culture of common sense are all reproduced. This reproduction implies negotiations and bargaining over redistribution. In the *kampung*, such systems of redistribution comprise the exchanges between kin through houses, the organization of informal labour and reproduction through households, and the prestige and status differentials symbolized by the home. The resource flows that are involved in this redistribution are "partial outcomes of conventional understandings of rights and needs of particular sorts of individuals. These conventional understandings can be seen as local theories of entitlement"(Moore 1994:104). These local theories of entitlement and local ideologies of gender and class are the resources used in negotiation and bargaining, and it is the engagement with the system of redistribution that they represent which provides individuals with the experience of the meaning of gender and community. In this process, local theories of entitlement and gender are coloured by state ideals as the alignment of the two regimes of value is effected.

When Bu Sae and Bu Apik approached Pak Sastro to put an end to the gambling threatening their families and community, they might be said to have engaged a long-standing set of ideas about appropriate community conduct. When Bu Apik takes on more and more roles within PKK, she might be said to be activating the power of state-sponsored domesticity to improve her own status as well as that of her community's. It matters less here whether *kampung* dwellers are imagining that they are involved in traditional patterns of *gotong-royong* or that the state perpetuates an imagined role for women. The effect is the same. Women and community are reproduced through the local-level use of state resources, and the state and state rule are reproduced through the action of women in giving credible accounts of themselves by calling on these same resources. The result of this zig-zag between the state and the local is what constitutes state formation.[12]

EVERYDAY FORMS OF STATE FORMATION REDUX

The ideology of PKK is evident in its programs. Women as housewives are placed within a moral sphere shaped by Western Victorian debates on separate spheres, by colonial racial boundaries, and by nationalist social welfare programs. The effects of these moral outlines for my neighbours was mitigated by the moral universe of the *kampung*. While the ideal of home with its mother as domestic angel is the legacy of a Western tradition, the *ibu rumah tangga* of PKK performs her duties within a nexus of moral demands that conform to a different logic of mutual cooperation, sharing, and mutuality between neighbours.

What an ethnomethodologist's attention to accountability provides us analytically is a way to understand how *kampung* women use and reproduce both moral spheres. In this case, what we are directed to see is that *kampung* women as housewives and as neighbours are seeking to conform to the constraints of both state-sponsored domesticity and local ideas of propriety. These "taken for granted' understandings" (Giddens 1995:237) form part of the resources used in the negotiation and bargaining that takes place not only within homes but within the neighbourhood. That these different moral dictates are managed and used by local, neighbourhood women attests to the reality of these visions of morality even as it suggests how disputed images are reproduced. In managing accounts in this way, denigrated and disputed categories of experience, such as housewife, are reproduced and maintained. Even more, in the case of PKK ideology, the reach of the state is extended.

Sheldon Garon's work on women's associations in Japan (1993, 1997) describes how these associations emerged, at times at odds with a nascent feminist movement, and at times in step with its leaders. As Garon suggests in his account of Japan, "we cannot hope to comprehend relations between the Japanese state and civil society without examining the roles of women, sexuality, and other aspects of gender" (1993:6; see also 1997). The establishment and support of PKK reflects an extension of the domestic sphere to social management of communities more generally, and especially to the configuration of local community as an extended household subject to women's management. As Garon documents for Japan, this extension of domestic duties into a public sphere was the only public manifestation of women's politics allowable under some regimes and in some periods. As in Japan, the Indonesian government used—indeed, continues to use—the offices of PKK and its members as part of a campaign of moral suasion (Garon 1993; 1997), to inculcate and convince the populace of a particular set of moral values. In the case of Indonesia under Suharto, these values followed upon the wholesale adoption of modernization theory and the logic of development.

And yet, for Indonesia, and for Japan as described by Garon, this is less a story about government domination and collaboration, than it is an example of how organizations sponsored by the state and aimed at the social management of civil society are not the end of the story but the beginning. The staging of neighbourhood rituals in the guise of government meetings or the staging of government meetings in the guise of neighbourhood rituals illustrate how women's roles in small, densely lived communities work in and around such organizations. The reach of the official government is incomplete, and the popular, positive practice of neighbourly exchange is in circulation with government-provided ideologies of community organisation.

Recent attention to governmentality and the forms of rule and subjection that follow from the modern liberal state have encouraged anthropologists to consider these taken-for-granted meanings of daily life as constitutive of particular modalities of political rule. The attention to governmentality has been fostered in part by the work of Foucault (1979) whose description of the art of government focuses on the dispersed and dispersive nature of state power through the practises of government. A second approach is couched in post-structural, cultural Marxian theories of state formation (Corrigan and Sayer 1985; Joseph and Nugent 1994; Nugent 1993). While complementary in some ways, the state formation literature shifts the focus to the emergence and reproduction of particular forms of rule and their association with moral regulation. In both instances, the reality of the state as a political form is questioned even as state rule is brought to the fore. Beginning with the word, state, often circumvents the analysis of what this form of rule includes, particularly its daily expression in the lives of subject citizens. By emphasizing its onto- logical reality rather than beginning with a question of what constitutes such rule and how it is accomplished, standard political analyses of the state elide its most powerful manifestations.

Taking the title of Joseph's and Nugent's 1994 book seriously, it is the everyday forms of state formation that are of interest here. State-level rule is a virtual accomplishment in much the same way that accountability is, and in this case, using some of the same resources. When a judgement is made against a neighbour using the ideology of PKK, the rule of the state is made real in the everyday life of *kampung* residents. Simultaneously, neighbourhood women move in and through the gendered categories of experience made available both through the state and through the logic of making do in *kampung* community. Attention to these multiple, shifting experiences of housewife is an unexpected but profoundly important way to understand how rule is produced and reproduced. The state is formed through everyday acts such as these.

This chapter ends with the words of an Indonesian who played a prom- inent role in the early nationalist women's organizations in the country. She gave a talk to a group of young language students from the US in 1992. After her introduction in which her many political connections and accomplishments were cited, she began her speech by defining the basis of her authority to speak that day:

> Saya sebenarnya hanya seorang ibu rumah tangga biasa.
> I actually am only an ordinary housewife.

NOTES

1. Rybczynski (1986) dates the emergence of the private family home to the 17th century when the public, feudal home was replaced, while Oakley (1974) for example, does not see its spread until the 1840s and after, with its gradual penetration downward to the working classes.
2. See Boris and Bardaglio (1983), Callaway (1987), Chatterjee (1989), Cott (1977), Donzelot (1979), Harris (1984), Harrison and Mort (1980), Jolly and Macintyre (1989), Knapman (1986), Matthews (1987), Scott and Tilly (1975), Tilly (1993), Strobel (1993), and L.White (1990).

3. "According to evolutionism, Victorian women retained their animal natures, despite the veneer of domesticity. Moreover, there was no place for the civilized woman to go, except backwards. Yielding to the passions inherent in female nature constituted downfall" (Tiffany and Adams 1985:9).

4. The topic of TKW, or *Tenaga Kerji Wanita*, the national program to export Indonesian women as maids is beyond the scope of this project, and yet, it is clear that this is based on a continued subordination of Third World women as domestic servants (see Chin 1998, for example).

5. Jayawardena points again to the invented nature of the past that was called upon: the glorified Asian civilization presented by the Orientalists (1986; cf. Said 1979).

6. Republican motherhood, a phrase coined by Linda Kerber (1980), referred to the role of the revolutionary house in following the trade embargoes against the British.

7. Although it can no longer be held to be distinctly American, home economics has a very American flavour, and it appears to have begun in that country in early 1899 (Matthews 1987).

8. Kartini's place in Indonesia history is assured, although controversy over her legacy continues. While some argue that her impulses were democratic despite the co-optation of her symbolically by the New Order government of Suharto (Tiwon 1996), others have noted that her own privileged status necessarily restricted her perspective to that of the ruling class (Gouda 1995).

9. Wieringa (1993) provides a telling comparison of PKK with GERWANI. In program goals, the two organizations were much alike, emphasizing literacy, cooperatives, handicraft courses, and assistance to women. It was in the political character of the two organizations that the difference lay (see Kasza on administered mass organizations; 1995). After the fall of Sukarno, the independent GERWANI was banned while PKK became the focus of the government's goals regarding women. This shift was part of a larger attempt to depoliticize the successful women's organizations associated with the Indonesian revolution while capturing their momentum for change.

10. The pseudonyms chosen for these two women both translate as "good mother." *Apik* is a term from the lower register of Javanese, and *sae* is from a higher register.

11. See Brenner (1995, 1998), Errington (1990), Keeler (1990), Papanek and Schwede (1988), Peletz (1996).

12. Thanks to Daniel Nugent for the zig-zag metaphor.

Chapter Six

Through the Back Door of Domesticity: An Exit

JERO KUNCI: THE KEY TO FERTILITY

I was on another interminable trip with the women of *Kampung Rumah Putri*. After months of working with and alongside women, this was another one of countless excursions to hospitals, shops, markets, neighbours' houses and other trips inside and outside the *kampung*. Like most Westerners, I struggled early on with the intensity of bodily contact involved in public transportation but then grew to count on the support of all that warm flesh as vans, cars, and buses bounced and lurched down the road. On this day, I was wedged between Mbak Yeni, Bu Sae's oldest daughter, and her aunt. Her uncle and another older woman from the *kampung* were sitting in front of us.

We were going on this long, hot trip to get to Imogiri, the small town at the foot of the mountains south of Yogyakarta that housed the graves of most of its sultans. I had visited Imogiri before, walked up the many steps to enter the sacred site of the graves, after having changed to traditional dress and assuring everyone that I wasn't menstruating. Today, I wasn't very clear on our destination; I was going along mostly to please Mbak Yeni. She and I shared a common problem: we were both having trouble getting pregnant.

Mbak Yeni had enlisted me to *ikut* or follow on this expedition so that she wouldn't alone be subject to the ministrations of her aunt, uncle and their powerful friend, all followers of an old form of Javanese mysticism known as *kejawenan*. Her aunt had decided to take Mbak Yeni's case on. Perhaps she had heard that Mbak Yeni and I had already visited the famous healer, Pak Gembong, just outside the *kampung*, as well as having tried to visit another famous healer inside the walls of the Sultan's palace, who was known for being a masseuse capable of manipulating an infertile woman's uterus so that she could conceive. Of course, her expertise was such that she could achieve the opposite as well. We never managed to see this particular healer, and I was not particularly regretful about the missed opportunity.

I had made other such trips without Mbak Yeni, typically with Steve who was using my "treatments" as cases for his own work. Together, we visited a healer and friend known for using reflexology and foot massage to diagnose and treat illness. She supplemented her massage with *jamu* of various concoctions. And then there was the *para-psikolog* who used a divinatory technique using pendulums and divining rods (Ferzacca 2001:183).

Yet another diagnosis and treatment was offered through a visit to a Balinese *balian* arranged by a friend. On that occasion, I had to don Balinese dress late in the day before we drove to the *balian*'s house. As Steve and I waited our turn to speak to the *balian*, I was read by the *balian*'s colleague, a psychic, who located a problem between my left shoulder and right hip. He also suggested that perhaps a woman I had known had meant me harm. The number seven was quite important in this matter. After my reading, Steve and I were taken to stand in front of the *balian*, who sat on his raised temple platform surrounded by offerings and religious paraphernalia. We were then sent to stand a little away from him in a dark part of the courtyard. Beneath a full Balinese moon, I was bathed in sanctified water and instructed to turn in a circle several times. Steve and I were later sent home with a bottle of pure water to continue to drink and use. This treatment was the most romantic of all, but it was Pak Gembong who was the most famous healer.

At Pak Gembong's clinic I made my way to the front of the crowd to put Steve's and my names on the list of those waiting to see him. We had not been sitting long when I was called ahead of many that had waited longer, presumably because of Pak Gembong's growing relationship with Steve. When it was my turn, I stepped from his outdoor waiting area into his small office, he greeted me warmly as I took a seat. We talked for only a moment or so before he asked to hold the middle finger of my right hand. After a few seconds and with no apparent hesitation, Pak Gembong delivered up his diagnosis: endometriosis. He prescribed a *jamu* health tonic. Because Pak Gembong and his "clinic" were such a bustling enterprise, after I got my diagnosis, I was taken to the back where I was given a large jug of *jamu* to drink and a set of gelatin capsules with dried *jamu* inside.

So now my trip to Imogiri seemed just another of many fertility pilgrimages. I no longer knew why I was doing it. Was it really to conceive? Was it to supply Steve with interesting information for his ethnography on medical pluralism? Like most anthropologists, my skepticism about any specific belief system was balanced by optimism about the power of human meaning and belief.

On this particular day, we were dropped off halfway up a mountain, miles from the actual town of Imogiri. Our group then straggled up a narrow stony path leading away from the road. Mbak Yeni and I in our western-style skirts were unencumbered in our climb, except by loose sandals. It was the two older women wearing slippers, tight sarongs, and carrying umbrellas who were really at a disadvantage, although their steady progress up the hill didn't show it. After what seemed a two-mile walk at least, pausing only once for a drink of water, we stopped in a clearing overlooking a small house in an isolated valley. Not knowing our ultimate goal here, I was led down to the house which appeared at first glance to be deserted. We announced our presence several times, apparently only for the benefit of several chickens scratching around the open door.

Moments later, from around the corner of the house, appeared a small old man, blind in one eye, who bade us enter. The dark interior of his house was dusty, open as it was to the outdoors and the wandering chickens. I could not follow the high Javanese that was spoken, and I sat nervously on my seat. It seemed to me that the old man fixed me with his one good eye and saw through all of my guises as anthropologist, friend, patient, and supplicant. Despite the bright midday sun outside the house, I was positively chilled by his careful consideration of me, and although I can hardly credit it now, it seemed that this particular pilgrimage was into the heart of something quite different than the waiting rooms and homes of the healers I had visited.

Finally, it seemed we passed inspection, and our group, along with the old man, left his house and continued to climb higher along the rough track. Not far above the house, we found a small, roofed concrete platform in a grove of trees. Nearby there was a blackened spot of earth that looked like an abandoned campfire. At this point, the elaborate banana and flower offerings we had purchased in Yogya were placed on the platform. I sat down to wait. The old man finally took his leave of us, and I was able to ask Mbak Yeni who he was. As it turns out, he was the *Jero Kunci*, the keeper of the keys, to this site (*jero* also means inside in Javanese, so one might translate this as the keys to the inside). Looking around at the nondescript clearing, marked only by the small platform and the black-ened and burned spot, I didn't understand his purpose, although it was clear that he would have use of the offerings after we were done with them as partial payment for guarding the site. This was in addition to the money slipped to him by the leader of our group, Bu Atmo.

After the departure of the *Jero Kunci*, Bu Atmo called us over to sit in front of the blackened spot and pray. We arranged ourselves in front of the area and each applied a spot of fragrant oil to our wrists. We then bowed our heads as Bu Atmo began to pray aloud. As her Javanese was difficult for me to follow, I resigned myself to being quiet with my thoughts. And so I was completely taken by surprise when the voice next to me changed completely in timbre and pitch. I was so startled that I whipped my head up and looked at her. Bu Atmo was a spirit medium, I understood then. She had been entered by the spirit who inhabited this small spot in the woods. I quickly composed myself and bent my head again.

After speaking at length, Mbak Yeni's aunt repeating everything she said, Bu Atmo finally came out of the trance. She had been entered by the spirit of Sultan Agung who had given us detailed directions about how to conceive and also given us names for the children to be born. In my case, it was Agung Wusono. We then walked a little further up the trail to a spring to gather water before we began our descent back to the main road.

One of our directives from Sultan Agung was to eat young pineapple grown on this very mountain. The importance of this directive became quite clear when Mbak Yeni's diminutive aunt gave a cry and darted to the edge of the path. She had spotted a pineapple growing a little below the path. She tried to grab it but found it too far below the edge of the path on this steep part of the mountain. Ignoring our protests, she promptly up-ended herself, no mean feat in a sarong, and reached to grab the pineapple with the crook of her umbrella. She was eventually successful, although her niece and husband had to reach down below the edge of the path to retrieve her.

Still reeling from the sight of a proper Javanese *ibu* upside-down in pursuit of a pineapple, I was following the others down the path, when there was a shout above us. The pineapple plant belonged to someone who lived on the mountain and we had been seen taking the fruit. I was beyond surprise when our little group, rather than turning to apologize and return the fruit, instead picked up speed and hurried down the path off the mountain.

CULTURE IS ORDINARY

> There is a distinct working-class way of life, which I for one value—not only because I was bred in it, for I now, in certain respects live differently. I think the way of life with the emphases of neighbourhood, mutual obligation, and common betterment, as expressed in the great working-class political and industrial institutions, is in fact the best basis for any further English society. (Williams 1989:8)

By following *kampung* women in their daily tasks of reproduction and production, I was given a guided tour of domestic space in urban Java, and that space extended from inside the structures of houses to the tops of magic mountains, making it difficult to draw the boundaries of domestic space. My trip to the mountain with my neighbours, a young married woman trying to conceive and a set of retired people devoted to the older spiritual beliefs of Java, illustrates that the topography of reproduction and domestic work stretches far beyond the doors of the house, or even the *kampung*. In a sense, our approach to Sultan Agung up the back side of a mountain rather than directly through the gates of the Imogiri cemetery was another view through the back door of domesticity.

My goal here has been to expand "the domestic" from its tight circumscription in scholarly literature. My own position as a housewife-ethnographer gave me, not only a sense of the immutability of the daily reproductive work of the household, but also a sense of the invisibility of that work. Not only that, my discomfort with the role I chose in the field— apprentice housewife—also afforded a clear view of how uncomfortable social categories are reproduced despite their ambivalent fit. When I acted as a housewife, just as it happened for my neighbours, a particular gendered and classed social category was reproduced. This reproduction is tied up not only with the making of houses, households, and homes, but the *kampung* community as a form of state rule.

The ordinary culture of the *kampung* is often overlooked. Ethnographies of the marginal, now balanced by ethnographies of the powerful, leave out those whose class position belies their association with the dominant culture of Java. The lack of attention to *kampung* culture leaves unexplored its multiply construed reality as a community: as ethnic enclave, guild neighbourhood, royal protectorate, village administrative unit, "stated" community, and home community. Borrowing from Corrigan and Sayer the idea of the long-making of the English state, the *kampung* can be seen as social formation, emergent over time, congruent with changes in the settlement and administration of Indonesia. Its usefulness to cultures of administration (Adorno 1990) should not mask its reality as a structure of feeling in the lives of its inhabitants. If a culture is the "common meanings, the product of a whole people" and the individual meanings that are a product of "whole committed personal and social experience," as Williams describes (1989:87), then the *kampung* is a kind of culture, distinct from other cultural forms and class fragments. It is made up of the various dimensions of domestic space described here: the house, the household, and the home.

The *kampung* as a house is made through the flows of kin, labour, and resources over thresholds of domestic space. *Kampung* kinship shows the limits of any ideal model of nuclear family and bilateral descent, even as it proves itself to be a language of shared commitment, exchange, and transformation. My neighbours in the *kampung* live in extended and joint family compounds, sharing children, tasks, and values. The physical structure of the house, its architecture and its symbolic values, is perhaps best conceptualized as Waterson describes: "metaphorical chains of association linking women, houses, kin groups, ancestors, the earth, and so on" (1990:196). The *kampung* house is defined less by its walls than by the paths, connections, and flows between houses. In a very meaningful sense, the house is the community in miniature and the community is a model of the house, transforming the opposition between the equality of shared exchange and the hierarchy of, marriage and gender.

The reproduction of the household as an economic unit of production, reproduction, and consumption is overdetermined by the state-sponsorship of the *kampung* as a reserve army of labour.[1] *Kampung* inhabitants make-do by mixing formal sector work with informal sector work, often done out of the house by women, and promoted by the Republic of Indonesia through programs such as PKK. Rather than see the householding strategy of many *kampung* households as the direct result of government policies and programs, it is more appropriate to see PKK as providing the ideological vocabulary for producing and sustaining a domestic community—the *kampung*—and for organizing support for large numbers of low-waged, low-skilled labour. According to the official government ideology this should be accomplished through a bio-social group—the household—focussed centrally around unpaid work of the housewife.

The home, like the moral universe of the *kampung*, signifies warmth, acceptance, shared burden, and cooperation. Morality in the *kampung* taps into both national and local systems of value and meaning, making any single understanding of gender and power, or community and power, impossible. In the daily working out of *kampung* community, resources are called upon, identities are negotiated, and the redistribution of status and power are bargained over and accomplished. The home, the house, and the household, are made and remade in the use of material and ideological resources available in regimes of value at the local level as well as resources from the state.

The housewife as the domestic angel, as the handmaiden of colonialism, as the nation's moral pillar, certainly haunts the houses, households and homes of *Kampung Rumah Putri*, but logic of making do, the structure of kin and exchange, and the moral universe of the *kampung* help maintain the house she haunts.

STATE FORMATION ON MY STREET

The *kampung* is a "stated" community in that it was been formed and reformed around the administrative and political needs of successive regimes: colonial, war-time, republican, and nationalist. Yet as Adorno (1990) writes, (in some contrast to Pemberton [1994]), "[a]dministration ... is not simply imposed upon the supposedly productive human being from without. It multiplies within this person himself" (1990:41). The inevitable reach of administration to take over culture does not mean its end: there remains the active play of culture within and without administration.

It is the daily living out of these structures of feeling (Williams 1977) by *kampung* dwellers and government-sponsored housewives that produces a particular social—and political—formation that is both question and response to how a people are organized in response to rule. State rule is always and forever a domestic project, aimed at the control of reproduction as much or more than it is at production. The control of domestic reproduction in its expanded sense—humans, social relations, society—is integral to state rule, and not the feminized adjunct of real politics. It would be a mistake, however, to see this project as complete, successful or comprehensive. Instead, the reach of administration is virtual, always almost accomplished but never fully achieved, filled with misunderstandings, gaps and absences. Likewise, the lived practice of *kampung* community and family is incomplete, filled with struggles, arguments, and competing claims within and between houses, men and women.

The foregoing consideration of the *kampung* as a particular kind of domestic community could be described as a study in popular culture, by which I mean, the culture of the popular classes and the long-making of the Indonesian state and *kampung* culture. That this culture is also a form of state imposed ideology is also true. Yet it is the daily practice of these cultural forms in the mundane domestic moments of *kampung* life that should direct our attention to how state rule is formed and reformed on the side streets and back alleys of this working class *kampung*. Given that this work is based on experience before the dramatic political changes begun in Indonesia in 1998, it might be suggested that its conclusions no longer hold, but instead I argue just the opposite here. Households are still run, houses and kin are still built, PKK meetings are still held, and *kampung* values still hold.

NOTE

1. The concept of overdetermination is often associated with Althusser (1962). It refers, in its simplest form, to social phenomena which result not from one cause, but many, the result of a number of interlocking effects.

Epilogue

Housewife Ethnographer

The image of the self projected in women's memoirs and autobiographies reveals a need to sift through their lives for explanation and understanding. The female autobiographical intention is often powered by the motive to convince readers of the author's self-worth, to clarify and authenticate her self-image. (Tedlock 1995:275)

THE DINGHY DEPARTS

I went to the field confused. There was, of course, the much discussed and overly romanticized confusion of cultural disorientation and student self-consciousness. But there was also the bewilderment, the stupefaction, of having come to the field at the time in anthropology when I did. I had been "posted" to the field—postmodern, post-structural, post-textual, post-narrative, post-science, and on and on, at a difficult time. The worm had turned and few of my friends felt confident about how to "do" fieldwork. There were those who militantly insisted on a traditionalist framework of measurement and structured interview with a formally designed plan. And there were those who felt free—if not entirely confident—to pursue a modified program of travel and experience with a personal journal as the most formal of instruments.

So it was with some chagrin that I came to find myself sitting in my house in an urban neighbourhood in Yogyakarta, Central Java, hosting a meeting of the national housewives organization, confounding my expectations as both ethnographer and wife. My choice to do fieldwork in Indonesia with my husband, had been based partly on economic and logistical realities, but I did not make this decision to be part of a fieldwork couple easily. The weight of the unhappy history of married couples in anthropology was no small obstacle. I knew without being reminded—although indeed I was—about the phenomenon of the husband who is the centrepiece of the field experience, using the wife as *aide de camp*, later discarding her to go on to anthropological fame and a trophy wife. Languishing in academic obscurity, the first wife's insightful work is overlooked until the posthumous publication of her fieldwork reveals her as the brilliant one of the pair. Facing fieldwork in the 1990s, I was caught between this history and

159

the exhortations of feminist colleagues that a choice to go to Java with Steve was the equivalent of long-term academic suicide. My initial discomfort was compounded by my ultimate positioning in the field: I became a housewife. My own double position as housewife and ethnographer gave me some insight into the embodied experience of subjectivity and the role of ethnographic fieldwork in understanding the constitution and experience of the everyday. Equally important, this experience demonstrated that the critical job of household reproduction and women's part in household management remain under-theorized and often unmentioned, not only in terms of the practicalities of fieldwork but in terms of ethnographic analysis because researchers find it (1) boring, (2) of secondary importance, or (3) troubling.

BECOMING A HOUSEWIFE

Anthropologists have all been affected by those singular moments of fieldwork characterized by fear, confusion, and epiphany: running from the cockfight, watching the dinghy depart, seeing the green snot ooze over drawn arrows, and so on. It was humbling but no less transforming when my own fieldwork began, not with our arrival in Java or even with our taking up residence in the *kampung*, but with my first walk down the street, grocery basket clutched in hand, to do my own shopping. The absurdity of my terror at accomplishing the most mundane of daily tasks was not lost on me. After all, millions of Javanese managed to feed themselves every day. Surely, I could manage it too. But at the same time, there was an enormity to that walk down the alleyway to the neighbourhood market that I did not understand even then. I did realize that my daily shopping required me to traverse the two short "blocks" to the *Rumah Putri* market. On the way, I would have to greet and converse with many of my neighbours, some on their way to or from the market, some doing yard work or laundry, some walking babies, some selling goods from small *warung* (food and/or dry goods stalls). I would then have to enter the market and negotiate not only what I was going to get, but also from whom, for how much, and then I would have to carry the whole batch back home under the watchful eyes of my neighbours to cook it. At every step I would be involved in sets of social relations that determined not only the success of my fieldwork but in many real ways, our social survival in the *kampung*.

Somehow the one-on-one interview seemed vastly preferable to this long walk to the market. I became something of a joke to my neighbours, who delighted in pinning me against the nearest fence and questioning me about my plans for dinner, the ingredients required, the method of cooking, and so on. And the return from the market meant that the purchases in my basket were thoroughly inspected to assess the amount of money I was spending as well as what was for dinner. The intense scrutiny of trying to keep house caused me some of the greatest discomfort I have ever experienced, but it also afforded a perspective on daily *kampung* life not often available to those fed by others. Not only did the fact that we ate *nasi* (cooked rice) and not *roti* (bread) help to convince our neighbours that we were trying to fit in and live like them, but cooking also involved me most directly in the social exchange system of the *kampung*. The way my cooking was treated was also one of the clearest illustrations that the domestic and private are quite public in the *kampung*. I was quizzed repeatedly and in front of others about my cooking, and my failures were the regular stuff of neighbourhood gossip. For example, my first attempt at sharing food was kindly accepted only for me to hear later that I had used the wrong ingredients and added too much salt. Another time, I shared some *sambal tempe goreng*—a sweet, hot mixture of *tempe* (fermented soybean cake), tamarind, and sugar cooked with hot peppers—and this time the report came back that it tasted like *empiyang*, a peanut candy.

Any day that I failed to cook was noted by my neighbours. The oppressiveness of constant *kampung* facework (Goffman 1959) was compounded by being judged on the house I kept.[1] Doors are left open in the *kampung* unless people are sleeping, not home, or just rude. So like my market basket, my house cleaning was very public and subject to scrutiny. Beyond our need to eat, there was a very social compulsion to make certain that the other *ibu* (adult women) did not think I was doing a poor job of feeding us, and specifically, taking care of Steve. This worry was no small one, since I witnessed the critical social importance attached to this ability when other women came under community scrutiny and were accused of keeping poor house. I knew, as the keeper of household books, that we paid socially every time we answered the standard *mau ke mana* (where are you going) with "out to eat."

Cooking in Java requires shopping each day, if you have money, because there is little or no refrigeration. I will offer no complaints about my two kerosene burners since they were more than most people had, and at least I had an electric pump for water. But I was overwhelmed with the feeling every morning that the first thing I must do was cook rice and boil water, not because this task was arduous, but because it must always be done. It was the sheer relentlessness of housework that was so inescapable (de Beauvoir 1952).[2] Indeed, the key thing for me was the realization that the work of feeding your family, when not supported by labour-saving devices, packaged food, and take-out restaurants, is the central feature of life. All else becomes secondary, especially when that work falls completely to you and/or your resources are limited in some fashion. It was these kinds of difficulties that I experienced first-hand and saw in the lives of others that lead me to think not only of how one must give a good account of oneself domestically, but about how difficult it was to be a credible housewife in the *kampung* (Garfinkel 1967).

Initially, I hoped to do work in the Javanese countryside on peasant communities, while Steve would look at health practices across clinics and hospitals in Yogyakarta. I had planned to consider the evidence for the so-called closed corporate peasant community (Greenberg 1981; Roseberry 1989; Wolf 1957) in Java and the formation and persistence of such communities in the Javanese countryside. In Yogya, Steve and I set up an office at the Clinical Epidemiology and Biostatistics Unit (CEBU) of the Rumah Sakit Sardjito (Sardjito Hospital). This public teaching hospital connected to Universitas Gadjah Mada served as our official sponsor. Steve's work required his collaboration with the doctors of the hospital, and I hoped to take part in their rural research program as a means to begin fieldwork in the areas outside Yogya. Eventually it became clear that we would be held at some distance from the actual research being conducted. These obstacles were compounded by the heart attack of our main sponsor and the restrictions on work in the countryside during the time of the election. In frustration, I decided to change the focus of my work to my own neighbourhood in Yogya. It was at this point that my research interests turned to the *kampung* itself and to its formation through state ideologies and the local, popular practice of housework and community.

I chose as my focus the seemingly ubiquitous PKK program, and I decided beyond attending the meetings (see Figure 7.1) and interviewing women about their work and birth histories and their involvement with PKK, I would also work as a housewife. And so began my long walk to the market. The results of my choices in fieldwork ramify not only in the research that I did but in the ethnography that follows from it. By focussing on the taken-for-granted in the everyday domestic life of working class urban Javanese, I discovered the centrality of the domestic to the reproduction of social life as well as state rule in Indonesia. This work also demonstrated to me that despite the importance of the reproductive and domestic labour identified by feminist anthropologists as early the 1970s (Ortner 1974; Rosaldo 1974, 1980; Yanagisako and Collier 1987, 1989), this part of social life remains under-documented and overlooked.

Figure 7.1
A farewell PKK meeting in my rented house. (Photo by S. Ferzacca.)

HUSBANDS AND WIVES

Barbara Tedlock, in her *Works and Wives: On the Sexual Division of Textual Labour* (1995), discusses the incorporation of wives in their husbands' fieldwork, citing the infamous examples of Margery Wolf, Elizabeth Fernea, Daisy Dwyer, Carobeth Laird, and Edith Turner, to name but a few. She notes the tendency for these hidden ethnographers, who typically supported their husbands in a variety of ways in the field, to produce ethnographies in the narrative mode rather than the expository mode of the heroic male anthropologist. These wives produced writings, whether strictly ethnographies or not, that focus on the frustrations of fieldwork, that are fragmentary, disconnected, not strictly chronological, and that are often more personal and marked by conflicts between the personal and professional. According to Tedlock, women more often emphasize their lack of rapport, the bad faith of fieldwork, their un-professionalism and un-premeditatedness, in contrast to male writers who tend to construct more coherent, linear accounts that admit no confusion or contradiction (although there are obvious exceptions to this now: Rabinow 1978; Crapanzano 1985; Desjarlais 1997).

The different styles of ethnographic writing, Tedlock seems to suggest, come from the different fieldwork experiences of husbands and wives but also from what might be called a kind of feminine sensibility in writing. My own fieldwork experience contradicts this model in many ways and suggests that more recent experimental ethnographies may emphasize

fragmentation, reflexivity, and conflict but still founder on unacknowledged gender inequalities. To begin with, Steve, in contrast to the hus-
bandly ethnographers criticized by Tedlock, consciously attempted to
incorporate me in his ethnography. He explicitly deals with my presence
in the field, our household situation, and the effect of our relationship
on his own work. Unfortunately, this attempt to be more forthcoming
about the personal realities of his own fieldwork yielded paradoxical
effects. Let me begin first with a passage from Theron Nuñez's Mexican
research quoted in Tedlock:

> "One day, after almost fourteen months in the field, I rode my horse into
> the plaza and dismounted in front of the café." There he heard the story of
> the arrest of a woman he knew for cursing a man who had told her to sweep
> debris out of the street.... "Upon hearing the full story of Dona Augustina's
> dilemma, I remounted my horse, galloped across the cobblestone plaza,
> reined up sharply in front of the town hall, dismounted, and entered, my
> spurs jangling as I walked.... I was angry and arrogant." (quoted in Tedlock
> 1995:273–74)

And then a quote from Steve's dissertation:

> One day as I was standing with a neighbour woman who was the local maker
> and seller of the health elixirs known as *jamu* that people drink on a daily
> basis, we watched my wife as she walked off down the lane to an interview.
> Bu Jamu jabbed me in the side with her elbow and said that my wife really
> did fit in here in Java—that she could tell my wife liked Javanese life. I asked
> her how could she tell. She turned to me and with her arm raised pointing
> down the lane toward my wife she exclaimed, "Look at how fat she is!" I
> turned to Bu Jamu and chuckled, "Don't tell Mbak Janice she's getting fat."
> Looking perplexed Bu Jamu turned and walked back to her house. (Ferzacca
> 1996:72–73)

Comparing the two quotes one can easily see the difference between the
dauntless male ethnographer of 1970s and the more sensitive, domesti-
cated male ethnographer of the 1990s. Nuñez appears as the heroic male
ethnographer, not only bravely challenging local authorities but doing so
in the name of a woman wrongfully accused, and from horseback no less.
Steve's account shows the more homely side of fieldwork. He is described
as chatting with neighbours and fondly watching his wife. But the second
quote drawn from Steve's work is reminiscent of Elizabeth Fernea's self-
portrait in the field: "They talked loudly about me, indifferent to my
presence or possible comprehension" (1965:46–47). As Tedlock goes on
to say, Fernea's description of how the harem women she worked among
saw her, breaks down any unified, authoritative speaker—"shoes (horri-
ble); my skin (white); my husband (not bad); my skirt, visible when I sat
down even though I keep my abayah around me (good wool, but too
short): and my cut bangs (really strange, quite awful in fact)" (ibid.). As
Tedlock puts it: "The self sees, it sees itself seeing, it sees itself being seen,

and it parodies itself" (1995:269). But in my own case, the quote from Steve's dissertation does not split me into protagonist and narrator, as Tedlock describes for Fernea's work. Instead, Steve's postmodern ethnography describes him watching the Javanese watch me.

Not surprisingly, my trouble with this portrayal is the lack of control over my own representation, which puts me in a position not dissimilar from that of any ethnographic subject. Although, as part of a husband and wife team of ethnographers, I at least had the tools to insist on the acknowledgment of the unsaid. Still, this portrayal of me filtered through my husband's ethnography represents not only the specific dilemma of my own fieldwork and its presentation but goes to some of the issues of my ethnography, such as the reproduction of the housewife as a social category.

Despite years of work on gender and anthropology and the emergence of a rich literature on the gendered division of labour, the effects for fieldwork remain only half-acknowledged. The female ethnographic voice of the late 1980s and early 1990s is as heroic and singular as the male voice of the preceding decades (LaVie 1990; Boddy 1989; Tsing 1993; Behar 1993), and more easily ignored mundane worlds still remain hidden in plain sight. A colleague in the field at the same time as Steve and me reported her frustration at not being able to sit with men in the road in the middle of the night. She was certain that she was missing important information. After my time in kitchens and front stoops watching food, gossip, and support flow in and out, I'm not so certain, but I find it revealing that a female ethnographer in the 1990s is still convinced that the men in the middle of the road still are the real ethnographic subjects, in contrast to the women's worlds to which she had access.

Dorothy Smith's admonition—that women's standpoint is a point of analytical access to the constitution of sociology as a particular form of knowledge—is useful here. Her consideration of the everyday as a problematic directs our attention both to the constitution of the female sociological object through our knowledge practices as well as to the consequent possibilities for "a systematically developed consciousness of society" (Smith 1974:107). Indeed, my choice of the everyday worlds of women as the focus of ethnographic study substantiates Smith's contention that women's standpoint is one "outside textually mediated discourses in the actualities of our everyday lives. This is a standpoint designed in part by our exclusion from the making of cultural and intellectual discourse and the strategies of resorting to our experience as the ground of new knowledge, a new culture" (Smith 1974:107). My own experience as ethnographic subject and object illustrates this.

The contradictory effects of this unresolved gender tension in fieldwork and writing were clearly played out between Steve and me. While Steve's ethnography (1996) is experimental in some sense, devoted to portraying the sensual experience of living in a Javanese city in the 1990s and dealing with the hybridity of medical practices there, his portrayal of me in his ethnography—while more sensitive than the male ethnographers singled out by Tedlock—fails to overcome some of the basic problems of husband and wife research, i.e., how to do full justice to both ethnographers and their contributions to collaboration.

Setting up house in the *kampung* meant that Steve and I had to struggle with more than the division of labour in research, there was also the division of labour in our house. Both of us assumed roles not entirely consistent with those we occupy in the United States. I did not and do not consider myself a housewife, and my choice to live and work as a housewife was not always comfortable for me or for Steve. In terms of our identity as a couple within the *kampung*, it was necessary that we convince our neighbours that we were not just rich *orang asing* (foreigners). Steve and I had to overcome this not only to justify our living in the *kampung* and our interest in being part of the *kampung*, but to get past the perception that any social relationship with us would eventually become one of benefactor and client. Many researchers appear untroubled by such issues, and indeed, during our own fieldwork we knew people who chose to live in hotels and in the expat communities, doing their fieldwork through visits they largely controlled. We were, perhaps not even consciously, pursuing an older notion of fieldwork that includes daily participation in life. Our attempt to become part of the *kampung* was one of the most challenging things we tried to do, yet it yielded the richest results, both personally and analytically.

As a couple we fitted categorically into the neighbourhood in ways that afforded us easy acceptance. And it is clear that two ethnographers are able to "see" much more. For Steve and me this was often as simple as comparing notes to find out that one of us had read the verbal signals in a conversation and the other the nonverbal signals only to come to very different interpretations of what had transpired (cf. Gudeman and Rivera 1990). Our work was complementary in many ways. While my own work tended to be socially embedded in the neighbourhood, Steve was freer to see difference across sections of the city in his clinic-based research. So the very middle-class Western model of husband outside the house and wife inside was central to how we did our fieldwork.

The importance of the information I gathered by staying in the neighbourhood and apprenticing as a housewife, for the completion of Steve's work challenges the notion of the partial or muted view of women, whether as subjects of ethnography or ethnographers themselves (cf. Ardener 1975; Keeler 1990; Keesing 1985). The holism of my work based out of a house in the *kampung*, looking at a whole way of life, served as a touchstone for Steve's own peripatetic ethnography, even as it reiterated the middle-class ideal of woman at home and man outside the home.

The interesting thing is that it is Steve's "experimental" ethnography that could be characterized as fragmentary, not strictly chronological, personal, disconnected, and marked by conflicts between the personal and professional. Perhaps this is what Catherine Lutz means when she suggests that the postmodern theorist is not a feminist but a drag queen, or in her words, "the postmodern is a man in woman's clothing" (Lutz 1995:257), or again as de Lauretis describes, "the 'flickering' of the post-humanist Lacanian subject, which is too nearly white and at best (fe)male" (1986:9). This is not to pillory my husband in his attempt to represent the disjointed nature of fieldwork. I only point out that the luxury of no attention to the requirements of daily life that seems characteristic of many postmodern ethnographies is often the result of an unrevised practice of gender asymmetry. Perhaps another example is in order.

One afternoon I got word that a near neighbour had become dizzy and taken a fall. She was an older woman and so the fall was of some concern; in fact, it was originally reported that she had had a heart attack. As is expected between close neighbours, Steve and I made an evening call. We were visiting and hearing that the spell was not that serious when Steve pulled out his notepad and pen and got ready to take notes. I was appalled and quickly kicked his ankle to get him to stop. As I thought about this scenario in the months afterward, I came to see that our differing responses had much to do with the way we were doing fieldwork. While Steve was comfortable in his role as ethnographer and note-taker, quickly in and out, my work thus far had been about establishing community ties and trust, about becoming embedded in the community, about being not only a researcher (although that was part of my identity) but also a neighbour. For my own work, I had to worry about the repercussions of acting in this disinterested way. Steve could walk away from the situation with "data," while my own success in fieldwork was based on my ability to come back as a neighbour again and again.

This constant and contingent reinforcement of *kampung* relationships resembles Keeler's description of the inappropriate use of a final thank you by Javanese speakers (Jv. *matur nuwun*) in transactions (Keeler 1984). *Matur nuwun* signals the end of the relationship, while many social relationships are extended through the unsaid thank you and the implied need to recompense the largess of a friend. By saying "thank you" one suggests that the relationship is over and no future exchange is implied. My fieldwork in the *kampung* was successful in so far as I was able to keep such relationships open and ongoing.

It was this work that provided Steve with access to the *kampung* data that he used in his own work. The success of his fieldwork was therefore dependent to some extent on my success as a household manager and community member. My identity as a housewife made his work possible, much like Tedlock's incorporated wives. Even more, as a subject of his ethnography—as he now is of mine—my own position as housewife ethnographer gave me some sense of the politics of subjectivity.

The difficulties with husband and wife ethnography have become clearer since we returned from the field. Steve has consistently and self-consciously included me in his ethnography and his analysis of Java. I figure prominently not only in his personal experience but in his research. But like the metaphor of the mirror in so much feminist analysis (MacKinnon 1983; Berger 1977), I serve to reflect for Steve issues of culture and conflict. My quibble with Steve's ethnographic representation is the unacknowledged division of labour within our house that made his work possible, as well as my own. That is, Steve was able to work out of the clinic and return to a *kampung* home because of my work as a housewife. Moreover, while his references to his wife grant him the aura of enlightened awareness of the problems of past couples, any mention I make of him does not grant me the same cachet. Indeed, by acknowledging that I worked as a housewife as part of a husband and wife team, recreating a very middle class ideal, my own work is immediately suspect.

My double position, as subject in Steve's ethnography and ethnographer in my own right, goes beyond anxiety about academic standing to how the experience of women forms a subject for sociological and ethnographic inquiry. Dorothy Smith proposes women's experience as a means to consider both the epistemological and ontological character of sociological analysis as well as the everyday as a problematic. She draws our attention to how the standpoint of women directs attention to an "embodied" subject located in a particular actual local historical setting (1974:108). Smith's location of textually mediated discourses as inherently separated and separating from women's experience prompts a reconsideration of my own position as inside and outside Steve's ethnography and my own. Taking seriously her dictum that we must start with women's experience, my own fieldwork as a housewife ethnographer made it apparent, both for me and the women I studied, that the "the available concepts and frameworks do not work because they have already posited a subject situated outside a local and actual experience, a particularized knowledge of the world" (ibid.: 109).

My choice to do participant observation as a housewife has also netted me several insights into the perception of housework as a field of study, from the worried condescension of some colleagues and the marginalization of my work by others, to the representation of this work by my distaff side. I want to argue here that these reactions reveal just how critical it is that we continue to consider the centrality of reproduction and domestic production to human social life despite our society's notions of its unimportance.

REPRODUCING HOUSEWIVES

Indonesia's national economic policy depends in large part on the unacknowledged labour of housewives, and in many ways the logic of this relationship is the same as that in the production of many ethnographies. The contradictions in my field position and the creation of PKK housewives follow from a failure to solve the dilemmas about household reproduction and it is reiterated in the "familiar overvaluing and overestimation of production in relation to reproduction" (Moore 1994:88). That is to say, in our ethnographies and our lives alike, anthropologists have failed to adequately theorize and describe the reproductive work,[3] and I mean reproduction beyond the sense of reproducing biological bodies but short of reproducing capitalism, for example. I am seeking here to investigate the middle ground: how the daily reproduction of housewives and appropriate domesticity illustrates the day-to-day reproduction of the *kampung* as a social formation, the community as a nationalist ideal, and the state as a lived political project.

So in my own work I have chosen quite deliberately to reverse the transit documented for other wifely ethnographers by Tedlock (1995:271): "a silent wife-ethnographer may undergo a metamorphosis, moving from housewife and participant informer to active, professional, ethnographer." I am an active, professional ethnographer who chose to work as a housewife and participant informer, and my own positioning in the field reveals some of the postmodern male and female ethnographers to be unreconstructed in their treatment of the household and its continued relegation to a woman's world. This is evident in Tedlock's own description of Ruth Behar whose field site was the kitchen table built by her husband and who, "like the Norwegian ethnographer Marianne Gullestad in *Kitchen Table Society*, evokes her kitchen table" (1984). But Tedlock goes on to say that "neither of these women is an innocent housewife whiling her time away" (1995:280).

What I saw daily in the *kampung* challenges the existence of any *innocent* housewife. Those who either dismiss the housewife, or romanticize her, fail to understand her role in social life. I have come to see that avoiding the reproductive work of women because of fears of academic marginalization reproduces the error of most traditional anthropology, that is, the assumption that this work could somehow be sorted out of the web of social life. So while I did not initially go to the field to work as a home-based ethnographer of housewifery, I stake that claim now.

My attempt to pass as a housewife was no different than if I had chosen to apprentice with a sorcerer or a puppetmaker, except in the lack of prestige associated with it. After all, I am not a housewife when in the US, and chores around our house are in a constant state of negotiation—who is cooking, who is cleaning, who is paying attention. The difficulty I had in giving a credible account of myself as a wife and homemaker was not that different from the difficulty of the women in the neighbourhood, although they had less room for failure. This notion of passing, of giving a credible account resonates with the ethnomethodologist's notion of accountability (see Chapter Five). I take this idea of accountability along with Goffman's idea of facework, not just because it dovetails so nicely with the ethnomethodologist's "theme of tacit or 'taken for granted' understandings" (Giddens 1995:237), but because it offers a micro-level tool for understanding the connection between everyday action and the production of common sense, as well as the reproduction of gendered subjectivity.

Whereas my broader theoretical perspective is on the long-term emergence of a working class culture (Williams 1961; Willis 1977), this perspective does not necessarily provide a technique for relating the emergence of this culture to everyday interaction. While the notion that the working class makes itself is appealing, how that is accomplished at the level of the individual is usually left to the imagination in retrospective treatments such as Williams's. I would like to suggest here that it is in the everyday accountability between *kampung* dwellers that such common sense is built up and modified, and for that reason the ethnomethodologist's frame is a useful one. And the emphasis on credible accounts and on facework (Garfinkel 1967; Goffman 1959) can be related to the more recent work on subjectivity. According to Moore (1994), it is individual women's engagement with and investment in particular subject positions among "several competing, possibly contradictory discourses on femininity and masculinity" that works to reproduce dominant cultural discourse even as these same individuals may stand at some remove from the discourse itself. This involvement is not about emotional satisfaction alone, but the "very real, material social and economic benefits which are the reward of the senior man, the good wife, the powerful mother or the dutiful daughter in many social situations." (Moore 1994:65)

The official PKK discourse on *ibu rumah tangga* (housewives) is a relatively recent one with a clear affinity with middle class and Dutch colonial ideas of a woman's proper place. The entrance of the good woman into a national dialogue and its dissemination to the most local level through this national housewives organization has forced women to pay some heed to its message. While the historical and class contents of this category, housewife, are limited, they are now taken to apply to all women, regardless of their family or occupational status. In other words, those working class Javanese women with whom I lived and worked were trying to pass, too. Like me, they were daily involved in giving a credible account of themselves in terms of the commonly understood official role of women and mothers, although tellingly, this had to be balanced continuously with the other modes of *kampung* membership and gendered identity.

While management of face was critical to my ability to complete my fieldwork and was the most difficult thing I did, it was of limited duration and my incompetence threatened only my ethnographic project. In contrast, those women unable to give credible accounts of themselves as household managers, as well as PKK workers, suffered not just the sting of gossip, but the very real cut of not receiving mutual aid and community support.

It is the daily work of women attempting to conform to the PKK ideal of womanhood that makes that policy manifest in daily life. Only when women feel compelled to acknowledge this discourse, or to gesture to it by acknowledging its credibility in their daily accounts, does it enter the realm of common sense and the daily life of culture (Goffman 1959). PKK becomes real in everyday life when *kampung* women feel embarrassed about their non-attendance or non-conformity to the extent that they maintain their reputation by apologizing, temporizing or avoiding the behaviour in the first place. My neighbours were managing accounts in more ways than one. My methods and my fieldwork came to be focussed on the ways in which *kampung* women unself-consciously, unreflexively, uncritically went about producing accounts of themselves as credible women. And so, I apprenticed as a housewife, cooking, shopping, and cleaning, trying to give a credible account of myself as a housewife, too.

SEEING HOUSEWIVES

Being watched (as I was by Steve and our neighbours) rather than seeing for oneself, has been suggested to have a role in gendered subjectivity. Lacan (1977) offered the *imago* or mirror stage of human psychic development in which the self is seen as whole but experienced as fragmented. Nancy Chodorow (1978) reworked Lacan in her object-relations theory so as to explain the development of gendered identity, and feminist theories have considered women's sexual objectification as part of male viewing of pornography (MacKinnon 1983). Subjectivity then, has been analysed as the result of the mirroring central to the emergence of self and identity. John Berger suggests yet another step:

> [M]en act; women appear. Men look at women. Women watch themselves being looked at. This determines not only most relations between men and women but also the relation of women to themselves. The surveyor of woman in herself is male: the surveyed, female. Thus she turns herself into an object—and most particularly an object of vision: a sight. (Berger 1977)

Although I read this long before I went to the field, I did not fully understand its meaning until I experienced being a housewife who plays a secondary role in her husband's ethnography while also being the housewife ethnographer of her own writing. Much as Berger (and Tedlock) say, my experience of fieldwork included the split self of surveyed and surveyor, but not only was I watching myself be watched, I was watching others too.

And as I served to refract the images of the neighbourhood for Steve, my own sense of being watched gave me some insight into how our neighbours might have felt—not just as people who were studied by us but most particularly how women feel as mirrors.

Javanese housewives, in their roles as mediators in community and national development, in effect mirror social relations to the state apparatus, but also serve to refract state directives to the local community. While the comparison of my personal experience of fieldwork and ethnography with that of Javanese women as mediators of state and community relations would appear to dislocate and confuse the level of experience considered, the two levels are indeed related in ways that light up the connection between the personal and the public. Javanese women are subjected to higher levels of conventional government surveillance than men because of the need to control population through their bodies and because of their officially sanctioned roles in PKK. This heightened surveillance of individual women was played out in the community in the surveillance of their abilities as housewives by other neighbours. So my own seeming double subjectivity finds a parallel in the way Javanese working class housewives have been split into watchers of one another, and perhaps more importantly, of themselves.

But beyond this, the perception of being watched, and watching yourself be watched, but also watching others as I experienced in Java, had much to do with the identity I created in the kampung and the development of my personal social relations. As de Lauretis suggests, identification is neither single nor simple but a relation, "part of the process of becoming a subject, and it involves the identification of oneself with something other than oneself, so that subjectivity is constituted through a series of such identifications (de Lauretis 1984:141). And this was another aspect my own positioning in the field as subject/object in Steve's ethnography and writer of my own: that my identity slipped between these positions. I was at once a researcher studying housewives and a housewife (at least during fieldwork) in my own marriage—at least insofar as I maintained Steve and myself in the field as a functioning household—which established not only my own gendered identity in the field but Steve's as well. Not only did Steve's use of me in his ethnography give me the experience of what it might be like to be an ethnographic subject and the consequences of ownership and control, but my own position as an extension of Steve meanwhile reproduced the conventional gender roles in a Western heterosexual marriage. So indeed my position was never singular.

My understandings of what it means to be a housewife in Java were very directly affected by how I figured in Steve's study, along with how I did my own. Similarly, the experience of being a housewife in Java for the female residents of the kampung has effected and is affected by the social relations of community. Yet the critical role of inter-subjectivity, the self created in social relations, has not been well translated into theories of subjectivity in anthropology. Anthropologists thus tend to see gender identity and subjectivity in overly rigid ways, reifying Western dichotomies and losing sight of the possibility of multiple subject positions (Moore 1994). Moore asks: "Do any of us really believe that we identify wholeheartedly with the dominant gender categories of our own societies" (1994:51). It often seems that the problem for anthropologists, as for social scientists in general, is to explain how dominant discourses and categories get reproduced when so few people are prepared to acknowledge that they support or believe in them.

My experience in the field as a housewife ethnographer was a project not only in seeing housewives as legitimate subjects of research, but also, in understanding how they are reproduced. That is, not only how a social category is reproduced, but why are roles that are at least partially disagreeable reproduced? For example, in Java, I reproduced in my daily life the category of experience termed housewife—one that I do not necessarily feel comfortable with in the United States. At the same time, I was able to contest this role inside my own home, sometimes vehemently. Still, the gender trouble I experienced among my own cultural cohort helps show how uncomfortable and incompletely integrated roles are nonetheless reproduced. Likewise, the women I worked with in Java reproduce the PKK *ibu* even while this role does not apparently match their feelings or all of their experiences. They are quite capable of cynicism about their roles in the organization known as "women without enough work to do" while effectively fulfilling their positions in the organization, and thereby reproducing the category of community-oriented housewife.

And so despite my own anger, confusions and discomfort at some parts of my fieldwork, I do believe I gained some perspective on the double bind of Javanese housewives. This is not to say that I am in the same position as the Javanese people I studied, only that my own multiple subjectivity has given me some insight into the reproduction of roles one is not completely comfortable with, and the unease of watching while being watched. It was in trying to act the part of a housewife, a role that was uncomfortable to me at home and nearly overwhelming in Java, that I learned the most about the complexities of reproduction, the delicacy of social relations, and the immutability and density of daily routine.

NOTES

1. Goffman's notion of facework relates to the everyday presentation of self in social situations. Face, in this sense, refers not just to actual faces but to the image of self that is projected. The concept of facework draws particular attention to the presentation of positive face in public settings of co-presence, as well as loss of face and the technologies of self that can mend this loss.

2. The cyclical quality of housework and its relationship to creativity have been considered by Simone de Beauvoir (1952) in the contrast between immanence and transcendence and by Arendt (1958) in the contrast between work versus labour. See Iris Marion Young (1995) for a attention to the preservation involved in housework.

3. By housework, I refer to the unpaid reproductive work in the home, and not factory work (Ong 1987; Wolf 1992) or paid domestic worker (Chin 1998) or colonial domestic work (Stoler 1996; Locher-Scholten 2000) which have been studied extensively.

References

Abdullah, Drs. Wuryanto, Drs. Salamun, Dra. Emiliana Sadilah, and Dra. Isyanti. 1985. *Perkampungan di Perkotaan Sebagai Wujud Proses Adaptasi Sosial Daerah Istimewa Yogyakarta.* Jakarta: Departemen Pendidikan dan Kebudayaan, Proyek Inventarisasi dan Dokumentasi Kebudayaan Daerah.

Abrams, Philip. 1988. [1977] Notes on the Difficulty of Studying the State. *Journal of Historical Sociology* 1(1):58–88.

Adas, Michael. 1981. From Avoidance to Confrontation: Peasant Protest in Precolonial and Colonial Southeast Asia. *Comparative Studies in Society and History* 23(2):217–47.

Adorno, Theodor. 1990. Culture and Administration. In *Philosophical Streets: New Approaches to Urbanism,* edited by Dennis Crow, pp. 27–51. Washington, DC: Maisonneuve Press.

Alexander, J. and P. Alexander. 1982. Shared Poverty as Ideology: Agrarian Relationships in Colonial Java. *Man* 17:597–619.

Althusser, Louis. 1962. *For Marx.* Ben Brewster, trans. New York: Penguin Press.

Anderson, Benedict. 1987. How did the Generals Die? *Indonesia* 43:109–13.

—. 1990. *Language and Power: Exploring Political Cultures in Indonesia.* Ithaca: Cornell University Press.

—. 1991. *Imagined Communities: Reflections on the Origin and Spread of Nationalism.* 2nd Edition. New York: Verso.

Antlov, Hans. 1995. *Exemplary Centre, Administrative Periphery: Rural Leadership and the New Order in Java.* London: Curzon Press.

Appadurai, Arjun. 1986. *The Social Life of Things: Commodities in Cultural Perspective.* Cambridge: Cambridge University Press.

Ardener, Edwin. 1975. The "Problem" Revisited. In *Perceiving Women,* edited by Shirley Ardener, pp. 19–27. London: Malaby.

Arendt, Hannah. 1958. *The Human Condition.* Chicago: University of Chicago Press.

Barrett, Michèle. 1988. W*omen's Oppression Today: The Marxist/Feminist Encounter.* Revised Edition. London: Verso.

Barry, Andrew, Thomas Osborne, and Nikolas Rose. 1996. *Foucault and Political Reason: Liberalism, Neo-Liberalism and Rationalities of Government.* Chicago: University of Chicago Press

Bartlett, Peggy. 1989. Introduction: Dimensions and Dilemmas of House-holding. In *The Household Economy: Reconsidering the Domestic Mode of Production*, edited by Richard Wilk. Boulder: Westview.

Beatty, Andrew. 1999. *Varieties of Javanese Religion: An Anthropological Account.* Cambridge: Cambridge University Press.

Becker, Gary. 1981. *A Treatise on the Family.* Cambridge: Harvard University Press.

Behar, Ruth. 1993. *Translated Woman: Crossing the Border with Esperanza's Story.* Boston: Beacon.

Benda, Henry, James Irikura and Koichi Kishi. 1965. *Japanese Military Administration in Indonesia: Selected Documents.* Southeast Asia Studies, Translations Series No. 6, Yale University.

Benedict, Ruth. 1946. *The Chrysanthemum and the Sword: Patterns of Japanese Culture.* New York: World Publishing, Meridian.

Bennholdt-Thomsen, Veronika. 1988. Why do Housewives Continue to be Created in the Third World too? In *Women: The Last Colony*, edited by Maria Mies, Veronika Bennholdt Thomsen, and Claudia von Werlhof, pp. 159–167. London: Zed Books.

Berger, John. 1977. *Ways of Seeing.* NY: Penguin Books.

Bestor, Theodore. 1989. *Neighborhood Tokyo.* Stanford: Stanford University Press.

Bianpoen, Carla. 2000. The Family Welfare Movement: A Blessing or a Burden. In *Indonesian Women: The Journey Continues*, edited by Mayling Oey-Gardiner and Carla Bianpoen, pp. 156–171. Canberra: RSPAS Publishing.

Biro Pusat Statistik. 1992. *Indikator Kesejahteraan Rakyat.* Jakarta, Indonesia.

Boddy, Janice. 1989. *Women, Men, and the Zar Cult of Northern Sudan.* Madison: University of Wisconsin Press.

Boris, Eileen and Peter Bardaglio. 1983. The Transformation of Patriarchy: The Historic Role of the State. In *Families, Politics, and Public Policy*, edited by Irene Diamond, pp. 70–93. New York: Longman.

Boon, James. 1990. Balinese Twins Time Two: Gender, Birth Order, and "Household" in Indonesia/Indo-Europe. In *Power and Difference: Gender in Island Southeast Asia*, edited by J.M. Atkinson and S. Errington, pp. 209–234. Stanford: Stanford University Press.

Bourdieu, Pierre. 1972. Marriage Strategies as Strategies of Social Repro-duction. In *Family and Society: Selections from the Annales, Économies, Sociétiés, Civilisations*, edited by Robert Forster and Orest Ranum, pp. 117–140. Baltimore: Johns Hopkins University Press.

—. 1977. *Outline of a Theory of Practice.* Translated by Richard Nice. Cambridge: Cambridge University Press.

—. 1984. *Distinction: A Social Critique of the Judgement of Taste.* London: Routledge & Kegan Paul.

Boutilier, James. 1982. European Women in the Solomon Islands, 1900–1942: Accommodation and Change on the Pacific Frontier. In *Rethinking Women's Roles: Perspectives on the Pacific*, edited by Denise O'Brien and Sharon Tiffany. Berkeley: University of California Press.

Bowen, John. 1986. On the Political Construction of Tradition: Gotong Royong in Indonesia. *Journal of Asian Studies* 45(3):545–561.

—. 1993. *Muslims through Discourse: Religion and Ritual in Gayo Society.* Princeton: Princeton University Press.

Branson, Jan and Don Miller. 1988. The Changing Fortunes of Balinese Market Women. In *Development and Displacement: Women in Southeast Asia*, edited by G. Chandler, N. Sullivan, and J. Branson, pp.1–16. Monash Papers on Southeast Asia, No. 18. Victoria, Australia: Monash University, Centre for Southeast Asian Studies.

Breman, Jan. 1980. *The Village on Java and the Early Colonial State.* Rotterdam: CASP, Erasmus University Rotterdam.

—. 1983. *Control of Land and Labour in Colonial Java.* Dordrecht: Foris. Publications.

—. 1988. *The Shattered Image: Construction and Deconstruction of the Village in Colonial Asia.* CASA, Dordrecht: Foris.

Brenner, Suzanne. 1995. Why Women Rule the Roost: Rethinking Javanese Ideologies of Gender and Self-Control. In *Bewitching Women, Pious Men: Gender and Body Politics in Southeast Asia*, edited by Aihwa Ong and Michael Peletz, pp.19–50. Berkeley: University of California Press.

—. 1998. *The Domestication of Desire: Women, Wealth, and Modernity in Java.* Princeton: Princeton University Press.

Buchori, Binny and Ifa Soenarto. 2000. Dharma Wanita: An Asset or a Curse? In *Indonesian Women: The Journey Continues*, edited by Mayling Oey-Gardiner and Carla Bianpoen, pp. 139–155. Canberra: RSPAS Publishing.

Budihardjo, Eko. 1998. *Percikan Masalah Arsitektur, Perumahan, Perkotaan.* Yogyakarta: Gadjah Mada Press.

Burchell, Graham, Colin Gordon, and Peter Miller, eds. 1991. *The Foucault Effect: Studies in Governmentality.* Chicago: University of Chicago Press.

Burger, D.H. 1957. *Structural Changes in Javanese Society: the Village Sphere.* Ithaca: Cornell University, Southeast Asia Program, Modern Indonesia Project.

Cain, Melinda. 1981. Java, Indonesia: The Introduction of Rice Processing Technology. In *Women and Technological Change in Developing Countries*, edited by R. Dauber and M. Cain, pp. 127–137. Boulder: Westview.

Callaway, Helen. 1987. *Gender, Culture and Empire: European Women in Colonial Nigeria.* Oxford: Macmillan Press and St. Antony's College.

Carey, Peter and Vincent Houben. 1987. Spirited Srikandhis and Sly Sumbadras: the Social, Political and Economic role of Women at the Central Javanese Courts in the 18th and early 19th Centuries. In *Indonesian*

Woman in Focus: Past and Present Notions, edited by Elsbeth Locher-Scholten and Anke Neihof, pp. 12–42. Dordrecht: Foris.

Carsten, Janet. 1995. Houses in Langkawi: Stable Structures or Mobile Homes? In *About the House: Levi-Strauss and Beyond*, edited by Janet Carsten and Stephen Hugh-Jones, pp.105–128. Cambridge: Cambridge University Press.

—. 1997. *The Heat of the Hearth: The Process of Kinship in a Malay Fishing Community.* Oxford: Oxford University Press.

Carsten, Janet and Stephen Hugh-Jones. 1995. Introduction. In *About the House: Levi-Strauss and Beyond*, edited by Janet Carsten and Stephen Hugh-Jones, pp.1–46. Cambridge: Cambridge University Press.

Chatterjee, Partha. 1989. Colonialism, Nationalism and Colonised Women: The Contest in India. *American Ethnologist* 16(4):622–633.

Chin, Christine. 1983. *In Service and Servitude: Foreign Female Domestic Workers and the Malaysian "Modernity" Project.* New York: Columbia University Press.

Chodorow, Nancy. 1978. *The Reproduction of Mothering: Psychoanalysis and the Sociology of Gender.* Berkeley: University of California Press.

Cobban, James. 1976. Geographic Notes on the First Two Centuries of Djakarta. In *Changing South-East Asian Cities: Readings on Urbanization*, edited by Y.M. Yeung and C.P. Lo, pp. 45–57. Singapore: Oxford University Press.

Collier, W. 1981a. Agricultural Involution in Java. In *Agricultural and Rural Development in Indonesia*, edited by G. Hansen. Boulder, CO: Westview.

—. 1981b. *Declining Labour Absorption (1978 to 1980) in Javanese Production.* Occasional Papers no. 2. Bogor, Indonesia: Agro Economic Survey.

Collier, Jane F. and Sylvia J. Yanagisako. 1989. Theory in Anthropology Since Feminist Practice. *Critique of Anthropology* 9(2):27–37.

Collier, W., Gunawan Wiradi and Soetono. 1973. Recent Changes in Rice Harvesting Methods. *Bulletin of Indonesian Economic Studies* 9(2):36–45.

Comaroff, Jean and John Comaroff. 1992. Home-Made Hegemony: Modernity, Domesticity, and Colonialism in South Africa. In *African Encounters with Domesticity*, edited by Karen Tranberg Hansen, pp. 37–74. New Brunswick: Rutgers University Press.

Cooley, Laura. 1992. Maintaining Rukun for Javanese Households and for the State. In *Women and Mediation in Indonesia*, edited by S. van Bemmelen, M. Djajadiningrat Nieuwenhuis, E. Locher-Scholten, and E. Touwen-Bouwsma, pp. 229–248. Leiden: KITLV Press.

Cooper, Frederick and Ann Laura Stoler. 1997. *Tensions of Empire: Colonial Cultures in a Bourgeois World.* Berkeley: University of California Press.

Corrigan, Philip and Derek Sayer. 1985. *The Great Arch: English State Formation as Cultural Revolution.* Oxford: Basil Blackwell.

Cott, Nancy. 1977. *The Bonds of Womanhood: "Woman's Sphere" in New England, 1780–1835.* New Haven: Yale University Press.

Crapanzano, Vincent. 1985. *Tuhami: Portrait of a Moroccan*. Chicago: University of Chicago Press.

Davidoff, Leonore and Catherine Hall. 1987. *Family Fortunes: Men and Women of the English Middle Class*. Chicago: University of Chicago Press.

de Beauvoir, Simone. 1952. *The Second Sex*. Translated by H.M. Parshley. New York: Random House.

de Certeau, Michel. 1984. *The Practice of Everyday Life*. Berkeley: University of California Press.

Dean, Mitchell. 1999. *Governmentality: Power and Rule in Modern Society*. London: Sage.

de Grazia, Victoria. 1992. *How Fascism Ruled Women: Italy, 1922–1945*. Berkeley: University of California.

Department of Information. 1984. *The Second Five-Year Development Plan* (1974/75–1078/79). Jakarta: Republic of Indonesia.

Desjarlais, Robert. 1997. *Shelter Blues: Sanity and Selfhood Among the Homeless*. Philadelphia: University of Pennsylvania Press.

de Lauretis, Teresa, editor. 1986. *Feminist Studies/Critical Studies*. London: Macmillan.

Dewey, Alice G. 1962. *Peasant Marketing in Java*. New York: The Free Press of Glencoe.

Dipodiningrat. 1956. Sedjarah Perkembangan Pemerintahan Kotapradja Jogyakarta in Kota Jogyakarta 200 Tahun, edited by Darmosugito, Dipodiningrat, Notojoedo, et al. Panitya Peringatan Kota Jogyakarta 200 Tahun, Yogyakarta.

Djajadiningrat-Nieuwenhuis, Madelon. 1987. Ibuism and Priyayization: Path to Power? In *Indonesian Woman in Focus: Past and Present Notions*, edited by Elsbeth Locher-Scholten and Anke Neihof, pp. 43–51. Dordrecht: Foris.

Donzelot, Jacques. 1979. *The Policing of Families*. New York: Pantheon Books.

Dumont, Louis. 1966. The 'Village Community' from Munro to Maine. *Contributions to Indian Sociology* 9(December):67–89

Echols, John and Hassan Shadily. 1990. *Kamus Indonesia-Inggris: An Indonesian-English Dictionary*. Third Edition. Jakarta: Penerbit PT Gramedia.

Errington, Shelly. 1990. Recasting Sex, Gender, and Power: A Theoretical and Regional Overview. In *Power and Difference: Gender in Island Southeast Asia*, edited by Jane Monnig Atkinson and Shelly Errington, pp. 1–58. Stanford: Stanford University Press.

Falconeri, G. Ralph. 1976. The Impact of Rapid Urban Change on Neighbourhood Solidarity. In *Social Change and Community Politics in Urban Japan*, edited by J.W. White and F. Munger. Chapel Hill: University of North Carolina Press.

Fernea, Elizabeth. 1965. *Guests of the Sheik: An Ethnography of an Iraqi Village*. Garden City: Doubleday.

Ferzacca, Steve. 1996. *In this Pocket of the Universe: Healing the Modern in a Central Javanese City.* Dissertation, Department of Anthropology, University of Wisconsin-Madison.

—. 2001. *Healing the Modern in a Central Javanese City.* Durham: Carolina Academic Press.

Folbre, Nancy. 1988. The Black Four of Hearts: Toward a New Paradigm of Household Economics. In *A Home Divided: Women and Income in the Third World,* edited by Daisy Dwyer and Judith Bruce, pp. 248–264. Stanford: Stanford University Press.

—. 1986 Cleaning House: New Perspectives on Households and Economic Development. *Journal of Development Economics* 22:5–40.

Foucault, Michel. 1979. Governmentality. In *The Foucault Effect: Studies of Governmentality,* edited by G. Burchell, C. Gordon, and P. Miller, pp. 87–104. Reprint. Chicago: The University of Chicago Press.

Fox, James J., editor. 1993. *Inside Austronesian Houses: Perspectives on Domestic Designs for Living.* Canberra, Australia: Department of Anthropology, Comparative Austronesian Project, Research School of Pacific Studies, the Australian National University.

Fox-Genovese, Elizabeth. 1991. *Feminism without Illusions: A Critique of Individualism.* Chapel Hill: University of North Carolina Press.

Furnivall, J.S. 1948. *Colonial Policy and Practice.* Cambridge: Cambridge University Press.

Garon, Sheldon. 1993. Women's Groups and the Japanese State: Contending Approaches to Political Integration, 1890–1945. *Journal of Japanese Studies* 19(10):5–41.

—. 1997. *Molding Japanese Minds: The State in Everyday Life.* Princeton: Princeton University Press.

Garfinkel, Harold. 1967. *Studies in Ethnomethodology.* Englewood Cliffs: Prentice-Hall.

Geertz, Clifford. 1960. *The Religion of Java.* Chicago: University of Chicago Press.

—. 1963. *Agricultural Involution: The Process of Ecological Change in Indonesia.* Berkeley: University of California Press.

—. 1980. *Negara: The Theater State in Nineteenth-Century Bali.* Princeton: Princeton University Press.

Geertz, Hildred. 1961. *The Javanese Family.* New York: Free Press of Glencoe.

Gerke, Solvay. 1992. *Social Change and Life Planning for Rural Javanese Women.* Saarbrucken: Verlag Breitenbach Publishers.

Gibson, Thomas. 1995. Having Your House and Eating It: Houses and Siblings in Ara, South Sulawesi. In *About the House: Levi-Strauss and Beyond,* edited by Janet Carsten and Stephen Hugh-Jones, pp. 129–148. Cambridge: Cambridge University.

Giddens, Anthony. 1995. *Politics, Sociology and Social Theory: Encounters with Classical and Contemporary Social Thought.* Stanford: Stanford University Press.

Gillespie, Susan D. 2000. Lèvi-Strauss: *Maison* and *Sociètè à Maisons.* In *Beyond Kinship: Social and Material Reproduction in House Societies,* edited by Rosemary Joyce and Susan Gillespie, pp. 22–52. Philadelphia: University of Pennsylvania Press.

Goffman, Erving. 1959. *The Presentation of Self in Everyday Life.* Garden City: Doubleday.

Goh, Taro. 1998. *Communal Land Tenure in Nineteenth-Century Java: The Formation of Western Images of the Eastern Village.* Canberra: Department of Anthropology, Research School of Pacific and Asian Studies.

Gouda, Frances. 1995. *Dutch Culture Overseas: Colonial Practice in the Netherlands Indies, 1900–1942.* Amsterdam: Amsterdam University Press.

Graaf, H.J. de and Th.G. Pigeaud. 1984. *Chinese Muslims in Java in the 15th and 16th Centuries: The Malay Annals of Semarang and Cheribon,* edited by M.C. Ricklefs. Monash Papers on Southeast Asia, No. 12. Melbourne: Monash University.

Greenberg, James. 1981. *Santiago's Sword: Chatino Peasant Religion and Economics.* Berkeley: University of California Press.

Grijns, Mies and Anita van Velzen. 1993. Working Women: Differentiation and Marginalisation. In *Indonesia Assessment 1993, Labour: Sharing in the Benefits of Growth?,* edited by C. Manning and J. Hardjono, pp. 214–228. Proceedings of the Indonesia Update Conference, August 1993, Indonesia Project, Department of Economics and Department of Political and Social Change, Research School of Pacific Studies, ANU. Canberra: Australian National University.

Grinker, Roy Richard. 1994. *Houses in the Rainforest: Ethnicity and Inequality among Farmers and Foragers in Central Africa.* Berkeley: University of California Press.

Gudeman, Stephen and Alberto Rivera. 1990. *Colombian Conversations: The Domestic Economy in Life and Text.* New York: Cambridge University Press.

—. 1992. Remodeling the House of Economics: Culture and Innovation. *American Ethnologist* 19(1):141–154.

Guinness, Patrick. 1986. *Harmony and Hierarchy in a Javanese Kampung.* Singapore: Oxford University Press.

—. 1991. Kampung and the Street-side: Yogyakarta under the New Order. *Prisma* 51:86–98.

Gullestad, Marianne. 1984. *Kitchen Table Society: A Case Study of Family Life and Friendships of Young Working-Class Mothers in Urban Norway.* Oslo: Universitetsforlaget.

Hadiz, Vedi. 1997. *Workers and the State in New Order Indonesia.* London: Routledge.

Halperin, Rhoda. 1994. *Cultural Economies Past and Present.* Austin: University of Texas Press.

Hansen, Karen Tranberg. 1992. *African Encounters with Domesticity.* New Brunswick, NJ: Rutgers University Press.

Hardjono, Joan. 1987. *Land, Labour and Livelihood in a West Java Village.* Yogyakarta: Gadjah Mada University Press.

Hareven, Tamara, editor. 1978. *Transitions: The Family and the Life Course in Historical Perspective.* New York: Academic Press.

Harris, Olivia. 1984. Households as Natural Units. In *Of Marriage and the Market: Women's Subordination Internationally and Its Lessons,* edited by K. Young, C. Wolkowitz, and R. McCullagh, pp.136–155. London: Routledge & Kegan Paul.

Harris, Olivia and Kate Young. 1981. Engendered Structures: Some Problems in the Analysis of Reproduction. In *The Anthropology of Pre-Capitalist Society,* edited by J. Kahn and J. Llobera, pp. 49–68. London: Macmillan.

Harrison, Rachel and Frank Mort. 1980. Patriarchal Aspects of Nineteenth-Century State Formation: Property Relations, Marriage and Divorce, and Sexuality. In *Capitalism, State Formation and Marxist Theory,* edited by Philip Corrigan, pp. 79–109. London: Quartet Books.

Hart, Gillian. 1993. Imagined Unities: Constructions of "the Household" in Economic Theory. In *Understanding Economic Process,* edited by Sutti Ortiz and Susan Lees, pp. 111–129. Lanham: University Press of America.

Hatta, Mohammad. 1971. *The Putera Reports: Problems in Indonesian-Japanese Wartime Occupation.* Translated by William Frederick. Ithaca, NY: Modern Indonesia Project, Southeast Asia Program, Cornell University.

Hayami, Yukiro and Masao Kikuchi. 1982. *Asian Village Economy at the Crossroads.* Tokyo: University of Tokyo Press.

Hayden, Dolores. 1981. *The Grand Domestic Revolution: A History of Feminist Designs for American Homes, Neighborhoods, and Cities.* Cambridge: The MIT Press.

Hayden, Sara. 2003. Family Metaphors and the Nation: Promoting a Politics of Care through the Million Mom March. *Quarterly Journal of Speech* 89(3): 196–215.

Headley, Stephen. 1987a. The Body as a House in Javanese Society. In *De La Hutte au Palais: Societes "A Maison" en Asie du Sud-Est Insulaire,* textes reunis par Charles Macdonald et les membres de l'ECASE, pp. 133–152. Paris: Editions du Centre National de la Recherche Scientifique.

—. 1987b. The Idiom of Siblingship: One Definition of "House" in Southeast Asia. In *De La Hutte au Palais: Societes "A Maison" en Asie du Sud-Est Insulaire,* textes reunis par Charles Macdonald et les membres de l'ECASE, pp. 209–218. Paris: Editions du Centre Naitonal de la Recherche Scientifique.

Heilbrun, Carolyn. 1989. *Writing a Woman's Life.* New York: Ballantine.

Hewison, Kevin, Richard Robison, and Garry Rodan. 1993. *Southeast Asia in the 1990s: Authoritarianism, Democracy and Capitalism.* New South Wales, Australia: Allen and Unwin.

Hill, Hal. 1991. *Multinationals and Employment in Indonesia.* Geneva: ILO.

—. 1994. The Economy. In *Indonesia's New Order: The Dynamics of Socio-Economic Transformation,* edited by Hal Hill, pp. 55–122. Honolulu: University of Hawaii Press.

Hilmy, Masdar. 1999. *Islam and Javanese Acculturation: Textual and Contextual Analysis of the Slametan Ritual.* Master's thesis, McGill University.

Hobsbawm, Eric. 1983. Introduction. In *The Invention of Tradition,* edited by E. Hobsbawm and T. Ranger, pp. 1–14. Cambridge: Cambridge University Press.

hooks, bell. 1990. Yearning: Race, Gender, and Cultural Politics. Boston: South End Press.

Horne, Elinor Clark. 1974. *Javanese-English Dictionary.* New Haven: Yale University Press.

Husken, Frans and Benjamin White. 1989. Java: Social Differentiation, Food Production, and Agrarian Control. In *Agrarian Transformations: Local Processes and the State in Southeast Asia,* edited by Gillian Hart, Andrew Turton, and Benjamin White, pp. 235–265. Berkeley, CA: University of California Press.

Hyde, Janet and Marilyn Essex. 1991. *Parental Leave and Child Care: Setting a Research and Policy Agenda.* Philadelphia: Temple University Press.

Indarti, Erlyn. 1988. Dharma Wanita dan Pembangunan Wanita. *Opini* 48:9–11.

Jay, Robert. 1969. *Javanese Villagers: Social Relations in Rural Modjokuto.* Cambridge: The MIT Press.

Jayawardena, Kumari. 1986. *Feminism and Nationalism in the Third World.* London: Zed Books.

Jolly, Margaret and Martha Macintyre, editors. 1989. *Family and Gender in the Pacific: Domestic Contradictions and the Colonial Impact.* Cambridge: Cambridge University Press.

Jones, Gavin. 1987. Labour Force and Labour Utilization. In *The Demographic Dimension in Indonesian Development,* edited by Graeme Hugo, Terence Hull, Valerie Hull, and Gavin Jones, pp. 244–297. Singapore: Oxford University Press.

—. 2000. The Social and Demographic Impact of the Southeast Asian Crisis of 1997–99. *Journal of Population Research* 38(5):1–17.

Joseph, Gilbert and Daniel Nugent. 1994. *Everyday Forms of State Formation: Revolution and the Negotiation of Rule in Modern Mexico.* Durham: Duke University Press.

Joyce, Rosemary A. and Susan D. Gillespie. 2000. *Beyond Kinship: Social and Material Reproduction in House Societies.* Philadelphia: University of Pennsylvania Press.

Kahn, Joel. 1985. Indonesia after the Demise of Agricultural Involution: Critique of a Debate. *Critique of Anthropology* 5:69–96.

—. 1991. Constructing Culture: Towards an Anthropology of the Middle Classes in Southeast Asia. *Asian Studies Review* 15(2):50–56.

Kano, Hiroyoshi. 1979. The Economic History of Javanese Rural Society: A Reinterpretation. *The Developing Societies* 17(4):3–22.

Kartini, Raden Adjeng. 1920. *Letters of a Javanese Princess.* Translated by Agnes Louise Symmers. New York: Alfred Knopf.

Kasza, Gregory. 1995. *The Conscription Society: Administered Mass Organizations.* New Haven: Yale University Press.

Keeler, Ward. 1983. *Symbolic Dimensions of the Javanese House.* Working Paper No. 29. Melbourne: Monash University.

—. 1984. *Javanese: A Cultural Approach.* Athens: Ohio University Center for International Studies.

—. 1987. *Javanese Shadow Plays, Javanese Selves.* Princeton: Princeton University Press.

—. 1990. Speaking of Gender in Java. In *Power and Difference: Gender in Island Southeast Asia,* edited by Jane Monnig Atkinson and Shelly Errington, pp.127–52. Stanford: Stanford University Press.

Keesing, Roger. 1985. Kwaio Women Speak: The Micropolitics of Autobiography in a Solomon Island Society. *American Anthropologist* 87(1):27–39.

Kemp, Jeremy. 1988. *Seductive Mirage: The Search for the Village Community in Southeast Asia.* Dordrecht: Foris.

Kerber, Linda. 1980. *Women of the Republic: Intellect and Ideology in Revolutionary America.* Chapel Hill: University of North Carolina Press.

Keyes, Charles. 1995. *The Golden Peninsula: Culture and Adaptation in Mainland Southeast Asia.* Honolulu: University of Hawai'i Press.

Knapman, Claudia. 1986. *White Women in Fiji, 1985–1930: The Ruin of Empire?* Sydney: Allen and Unwin.

Koentjaraningrat. 1989. *Javanese Culture.* Singapore: Oxford University Press.

Koonz, Claudia. 1987. *Mothers in the Fatherland: Women, the Family and Nazi Politics.* New York: St. Martin's.

Lavie, Smadar. 1990. *The Poetics of Military Occupation: Mzeina Allegories of Bedouin Identity under Israeli and Egyptian Rule.* Berkeley: University of California Press.

Levi-Strauss, Claude. 1983. *The Way of the Masks.* Translated by S. Modelski. London: Jonathan Cape.

—. 1987. *Anthropology and Myth: Lectures 1951–1982.* Oxford: Blackwell.

Locher-Scholten, Elsbeth. 1987. Female Labour in Twentieth Century Java: European Notions—Indonesian Practice. In *Indonesian Woman in Focus: Past and Present Notions,* edited by Elsbeth Locher-Scholten and Anke Neihof, pp. 77–103. Dordrecht: Foris.

—. 2000. *Women and the Colonial State: Essays on Gender and Modernity in the Netherlands Indies, 1900–1942.* Amsterdam: Amsterdam University Press.

Lutz, Catherine. 1995. The Gender of Theory. In *Women Writing Culture,* edited by Ruth Behar and Deborah Gordon. Berkeley: University of California Press.

Macdonald, C., editor. 1987. *De la Hutte au Palais: Societes "a Maisons" en Asie du Sud-Est Insulaire.* Paris: Edition du CNRS.

MacKinnon, Catharine. 1983. Feminism, Marxism, Method, and the State: An Agenda for Theory. In *The Signs Reader: Women, Gender, and Scholarship,* edited by Abel, E. and Abel, E., pp. 227–256. Chicago: University of Chicago Press.

Manderson, Lenore. 1983. *Women's Work and Women's Roles: Economics and Everyday Life in Indonesia, Malaysia, and Singapore.* Canberra: Australian National University.

Manning, Chris. 1988. *The Green Revolution, Employment, and Economic Change in Rural Java: a Reassessment of Trends under the New Order.* Singapore: ASEAN Economic Research Unit, Institute of Southeast Asian Studies.

Manning, Chris and Joan Hardjono, editors. 1993. *Indonesia Assessment 1993; Labour: Sharing in the Benefits of Growth.* Proceedings of Indonesia Update Conference, August 1993, Indonesia Project, Department of Economics and Department of Political and Social Change, Research School of Pacific Studies, ANU. Canberra: Department of Political and Social Change, Research School of Pacific Studies, Australian National University.

Marwan, Sihi Saudah. 1972. *Pendidikan Kesejahteraan Keluarga (PKK).* Surakarta, Indonesia: C.V. Ramadhani.

Mather, Celia. 1982. *Industrialization in the Tangerang Regency of West Java: Women Workers and the Islamic Patriarchy.* Working Paper no. 17. Amsterdam: Center for Sociology and Anthropology, University of Amsterdam.

Matthews, Glenna. 1987. *"Just a Housewife": The Rise and Fall of Domesticity in America.* New York: Oxford University Press.

McGee, T.G. 1967. *The Southeast Asian City: A Social Geography of the Primate Cities of Southeast Asia.* New York: Praeger.

—. 1984. *Urban Growth in Indonesia: Its Challenge to Environmental Policy.* Paper presented at the Indonesia-Canada Environment Conference, Mont Saint-Marie, Quebec.

McKinnon, Susan. 1995. Houses and Hierarchy: The View from a South Moluccan Society. In *About the House: Levi-Strauss and Beyond,* edited by Janet Carsten and Stephen Hugh-Jones, pp.170–188. Cambridge: Cambridge University.

Mead, Margaret and Gregory Bateson. 1993. *Balinese Character: A Photographic Analysis.* New York: New York Academy of Sciences.

Meillassoux, Claude. 1981. *Maidens, Meal and Money: Capitalism and the Domestic Community*, translated. [1975] London: Cambridge University Press.

Mies, Maria. 1986. *Patriarchy and Accumulation on a World Scale: Women in the International Division of Labour.* London: Zed Books.

Ministry of Home Affairs. 1983. *The Family Welfare Movement in Indonesia: PKK.* Mimeograph. Jakarta: Ministry of Home Affairs, Directorate General of Rural Development.

Moertono, Soemarsaid. 1968. *State and Statecraft in Old Java: A Study of the Later Mataram Period, 16th to 19th Century.* Ithaca: Cornell University Press.

Molyneux, Maxine. 1979. Beyond the Domestic Labour Debate. *New Left Review* (116) July-August: 3–28.

Moore, Henrietta. 1988. *Feminism and Anthropology.* Minneapolis: University of Minnesota Press.

—. 1994. *A Passion for Difference: Essays in Anthropology and Gender.* Bloomington: Indiana University Press.

Murray, Alison. 1991. *No Money, No Honey: A Study of Street Traders and Prostitutes in Jakarta.* Singapore: Oxford University Press.

Netting, Robert, Richard Wilk, and Eric Arnould. 1984. *Households: Comparative and Historical Studies of the Domestic Group.* Berkeley: University of California Press.

New Century Dictionary. 1948. New York: Appleton-Century-Croft.

Newberry, Janice. 1997. *Making Do in the Imagined Community: State Formation and Domesticity in Working Class Java.* Dissertation, Department of Anthropology, University of Arizona, Tucson.

—. 1999. The Good Terrorist: Domesticity and the Political Space for Change. In *Moral Issues in Global Perspective*, edited by Christine M. Koggel, pp. 302–317. Peterborough, ON: Broadview Press.

Nugent, Daniel. 1993. *Spent Cartridges of Revolution: An Anthropological History of Namiquipa, Chihuahua.* Chicago: University of Chicago Press.

Oakley, Ann. 1974. *Woman's Work: The Housewife, Past and Present.* New York: Pantheon.

Oey-Gardiner, Mayling. 1993. A Gender Perspective on Indonesia's Labour Market Transformation. In *Indonesia Assessment 1993, Labour: Sharing in the Benefits of Growth?*, edited by C. Manning and J. Hardjono, pp. 203–213. Proceedings of the Indonesia Update Conference, August 1993, Indonesia Project, Department of Economics and Department of Political and Social Change, Research School of Pacific Studies, ANU. Canberra: Australian National University.

O'Malley, Pat, Lorna Weir, and Clifford Shearing. 1997. Governmentality, Criticism, Politics. *Economy and Society* 26(4): 501–517.

Ong, Aihwa. 1987. *Spirits of Resistance and Capitalist Discipline: Factory Women in Malaysia.* Albany: SUNY Press.

Ong, Aihwa and Michael Peletz, editors. 1995. *Bewitching Women and Pious Men: Gender and Body Politics in Southeast Asia.* Berkeley: University of California Press.

Ortner, Sherry. 1974. "Is Female to Male as Nature is to Culture?" In *Women, Culture, and Society,* edited by Michelle Zimbalist Rosaldo and Louyise Lamphere, pp. 67–88. Stanford: Stanford University Press.

Papanek, Hanna. 1983. Implications of Development for Women in Indonesia: Research and Policy Issues. In *Women in Developing Countries: A Policy Focus,* edited by K. Staudt and J. Jaquette, pp. 66–87. New York: Haworth.

Papanek, Hanna, T. Omas Ihromi, and Yulfita Rahardjo. 1974. *Changes in the Status of Women and their Significance in the Process of Social Change: Indonesian Case Studies.* 6th International Conference on Asian History; International Association of Historians of Asia.

Papanek, Hanna and Laurel Schwede. 1988. Women are Good with Money: Earning and Managing in an Indonesian City. In *A Home Divided: Women and Income in the Third World,* edited by Daisy Dwyer and Judith Bruce, pp. 71–98. Stanford: Stanford University Press.

Peletz, Michael. 1996. *Reason and Passion: Representations of Gender in a Malay Society.* Berkeley: University of California Press.

Peluso, Nancy. 1982. *Occupational Mobility and the Economic Role of Rural Women: A Case Study of Women Working Outside Agriculture in Two Villages in Sleman, Yogyakarta.* Yogyakarta: Population Studies Center, Gadjah Mada University.

Pemberton, John. 1989. *The Appearance of Order: A Politics of Culture in Colonial and Postcolonial Java.* Dissertation. Department of Anthropology, Cornell University.

—. 1994. *On the Subject of "Java."* Ithaca: Cornell University Press.

Pigeaud, Th.G. 1960. *Java in the 14th Century: A Study in Cultural History. The Negara Kertagama by Rakawi Prapanca of Majapahit, 1365 A.D., Vol. III, Commentaries and Recapitulations.* Koninklijk Instituut Voor Taal-, Land- En Volkenkunde, Translation Series 4.3 and 4.4. The Hague: Martinus Nijhoff.

Pires, Tome. 1967. [1512–1515] *The Suma Oriental of Tome Pires and the Book of Francisco Rodrigues.* Translated by Amando Cortesao. Nendin/ Liechtenstein: Hakluyt Society, Krans Reprint Limited.

PKK TIM Penggerak Pusat. 1987. Peranan PKK Dalam Penyehatan Lingkungan Disajikan Dalam Semiloka Nasional dengan Judul "Peranan Ibu Rumah Tangga Dalam Penyehatan Lingkungan." Mimeograph. Jakarta: Pembinaan Kesejahteraan Keluarga.

Polanyi, Karl. 1944. *The Great Transformation.* New York: Holt, Rinehart and Winston.

188   Back Door Java

Poliman, B. A. Suratmin, Muljono, et al. 1977. *Sejarah Daerah Istimewa Yogyakarta, Proyek Penelitian dan Pencatatan Kebudayaan Daerah-Daerah Istimewa Yogyakarta.* Yogyakarta: Departemen P & K.

Pramoedya. 1991. *This Earth of Mankind.* New York: Penguin.

Prijotomo, Josef. 1995. *Petungan: Sistem Ukuran dalam Arsitektur Jawa.* Yogyakarta: Gadjah Mada Press.

Rabinow, Paul. 1978. *Reflections on Fieldwork in Morocco.* Berkeley: University of Chicago Press.

—. 1999. Artificiality and Enlightenment: From Sociobiology to Biosociality. In *Health Studies: A Critical and Cross-Cultural Reader,* edited by Colin Samson, pp. 50–60. Oxford: Blackwell.

Raffles, Thomas Stamford. 1978[1817]. *The History of Java, Volume 1.* Singapore: Oxford University Press.

Rassers, W.H. 1960[1925]. *Panji, the Culture Hero: A Structural Study of Religion in Java.* The Hague: Martinus Nijhoff.

Reid, Anthony. 1979. *The Structure of Cities in Southeast Asia, 15th to 17th Centuries.* Paper delivered at the ICIOS Conference, Perth, August.

—. 1988. *Southeast Asia in the Age of Commerce 1450–1680: Volume One, The Lands Below the Winds.* New Haven: Yale University Press.

Ricklefs, M.C. 1974. Jogjakarta Under Sultan Mangkubumi, 1749–1792: A History of the Division of Java. London: Oxford University Press.

—. 1981. *A History of Modern Indonesia, c. 1300 to the Present.* Bloomington: Indiana University Press.

Rigg, Jonathon. 1994. Redefining the Village and Rural Life: Lessons from South East Asia. *The Geographical Journal* 160(2):123–135.

Robison, Richard. 1986. *Indonesia: the Rise of Capital.* Singapore: Allen and Unwin.

—. 1993. Indonesia: Tensions in State and Regime. In *Southeast Asia in the 1990s: Authoritarianism, Democracy and Capitalism,* edited by Hewison, Kevin, Richard Robison, and Garry Rodan, pp. 39–74. New South Wales, Australia: Allen and Unwin.

—. 1996. The Middle Class and Bourgeoisie in Indonesia. In *The New Rich in Asia: Mobile Phones, McDonalds and Middle-Class Revolution,* edited by R. Robison and D.S.G. Goodman, pp. 77–101. London: Routledge.

Robson, Stuart and Singgih Wibisono. 2002. *Javanese-English Dictionary.* Hong Kong: Periplus Editions.

Rosaldo, Michelle. 1974. Woman, Culture and Society: A Theoretical Overview. In *Women, Culture and Society,* edited by Michele Zimbalist Rosaldo and Louise Lamphere, pp. 17–42. Stanford: Stanford University Press.

—. 1980. The Use and Abuse of Anthropology: Reflections on Feminism and Cross-Cultural Understanding. *Signs* 5(3):389–417.

Rosaldo, Renato. 1992. *Culture and Truth: Remaking of Social Analysis.* Boston: Beacon Press.

Rose, N. and P. Miller. 1992. Political Power Beyond the State: Problematics of Government. *British Journal of Sociology* 43(2):173–205.

Roseberry, William. 1989. *Anthropologies and Histories: Essays in Culture, History, and Political Economy.* New Brunswick: Rutgers University Press.

Rudini, Oddyana. 1988. *Peranan PKK dalam Peningkatan Kedudukan dan Peranan Wanita dalam Pembangunan.* Temu Karya dengan Wartawan Pengelola Media Massa dan Penulis tentang Pemasyarakatan Citra Wanita Indonesia, Peningkatan Peranannya dalam Pembangunan, 12–13 December 1988, Jakarta.

Rutz, Werner. 1987. *Cities and Towns in Indonesia: Their Development, Current Positions and Functions with Regards to Administration and Regional Economy.* Berlin: Gebrüder Borntraeger.

Rybczynski, Witold. 1986. *Home: A Short History of an Idea.* New York: Viking Penguin.

Sahlins, Marshall. 1972. *Stone Age Economics.* Chicago: Aldine.

Said, Edward. 1979. *Orientalism.* New York: Vintage Books.

Salamun, Drs. 1989/1990. Inventarisasi dan Dokumentasi Nama-Nama Jalan di Daerah Kotamadya Yogyakarta. In *Buletin Jarahnitra, Mengenal Bangunan Bersejarah dan Nama-Nama Jalan di Kotamadya Yogyakarta*, edited by Suwarno and Drs. Salamun. Yogyakarta: Departemen Pendidikan dan Kebudayaan, Direktorat Jenderal Kebudayaan.

Santosa, Revianto Budi. 1996. *Omah: The Spatial Structure of Javanese Houses.* Master's thesis, McGill University

—. 2000. *Omah: Membaca Makna Rumah Jawa.* Yogyakarta: Yayasan Bentang Budaya.

USC-Satunama. 2004. *USC-Canada Program Progress Report, Fiscal Years: 2003–2004.* Mimeograph. Sleman, Yogyakarta: USC-Satunama.

Schrauwers, Albert. 2004. H(h)ouses, E(e)states and Class: On the Importance of Capitals in Central Sulawesi. *Bijdragen tot de Taal-, Land- en Volkenkunde* 160–1:72–94.

Schulte Nordholt, Nico 1987. From LSD to LKMD: Participation at the Village Level. In *Local Leadership and Programme Implementation in Indonesia*, edited by Philip Quarles van Ufford, pp. 47–64. Amsterdam: Free University Press.

Scidmore, E.R. 1989[1899]. *Java: The Garden of the East.* Singapore: Oxford University Press.

Scott, Joan and Louis Tilly. 1975. Woman's Work and the Family in Nineteenth-Century Europe. In *The Family in History*, edited by Charles Rosenberg. Philadelphia: University of Pennsylvania Press.

Scott, James. 1985. *Weapons of the Weak: Everyday Forms of Peasant Resistance.* New Haven: Yale University Press.

—. 1998. *Seeing Like A State: How Certain Schemes to Improve the Human Condition Have Failed.* New Haven: Yale University Press.

Sears, Laurie, ed. 1996b. *Fantasizing the Feminine in Indonesia*. Durham, NC: Duke University Press.

Selosoemardjan. 1962. *Social Changes in Jogjakarta*. Ithaca: Cornell University Press.

Shapiro, Laura. 1986. *Perfection Salad: Women and Cooking at the Turn of the Century*. New York: Farrar, Straus, and Giroux.

Siegel, James. 1986. *Solo in the New Order: Language and Hierarchy in an Indonesian City*. Princeton: Princeton University Press.

Simanjuntak, Payaman. 1993. Manpower Problems and Government Policies. In *Indonesia Assessment 1993, Labour: Sharing in the Benefits of Growth?*, edited by C. Manning and J. Hardjono, pp. 45–60. Proceedings of the Indonesia Update Conference, August 1993, Indonesia Project, Department of Economics and Department of Political and Social Change, Research School of Pacific Studies, ANU. Canberra: Australian National University.

Smith, Dorothy. 1974. Women's Experience as a Radical Critique of Sociology. In *The Conceptual Practices of Power: A Feminist Sociology of Knowledge*. Boston: Northeastern University Press.

Soekarno. 1951. *Sarinah: Kewadjiban Wanita Dalam Perdjoangan Republik Indonesia*. Jakarta: Jajasan Pembangunan Djakarta.

Stack, Carol. 1983. *All Our Kin: Strategies for Survival in a Black Community*. New York: Basic Books.

Steinberg, Joel, editor. 1971. *In Search of Southeast Asia: A Modern History*. New York: Praeger.

Steinschneider, Janice C. 1994. *An Improved Woman: The Wisconsin Federation of Women's Clubs, 1895–1920*. Brooklyn: Carlson Publishing.

Stoler, Ann Laura. 1977. Class Structure and Female Autonomy in Rural Java. *Signs* 3(1):74–89.

—. 1981. Garden Use and Household Economy in Java. In *Agricultural and Rural Development in Indonesia*, edited by Gary Hansen, 242–254. Boulder: Westview Press.

—. 1985a. *Capitalism and Confrontation in Sumatra's Plantation Belt, 1870–1979*. New Haven: Yale University Press.

—. 1985b. Perceptions of Protest: Defining the Dangerous in Colonial Sumatra. *American Ethnologist* 12(4):642–58.

—. 1989a. Making Empire Respectable: The Politics of Race and Sexual Morality in 20th-Century Colonial Cultures. *American Ethnologist* 16(4):643–660.

—. 1989b. Rethinking Colonial Categories: European Communities and the Boundaries of Rule. *Comparative Studies in Society and History* (prepublication copy).

—. 1995. *Race and the Education of Desire: Foucault's History of Sexuality and the Colonial Order of Things*. Chapel Hill: Duke University Press.

—. 1996. A Sentimental Education: Native Servants and the Cultivation of European Children in the Netherlands Indies. In *Fantasizing the Feminine in Indonesia*, edited by Laurie Sears, pp. 71–91. Durham: Duke University Press.

—. 2002. *Carnal Knowledge and Imperial Power: Race and the Intimate in Colonial Rule*. Berkeley: University of California Press.

Strobel, Margaret. 1993. Gender, Sex, and Empire. In *Islamic and European Expansion: The Forging of a Global Order*, edited by Michael Adas, pp. 365–376. Philadelphia: Temple University Press.

Sullivan, John. 1980. Back Alley Neighbourhood: Kampung as Urban Community in Yogyakarta. *Monash University Papers on Southeast Asia*, No. 18.

—. 1986. Kampung and State: The Role of Government in the Development of Urban Community in Yogyakarta. *Indonesia* 41 (April):63–88.

—. 1992. *Local Government and Community in Java: An Urban Case-Study*. Singapore: Oxford University Press.

Sullivan, Norma. 1983. Indonesian Women in Development: State Theory and Urban *Kampung* Practice. In *Women's Work and Women's Roles: Economics and Everyday Life in Indonesia, Malaysia, and Singapore*, edited by Lenore Manderson, pp.147–172. Development Studies Centre, Monograph No. 32. Canberra: Australian National University.

—. 1994. *Masters and Managers: A Study in Gender Relations in Urban Java*. New South Wales, Australia: Allen and Unwin.

Sunindyo, Saraswati. 1996. Murder, Gender and the Media: Sexualizing Politics and Violence. In *Fantasizing the Feminine in Indonesia*, edited by Laurie Sears, pp. 120–139. Durham: Duke University Press.

Suratiyah, Ken and Sunarru Samsi Hariadi. 1991. *Wanita, Kerja, dan Rumah Tangga: Pengaruh Pembangunan Pertanian Terhadap Peranan Wanita Pedesaan di Daerah Istimewa Yogyakarta*. Yogyakarta: Pusat Penelitian Kependudukan, Universitas Gadjah Mada.

Suryakusuma, Julia. 1991. State Ibuism: The Social Construction of Womanhood in the Indonesian New Order. *New Asian Visions* 6(2):46–71.

—. 1996. The State and Sexuality in New Order Indonesia. In *Fantasizing the Feminine in Indonesia*, edited by Laurie Sears, pp. 92–119. Durham: Duke University Press.

Tambiah, Stanley. 1985. *Culture, Thought, and Social Action: An Anthropological Perspective*. Cambridge, MA: Harvard University Press.

Taylor, Jean Gelman. 1983. *The Social World of Batavia: European and Eurasian in Dutch Asia*. Madison: University of Wisconsin Press.

Tedlock, Barbara. 1995. Works and Wives: On the Sexual Division of Textual Labor. In *Women Writing Culture*, edited by Ruth Behar and Deborah Gordon, pp. 267–286. Berkeley: University of California Press.

Thompson, E.P. 1963. *The Making of the English Working Class*. New York: Pantheon.

—. 1967. Time, Work-Discipline, and Industrial Capitalism. *Past and Present* 38:56–97.

Tiffany, Sharon and Kathleen Adams. 1985. *The Wild Woman: An Inquiry into the Anthropology of an Idea.* Cambridge, MA: Schenkman.

Tilly, Louise. 1993. Industrialization and Gender Inequality. In *Islamic and European Expansion: The Forging of a Global Order,* edited by Michael Adas, pp. 243–310. Philadelphia: Temple University Press.

Tiwon, Sylvia. 1996. Models and Maniacs: Articulating the Female in Indonesia. In *Fantasizing the Feminine in Indonesia,* edited by Laurie Sears, pp. 47–70. Durham: Duke University Press.

Tooker, Deborah. 1996. Putting the Mandala in its Place: A Practice-Based Approach to the Spatialization of Power on the Southeast Asian "Perhipery"—the Case of the Akha. *Journal of Asian Studies* 55(2):323–358.

Tsing, Anna Lownhaupt. 1993. *In the Realm of the Diamond Queen: Marginality in an Out-of-the-Way Place.* Princeton: Princeton University Press.

Van Niel, Robert. 1979. From Netherlands East Indies to Republic of Indonesia, 1900–1945. In *The Development of Indonesian Society: From the Coming of Islam to the Present Day,* edited by Harry Aveling, pp. 106–165. Australia: University of Queensland Press.

—. 1992. *Java Under the Cultivation System: Collected Writings.* Leiden: KITLV Press.

Vreede-de Steurs, Cora. 1960. *The Indonesian Woman: Struggles and Achievements.* The Hague: Mouton and Company.

Waterson, Roxana. 1990. *The Living House: An Anthropology of Architecture in South-East Asia.* Singapore: Oxford University Press.

Weiner, Annette. 1992. *Inalienable Possessions; The Paradox of Keeping-while-Giving.* Berkeley, CA: University of California Press.

White, Benjamin. 1986. *Rural Non-Farm Employment in Java: Recent Developments, Policy Issues and Research Needs.* Geneva: Institute of Social Studies-UNDP/ILO.

White, Benjamin and Endang Lestari Hastuti. 1980. *Different and Unequal: Male and Female Influence in Household and Community Affairs in Two West Javanese Villages.* Working paper, Project on Rural Household Economies and the Role of Women, Centre for Rural Sociological Research. Bogor, Indonesia: Bogor Agricultural University.

White, Luise. 1990. *The Comforts of Home: Prostitution in Colonial Nairobi.* Chicago: University of Chicago Press.

Wieringa, Saskia. 1988 Aborted Feminism in Indonesia: A History of Indonesian Socialist Feminism. In *Women's Struggles and Strategies,* edited by S. Wieringa. Aldershot, UK: Gower.

—. 1993. Two Indonesian Women's Organizations: Gerwani and the PKK. *Bulletin of Concerned Asian Scholars* 25(2).

Wilk, Richard. 1989. Decision Making and Resource Flows within the Household: Beyond the Black Box. In *The Household Economy: Reconsid-*

ering the Domestic Mode of Production, edited by Richard Wilk, pp. 23–54. Boulder: Westview Press.

Williams, Raymond. 1961. *The Long Revolution*. New York: Columbia University Press.

—. 1973. *The Country and the City.* London: Paladin.

—. 1977. *Marxism and Literature*. Oxford: Oxford University Press.

—. 1989. *Resources of Hope: Culture, Democracy, Socialism.* London: Verso.

Williams, Walter. 1991. *Javanese Lives: Women & Men in Modern Indonesian Society.* New Brunswick: Rutgers University Press.

Willis, Paul E. 1977. *Learning to Labor: How Working Class Kids Get Working Class Jobs*. New York: Columbia University Press.

Wolf, Diane. 1992. *Factory Daughters: Gender, Household Dynamics, and Rural Industrialization in Java*. Berkeley: University of California Press.

Wolf, Eric. 1957. Closed Corporate Communities in Mesoamerica and Java. *Southwestern Journal of Anthropology* 13:1–18.

—. 1986. The Vicissitudes of the Closed Corporate Peasant Community. *American Ethnologist* 13:325–329.

Woodward, Mark. 1989. *Islam in Java: Normative Piety and Mysticism in the Sultanate of Yogyakarta*. Tucson: University of Arizona Press.

World Bank. 2004. World Development Indicators Database. <http://www.worldbank.org/data/countrydata/countrydata.html>. Accessed July 13.

World Health Organization. 1989. *World Health Organization Statistics Quarterly* 42(4):190.

Yanagisako, Sylvia and Jane Collier. 1987. Toward a Unified Analysis of Gender and Kinship. In *Gender and Kinship: Essays towards a Unified Analysis*, edited by S. Yanagisako and J. Collier, pp. 14–52. Stanford: Stanford University Press.

Young, Iris Marion. 1995. *Intersecting Voices: Dilemmas of Gender, Political Philosophy, and Policy.* Princeton: Princeton University Press.

Index

economy
   domestic, 112–13
   household, 97
   housewife role in, 107–08, 112–14,
      117–19, 120n1
   stability and dependencies in, 107–11
education, 76, 130–32, 131
elite class, 27, 33, 42–43, 65–66
ethnicity, 31–33
ethnography
   of becoming a housewife, 160–63
   fieldwork in, 159–60
   male and female styles of, 163–65, 172
   married couples in, 159–60, 163, 165
evenings (sore), 47
exports, 110

family, 13, 98. See also household; kinship
      system
   compound, 71–78, 88
   extended vs nuclear, 71–77, 90n11,
      101, 118
   head of, 21, 96, 98
   house and, 84–88. See also house.
   pooling of resources in, 95–98, 113
   in community, 17, 19
family planning, 15, 16, 40, 172
family wage, 113
Family Welfare Movement, 125. See also PKK,
      Pembinaan Kesejahateraan Keluarga
feasts. See slametan
feminist theory, 22, 96, 112, 125, 132, 168
fertility, 151–54
fetish, 89
food. See also cooking
   giving of, to others, 62–63, 68–70, 93
   women and, 96
   for slametan, 57–64
   symbolic uses of, 53–56, 62–64
foreign direct investment, 110

gandhok, 65–68
Garis Besar Haluan Negara (GBHN)
      (National State Guidelines), 15
Garon, Sheldon, 147
Geertz, Clifford, 37, 43, 53, 60, 116
Geertz, Hildred, 81, 82, 84, 86
gender. See also men; women
   household economics and, 95–98
   house symbolism and, 63–64,
      68–70

inheritance and, 74–77
separation by, 50–60
weddings and, 80–88
ghost stories, 12, 19
gift-giving, 68–69, 80, 93–95
gotong royong (mutual self-help), 40–44,
      142–44, 146, 171
government. See also state
   community governance and, 39–41,
      114. See also Pembinaan Kesejahteraan
      Keluarga
   households and, 98
   New Order, 35, 37, 39, 40–41, 44, 106,
      129–30, 133–34
   of kampung, 34–41, 43, 138–39
   small business development by, 112–17
   Suharto, 39, 107, 134, 147
   women's roles and, 17–18, 125–29,
      147, 172
governmentality, 18, 98, 147. See also
      state formation
governor, 35
guests, 20–21, 93
Guinness, Patrick, 42
Gullestad, Marianne, 169
Gyanti Treaty, 32

habitus, 56
Halperin, Rhoda, 117–18
Hamengkubuwana VII, 27
handbags, 115
handicrafts, 105, 108, 115
healers, 151–53
hearthhold, 96
home, 22. See also household; house
   as women's sphere, 125–27
   community and, 132
   morality and, 127, 135–44
   philosophies of, 125–35
   political function of, 129, 130, 144–46
   separate spheres of, 123–25
   state formation and, 144–48
home-based industries, 16–17, 100, 105–07,
      110–11, 113, 115, 138
home community, 41–44
home economics, 130–33, 149n7
hooks, bell, 129
house, 53–89
   as community, 88–89
   construction and rooms of, 19–20,
      61, 64–71